HISTORICAL AND POLITICAL ESSAYS

HISTORICAL

AND

POLITICAL ESSAYS

BY

WILLIAM EDWARD HARTPOLE LECKY

Essay Index Reprint Series

 BOOKS FOR LIBRARIES PRESS
FREEPORT, NEW YORK

First Published 1908
Reprinted 1970

INTERNATIONAL STANDARD BOOK NUMBER:
0-8369-1973-4

LIBRARY OF CONGRESS CATALOG CARD NUMBER:
76-99707

PRINTED IN THE UNITED STATES OF AMERICA

PREFACE

WHEN Mr. Lecky had finished his last work, ' The Leaders of Public Opinion in Ireland,' he did not intend to write another long book. His health was broken ; he had said most of what he wished to say. But he proposed collecting in a volume a few Essays which he had written at different times. As concentration was to him one of the first conditions of good work, he did not often allow his attention to be diverted from the book he was writing by giving addresses or contributing articles to reviews or magazines, unless he had some special reason for doing so. The number is, therefore, small. He began revising them ; and made some additions to ' Thoughts on History,' 'The Empire,' 'The Memoir of the Fifteenth Earl of Derby,' ' Queen Victoria as a Moral Force ' ; but he unfortunately did not live to complete the revision of the others.

In publishing this volume I have endeavoured to carry out his intentions. Besides the Essays which he had revised, I have included all that seemed to me to possess a permanent value. Even though some of them deal with questions of the day, the philosophic spirit in which they are treated may give them more than a transitory interest, and the forcible arguments that are adduced may still have weight in the future.

ELISABETH LECKY.

CONTENTS

HISTORICAL AND POLITICAL ESSAYS

THOUGHTS ON HISTORY

I DO not propose in this paper to enter into any general inquiry about the best method of writing history. Such inquiries appear to me to be of no real value, for there are many different kinds of history which should be written in many different ways. A diplomatic, a military, or a parliamentary history, dealing with a short period or a particular episode, must evidently be treated in a very different spirit from an extended history where the object of the historian should be to describe the various aspects of the national life, and to trace through long periods of time the ultimate causes of national progress and decay. The history of religion, of art, of literature, of social and industrial development, of scientific progress, have all their different methods. A writer who treats of some great revolution that has transformed human affairs should deal largely in retrospect, for the most important part of his task is to explain the long course of events that prepared and produced the catastrophe ; while a writer who treats of more normal times will do well to plunge rapidly into his theme.

Historians, too, differ widely in their special talents, and these talents are never altogether combined. The

B

power of vividly realising and portraying men, or societies
or modes of thought that have long since passed away ;
the power of arranging and combining great multitudes
of various facts ; the power of judging with discrimination,
accuracy, and impartiality conflicting arguments or
evidence ; the power of tracing through the long course
of events the true chain of cause and effect, selecting the
facts that are most valuable and significant and explaining
the relation between general causes and particular effects,
are all very different and belong to different types of mind.
It is idle to expect a writer with the gifts of a Clarendon,
a Kinglake, or a Froude to write history in the spirit of
a Hallam or a Grote. Writers who are eminently distinguished for wide, patient, and accurate research have
sometimes little power either of describing or interpreting
the facts which they collect. All that can be said with
any profit is that each writer will do best if he follows
the natural bent of his genius, and that he should select
those kinds or periods of history in which his special gifts
have most scope and the qualities in which he is deficient
are least needed.

It is the fashion of a modern school of historical
writers to deplore what they call the intrusion of literature
into history. History, in their judgment, should be
treated as science and not as literature, and the kind of
intellect they most value is not unlike that of a skilful
and well-trained attorney. To collect documents with
industry ; to compare, classify, interpret and estimate
them is the main work of the historian. It is no doubt
true that there are some fields of history where the
primary facts are so little known, so much contested or so
largely derived from recondite manuscript sources, that a
faithful historian will be obliged in justice to his readers

to sacrifice both proportion and artistic charm to the
supreme importance of analysing evidence, reproducing
documents and accumulating proofs; but in general the
depreciation of the literary element in history seems to
me essentially wrong. It is only necessary to recall the
names of Herodotus and Thucydides, of Livy and Tacitus,
of Gibbon and Macaulay, and of the long line of great
masters of style who have related the annals of France.
It may, indeed, be confidently asserted that there is no
subject in which rarer literary qualities are more demanded
than in the higher forms of history. The art of portraying characters; of describing events; of compressing,
arranging, and selecting great masses of heterogeneous
facts, of conducting many different chains of narrative
without confusion or obscurity; of preserving in a vast
and complicated subject the true proportion and relief,
will tax the highest literary skill, and no one who does
not possess some, at least, of these gifts in an unusual
measure is likely to attain a permanent place among the
great masters of history. It is a misfortune when some
stirring and momentous period falls into the hands of the
mere compiler, for he occupies the ground and a really
great writer will hesitate to appropriate and plagiarise the
materials his predecessor has collected. There are books
of great research and erudition which one would have
wished to have been all re-written by some writer of real
genius who could have given order, meaning and vividness to a mere chaos of accurate and laboriously sifted
learning. The great prominence which it is now the
fashion to ascribe to the study of diplomatic documents,
is very apt to destroy the true value and perspective of
history. It is always the temptation of those who are
dealing with manuscript materials to overrate the small

personal details which they bring to light, and to give them much more than their due space in their narrative. This tendency the new school powerfully encourages. It is quite right that the treasure-houses of diplomatic correspondence which have of late years been thrown open should be explored and sifted, but history written chiefly from these materials, though it has its own importance, is not likely to be distinguished either by artistic form or by philosophical value. Those who are immersed in these studies are very apt to overrate their importance and the part which diplomacy and statesmanship have borne in the great movement of human affairs.

A true and comprehensive history should be the life of a nation. It should describe it in its larger and more various aspects. It should be a study of causes and effects, of distant as well as proximate causes, and of the large, slow and permanent evolution of things. It should include, as Buckle and Macaulay saw, the social, the industrial, the intellectual life of the nation as well as mere political changes, and it should be pre-eminently marked by a true perspective dealing with subjects at a length proportioned to their real importance. All this requires a powerful and original intellect quite different from that of a mere compiler. It requires too, in a high degree, the kind of imagination which enables a man to reproduce not only the acts but the feelings, the ideals, the modes of thought and life of a distant past, and pierce through the actions and professions of men to their real characters. Insight into character is one of the first requisites of a historian. It is therefore, much to be desired that he should possess a wide knowledge of the world, the knowledge of different types of character, foreign as well as English, which

travel and society and practical experience of business
can give, and it will also be of no small advantage to him
if he has passed through more than one intellectual or
religious phase, widening the area of his appreciation and
realisations. He should also have enough of the dramatic
element to enable him to throw himself into ways of
reasoning or feeling very different from his own. One of
the most valuable of all forms of historical imagination is
that which enables a writer to place himself in the point
of view of the best men on different sides, and to bring
out the full sense of opposing arguments. All these
gifts or qualities are never in a high degree united, but
they are all essential to a great historian, and a true
school of history should widen instead of narrowing our
conception of it.

The supreme virtue of the historian is truthfulness,
and it may be violated in many different degrees. The
worst form is when a writer deliberately falsifies facts
or deliberately excludes from his picture qualifying
circumstances. But there are other and much more
subtle ways in which party spirit continually and often
quite unconsciously distorts history. All history is
necessarily a selection of facts, and a writer who is
animated by a strong sympathy with one side of a
question or a strong desire to prove some special point
will be much tempted in his selection to give an undue
prominence to those that support his view, or, even
where neither facts nor arguments are suppressed, to give
a party character to his work by an unfair distribution
of lights and shades. The strong and vivid epithets are
chiefly reserved for the good or bad deeds on one side,
the vague, general and comparatively colourless epithets
for the corresponding deeds on the other side; and in

this way very similar facts are brought before the reader with such different degrees of illumination and relief that they make a wholly different impression on his mind. In the history of Macaulay this defect may, I think, be especially traced. The characteristic defect of that great and in most respects admirable writer, both as historian and artist, was the singular absence of graduation in his mind. The neutral tints which are essential to the accurate shading of character seemed almost wanting, and a love of strong contrasted lights and shades, coupled with his supreme command of powerful epithets, continually misled him. But no attentive reader can fail to observe how unequally those epithets are distributed and how clearly this inequality discloses the strong bias under which he wrote.

The truth of an historical picture lies mainly in its judicious and accurate shading, and it is this art which the historian should especially cultivate. He will scarcely do so with success unless it becomes to him not merely a matter of duty, but also a pleasure and a pride. The kind of interest which he takes in his narrative should be much less that of a politician and an advocate than of a painter, who, now darkening and now lightening the picture, seeks by many delicate touches to catch with exact fidelity the tone and hue of the object he represents.

The degree of certainty that it is possible to attain in history varies greatly in different departments. The growth of institutions and laws, military events, changes in manners and in creeds, can be described with much confidence, and although it is more difficult to depict the inner moral life of nations, the influences that form their characters and prepare them for greatness or decay, yet when the materials for our induction are sufficiently large this field of history may be studied with great profit. Diplomatic history and the more secret springs of political history can only be fully disclosed when the archives relating to them have been explored and when the confidential correspondence of the chief actors in them has been published. The biographical element in history is always the most uncertain. Even among contemporaries the judgment of character and motives depends largely on indications so slight and subtle that they rarely pass into books and are only fully felt by direct personal contact, and the smallest knowledge of life shows how quickly anecdotes and sayings are distorted, coloured, and misplaced when they pass from lip to lip. Most of the 'good sayings' of history are invention, and most of them have been attributed to different persons. A history which is plainly written under the influence of party bias has the value of an advocate's speech giving one side of the question. When our only materials for the knowledge of a period are derived from such histories, the saying of Voltaire should be remembered—that we can confidently believe only the evil which a party writer tells of his own side and the good which he recognises in his opponents. In judging the historian we must consider his nearness to the events he relates, his probable means of information and the internal evidence in his narrative of accuracy, honesty, and judgment, and we must also consider the standard of proof and the methods of historical writing prevailing in his time. A modern writer who placed in the mouths of his personages speeches which he himself invented would be justly discredited, but in antiquity it was a recognised custom for a historian to embody in fictitious speeches the reflections suggested by his narrative and the motives which he believed to have actuated his heroes.

Different ages differ enormously in the severity of proof which they exact, in the degree of accuracy which they attain. The credibility of a statement also depends not only on the amount of its evidence, but also on its own inherent probability. Everyone will feel that an amount of testimony that would be quite sufficient to persuade him that a butcher's boy had been seen driving along a highway is wholly different from that which would be required to persuade him that a ghost had been met there. The same rule applies to the history of the past, and it is complicated by the great difference in different ages of the measure of probability, or, in other words, by the strong predisposition in certain stages of knowledge to accept statements or explanations of facts which in later stages we know to be incredible or in a high degree improbable. Few subjects in history are more difficult than the laws of evidence in dealing with the supernatural and the extent to which the authority of historians in relating credible and probable facts is invalidated by the presence of a mythical element in their narratives.

Connected with this subject is also the question how far it is possible by merely internal evidence to decompose an ancient document, resolving it into its separate elements, distinguishing its different dates and its different degrees of credibility. The reader is no doubt aware with what a rare skill this method of inquiry has been pursued in the present century, chiefly by great German and Dutch scholars, in dealing with the early Jewish writings. At the same time, without disputing the value of their work or the importance of many of the results at which they have arrived, I may be pardoned for expressing my belief that this kind of investigation is often pursued with an exaggerated confidence. Plausible conjecture is too frequently mistaken for positive proof. Undue significance is attached to what may be mere casual coincidences, and a minuteness of accuracy is professed in discriminating between the different elements in a narrative which cannot be attained by mere internal evidence. In all writings, but especially in the writings of an age when criticism was unknown, there will be repetitions, contradictions, inconsistencies and diversities of style which do not necessarily indicate different authorship or dates.

I have spoken of the uncertainty of the biographical element in history. It must, however, be said that when a historian is dealing with men who have played a very prominent part on the stage of life, the general acceptance of his judgment is a strong corroboration of its truth. It may be added that the later judgment of men is not unfrequently more true than the contemporary judgment. The wisdom of a teaching or of a policy is shown by its results, and these results are in most cases very gradually disclosed. Great men are like great mountains which are surrounded by lower peaks that often obscure their grandeur and seem to a near observer to equal or even to overtop them. It is only when seen from far off that their true dimensions are fully realised and they soar to heaven above all rivals. In the page of history men are judged mainly by the net result of their lives, by the broad lines of their characters and achievements. Many injudicious words, many minor weaknesses of conduct, are forgotten. Faults of manner, deficiencies of tact, awkwardnesses of appearance, which tell so largely upon the judgments of contemporaries, are no longer seen. The

conversational nimbleness and versatility of intellect, the
charm or assurance or magnetism of manner, the weight
of social position, all of which tend to secure to an
inferior man a pre-eminence in the circle in which he
moves, are equally evanescent, and the shy, rugged, and
tactless recluse often emerges on the strength of his
genuine and abiding performances to a position in the
eyes of the world which he never attained during his
lifetime.

That fine saying of Cardan, 'Tempus mea possessio,
tempus ager meus,' might be the motto of the historian.
Time is the field which he cultivates, and a true sense of
space and distance should be one of the chief characteristics of his work. Few things are more difficult to
attain than a just perspective in history. The most
dramatic incidents are not the most important, and in
weighing the joys and sorrows of the past our measures
of judgment are almost hopelessly false. The most
humane man cannot emancipate himself from the law of
his nature, according to which he is more affected by
some tragic circumstance which has taken place in his
own house or in his own street than by a catastrophe which
has carried anguish and desolation over enormous areas in
a distant continent. In history, too, there are vast tracts
which are almost necessarily unrealised. We judge a
period mainly by its great men, by its brilliant or salient
incidents, by the fortunes of a small class ; and the great
mass of obscure, suffering, inarticulate humanity, whose
happiness is often so profoundly affected by political and
military events, almost escapes our notice. It should
be the object of history to bring before us past events in
their true proportion and significance, and one of the
greatest improvements in modern history is the increased

attention which is paid to the social, industrial, and moral history of the poor. The paucity of our information and the difficulty of realising the conditions of obscure multitudes will always make this branch of history very imperfect, but it is one of the most essential to the just judgment of the past.

Another task which lies before the historian is that of distinguishing proximate from ultimate causes. Our first natural impulse is to attribute a great change to the men who effected it and to the period in which it took place, and to neglect or underrate the long train of causes which had been, often through many generations, preparing its advent. A faithful historian must especially guard against this error. He must study the slow process of growth as well as the moment of efflorescence, the long progress of decay as well as the final catastrophe. He will probably find that the part played by statesmen and legislatures is less than he had imagined, and that the causes of the movements he relates must be sought over a wider area and through a longer period.

Moral, intellectual, or economical movements very slightly connected with political life are often those which have most largely contributed to the good or evil fortunes of a nation ; and even in the sphere of politics it is not the events which attract the most vivid contemporary interest that have the most enduring influence. Few things contribute so much to the formation of the social type as the laws regulating the succession of property and especially the agglomeration or division of landed property. The growth of militarism in a nation, besides its direct and obvious consequences, forms a type of character which will sooner or later show itself in almost every department of legislation, and the tendency

of politics to enlarge or narrow the sphere of individual
liberty or of government control, will affect most deeply
the habits of the people. Laws regulating private enterprises, substituting State control or initiative for individual
action, encouraging or discouraging thrift, and above all
interfering with free contracts, have much more than
an immediate influence, for they become the prolific
parents of many further extensions. In the words of an
excellent observer, it will be found 'that our legislative
interference is but the first link of a long chain of repetitions, every subsequent interference being naturally
produced by the effects of the preceding.' It is by
studying such tendencies through long periods of time
that their good or evil influences may be best discovered,
and this should be one of the great tasks of the historian.

But, however large a part may be given to the im-
personal influences in history, he will still be largely
concerned with the record of individual achievements, and
the great men of the past will form the most conspicuous
landmarks of his narrative. I have often thought, however, that nations are judged too much by the great men
they have produced and not sufficiently by the way in
which they have discriminated among them and appreciated them. Genius is like the wind that bloweth where
it listeth, and it often appears in strangely uncongenial
quarters. The true nobility of a nation is shown by the
men they choose, by the men they follow, by the men
they admire, by the ideals of character and conduct they
place before them. Tried by such tests, there is often
much that is profoundly saddening in the history of
countries that have been far from poor in the number of
their great men.

In the judgment of historical characters there are two

cautions on which it may not be useless to dwell. There is a large class of public men who show little capacity in dealing with or directing the present conditions of their time, but who see clearly the bourne to which existing forces or tendencies are moving and who, judged by their distant forecasts, will appear much wiser than their contemporaries. It is the natural bias of the historian to place them perhaps higher than they deserve. This power of just speculative foresight is no very rare gift, and in public affairs it is often as much a hindrance as a help. Forms of government and other great religious or political institutions, like the products of nature, have their times of immaturity, of growth, of ripeness and of decay, and it by no means follows because they at last become indefensible, that they have not during many generations discharged useful functions and that those who first assailed and condemned them are deserving of praise. Not unfrequently, indeed, a public man must take his choice whether by fully identifying himself with the existing conditions around him and employing them to the best advantages he will lead a useful and practical life, or whether as an advanced thinker he will associate himself with the cause that is one day to conquer, place himself in the van of progress and at the sacrifice of much present influence deserve the credit of foresight.

Historians will probably always judge men and policies by their net results, by their final consequences, and this judgment is on the whole the most sure that we can attain. It is not, however, altogether infallible. Apart from the question of the moral character of the methods employed which a good historian should never omit from his consideration, success is not always a decisive proof of sagacity. Chance and the unexpected play a great part in human affairs, and a judgment founded on a perfectly just estimate of probabilities will often prove wrong. The result which was the least probable will come true, some wholly unforeseen and unforeseeable occurrence will scatter dangers that were very real and give a new complexion to events. The rise of some pre-eminently great or of some pre-eminently mischievous personage among the guiding influences of a nation will derange the most sagacious calculations, and the reckless gambler or the obtuse obstructionist may prove more right than the most cautious, the most skilful, the most farseeing statesman.

A fatal and very common error is that of judging the actions of the past by the moral standard of our own age. This is especially the error of novices in history and of those who without any wide and general culture devote themselves exclusively to a single period. While the primary and essential elements of right and wrong remain unchanged, nothing is more certain than that the standard or ideal of duty is continually altering. A very humane man in another age may have done things which would now be regarded as atrociously barbarous. A very virtuous man may have done things which would now indicate extreme profligacy. We seldom indeed make sufficient allowance for the degree in which the judgments and dispositions of even the best man are coloured by the moral tone of the time or society in which they live. And what is true of individuals is equally true of nations. In order to judge equitably the legislation of any people, we must always consider corresponding contemporary legislations and ideas. When this is neglected our judgments of the past become wholly false. How often, for example, has such a subject as the history of the penal laws against Irish Catholics been treated without the smallest reference to the contemporary laws against Protestants that existed in every Catholic nation and the contemporary laws against Catholics that existed in almost every Protestant country in Europe. How often have the English commercial restrictions on the American colonies been treated as if they were instances of extreme and exceptional tyranny, while a more extended knowledge would show that they were simply the expression of ideas of commercial policy and about the relation of dependencies to the mother-country which then almost universally prevailed.

It is not merely the moral standard that changes. A corresponding change takes place in the moral type, or, in other words, in the class of virtues which is especially cultivated and especially valued. To know an age aright we should above all things seek to understand its ideal, the direction in which the stream of its self-sacrifice and moral energy naturally flowed. Few things in history are more interesting and more valuable than a study of the causes that produced and modified these successive ideals. Thus in the moral type of pagan antiquity the civic virtues occupied incomparably the foremost place. The idea of a supremely good man was essentially that of a man of action, of a man whose whole life was devoted to the service of his country. The life and death of Cato were for generations the favourite model. He was deemed, in the words of an old Latin historian, to be of all men the one 'most like to virtue.' This pattern retained its force till the softening influence of the Greek spirit, permeating Roman life, made the stoical ideal seem too hard and unsympathising; till the corruption and despotism of the Empire had withdrawn the best men from political life and attached a certain taint or stigma to public employment; till new religions arose in the East, bringing with them new ideals to govern the world. Gradually we may trace the contemplative virtues rising to the foremost place until, about the fifth century, the ideal had totally changed. The heroic type was replaced by the saintly type. The supremely good man was now the ascetic. The first condition of sanctity was a complete abandonment of secular duties and cares and a complete subjugation of the body. A vast literature of legends arose reflecting and glorifying the prevailing ideal and holding up the hermit life as the supreme pattern of perfection, and this literature occupies a place in mediævalism very similar to that held by the 'Lives' of Plutarch in antiquity.

Ancient art was essentially the glorification of the body, a representation of the full strength and beauty of developed manhood. The saint of the mediæval mosaic represents the body in its extreme maceration and humiliation. The rhetorician, Dio Chrysostom, in a somewhat whimsical passage, which was suggested by a remark of Plato, found a special moral significance in the fact that Homer, though he places his heroes on the the banks of what he calls 'the fishy Hellespont," never makes them eat fish, but always flesh and the flesh of oxen, for this, as he says, is 'strength-producing food' and is therefore suited for the formation of heroes and the proper diet for men of virtue. Compare this judgment with the protracted, and indeed incredible, fasts which the monkish writers delighted in attributing to the saints of the desert, and we have a vivid picture of the change that had passed over the ideal.

But as time moved on the ascetic ideal gradually

declined and was replaced by the very different ideal of chivalry. It consisted chiefly of three new elements. The first element was a spirit of gallantry which gave women a wholly new place in the imaginations of men. It was in part a reaction against the extreme austerity of the saints, and this reaction was much intensified after the cessation of the panic which had risen at the close of the tenth century about the approaching end of the world. It was in part produced by the softer and more epicurean civilisation which grew up in the country bordering on the Pyrenees. It was especially represented in the romances and poems of the Troubadours, and the new tendency even received some assistance from the Church when the Council of Clermont, which originated the Crusades, imposed on the knight the religious obligation of defending all widows and orphans.

The second element was an increased reverence for secular rank, which grew out of the feudal system, when a great hereditary aristocracy arose and all European society was moulded into a compact hierarchy, of which the serf was the basis and the emperor the apex. The principle of subordination and obedience ran through the whole edifice, and a respect for rank was universally diffused. Men came to associate their ideal of greatness with regal or noble authority, and they were therefore prepared to idealise any great sovereign who might arise. Such a sovereign appeared in Charlemagne, who exercised upon Christendom a fascination not less powerful than that which Alexander had once exercised upon Greece, and he accordingly soon became the centre of a whole literature of romance.

The third element was the fusion of religious enthusiasm with the military spirit. Christianity in its first

C

phases was utterly opposed to the military spirit; but
this opposition was naturally mitigated when the Church
triumphed under Constantine and became associated with
governments and armies. The hostility was still further
qualified when many tribes of warlike barbarians embraced
the faith, and the military obligation which was an
essential element of feudalism acted in the same direction.
But, above all, the rise and conquests of Mohammedanism awoke the military energies of Christendom
and determined the direction it should take. In the
Crusades the two great streams of military enthusiasm
and of religious enthusiasm met, and the result was the
formation of a new ideal which for a long period mainly
governed the imagination of Christendom.

It for a time absorbed, eclipsed, and transformed all
purely national ideals. No poet was ever more intensely
English in his character and sympathies than Chaucer,
and he wrote when the dazzling glories of Crécy and
Poitiers were still very recent. Yet it is not on these
fields, but in the long wars with the Moslems, that his
pattern knight had won his renown. The military
expeditions of Charlemagne were directed almost exclusively against the Saxons and against Slavonic tribes.
With the Spanish Mohammedans he came but very slightly
in contact. He made in person but one expedition against
them, and that expedition was both insignificant and unsuccessful. But in the Karlovingian romances, which
were written when the crusading enthusiasm was at its
height, the figure of the great emperor underwent a strange
and most significant transformation. The German wars
were scarcely noticed. Charlemagne is surrounded with
the special glory that ought to have belonged to Charles
Martel. He is represented as having passed his entire life

in a victorious struggle with the Mohammedans of Europe, and is even gravely credited with a triumphant expedition to Jerusalem. The three romances of the Crusades which are believed to be the oldest were all written by monks, and they all make Charlemagne their hero. Even geography was transformed by the new enthusiasm, and old maps sometimes represent Jerusalem as the centre of the world.

In few periods has there been, so great a difference between the ideals created by the popular imagination and the realities that are recognised by history. Few wars have been accompanied by more cruelty, more outrage, and more licentiousness than the Crusades or have brought a blacker cloud of disasters in their train. Yet the idea that inspired them was a lofty one, and they were so speedily transfigured by the imaginations of men that in combination with the other influences I have mentioned they created an ideal which is one of the most beautiful in the history of the world. We may trace it clearly in the romances of Arthur and Charlemagne and of the " Cid ; " in the " Red-Cross Knight " of Tasso and Spenser ; in the old ballads which paint so vividly the hero of chivalry, ever ready to draw his sword for his faith and his lady-love and in the cause of the feeble and the oppressed. The glorification of military courage and self-sacrifice which had been so prominent in antiquity was again in the ascendant, but it was combined with a new kind of honour and with a new vein of courtesy, modesty, and gentleness. When we apply the epithet ' chivalrous ' to a modern gentleman, this is no unmeaning term. There is even now an element in that character which may be distinctly traced to the ideal of chivalry which the Crusades made dominant in Europe.

I do not propose to follow the history of other ideals that have in turn prevailed. What I have written will, I trust, be sufficient to illustrate a kind of history which appears to me to possess much interest and value. It will show, too, that a faithful historian is very largely concerned with the fictions as well as with the facts of the past. Legends which have no firm historical basis are often of the highest historical value as reflecting the moral sentiments of their time. Nor do they merely reflect them. In some periods they contribute perhaps more than any other influence to mould and colour them and to give them an enduring strength. The facts of history have been largely governed by its fictions. Great events often acquire their full power over the human mind only when they have passed through the transfiguring medium of the imagination, and men as they were supposed to be have even sometimes exercised a wider influence than men as they actually were. Ideals ultimately rule the world, and each before it loses its ascendancy bequeaths some moral truth as an abiding legacy to the human race.

THE POLITICAL VALUE OF HISTORY

WHEN, shortly after I had accepted the honourable task which I am endeavouring to fulfil to-night, I received from your Secretary a report of the annual proceedings of the Birmingham and Midland Institute,—when I observed the immense range and variety of subjects included within your programme, illustrating so strikingly the intense intellectual activity of this great town,—my first feeling was one of some bewilderment and dismay. What, I asked myself, could I say that would be of much real value, addressing an unknown audience, and relating to fields of knowledge so vast, so multifarious, and in many of their parts so far beyond the range of my own studies? On reflection, however, it appeared to me that in this, as in most other cases, the proverb was a wise one which bids the cobbler stick to his last, and that a writer who, during many years of his life, has been engaged in the study of English history could hardly do better than devote the time at his disposal to-night to a few reflections on the political value of history, and on the branches and methods of historical study that are most fitted to form a sound political judgment.

Is history a study of real use in practical, and especially in political, life? The question, as you know, has been by no means always answered in the same way. In its earlier stages history was regarded chiefly as a form of poetry recording the more dramatic actions of kings,

warriors, and statesmen. Homer and the early ballads
are indeed the first historians of their countries, and long
after Homer one of the most illustrious of the critics of
antiquity described history as merely 'poetry free from
the incumbrance of verse.' The portraits that adorned
it gave some insight into human character; it breathed
noble sentiments, rewarded and stimulated noble actions,
and kindled by its strong appeals to the imagination high
patriotic feeling; but its end was rather to paint than to
guide, to consecrate a noble past than to furnish a key
for the future; and the artist in selecting his facts looked
mainly for those which could throw the richest colour upon
his canvas. Most experience was in his eyes (to adopt an
image of Coleridge) like the stern light of a ship, which
illuminates only the path we have already traversed;
and a large proportion of the subjects which are most
significant as illustrating the true welfare and development of nations were deliberately rejected as below the
dignity of history. The old conception of history can
hardly be better illustrated than in the words of Savage
Landor. 'Show me,' he makes one of his heroes say,
'how great projects were executed, great advantages
gained, and great calamities averted. Show me the
generals and the statesmen who stood foremost, that I
may bend to them in reverence. . . . Let the books of
the Treasury lie closed as religiously as the Sibyl's.
Leave weights and measures in the market-place; Commerce in the harbour; the Arts in the light they love;
Philosophy in the shade. Place History on her rightful
throne, and at the sides of her Eloquence and War.'[1]

It was chiefly in the eighteenth century that a very
different conception of history grew up. Historians then

----

[1] *Pericles and Aspasia.*

came to believe that their task was not so much to paint a picture as to solve a problem; to explain or illustrate the successive phases of national growth, prosperity, and adversity. The history of morals, of industry, of intellect, and of art; the changes that take place in manners or beliefs; the dominant ideas that prevailed in successive periods; the rise, fall, and modification of political constitutions; in a word, all the conditions of national well-being became the subjects of their works. They sought rather to write a history of peoples than a history of kings. They looked specially in history for the chain of causes and effects. They undertook to study in the past the physiology of nations, and hoped by applying the experimental method on a large scale to deduce some lessons of real value about the conditions on which the well-being of society mainly depends.

How far have they succeeded in their attempt, and furnished us with a real compass for political guidance? Let me in the first place frankly express my own belief that to many readers of history the study is not only useless, but even positively misleading. An unintelligent, a superficial, a pedantic or an inaccurate use of history is the source of very many errors in practical judgment. Human affairs are so infinitely complex that it is vain to expect that they will ever exactly reproduce themselves, or that any study of the past can enable us to predict the future with the minuteness and the completeness that can be attained in the exact sciences. Nor will any wise man judge the merits of existing institutions solely on historic grounds. Do not persuade yourself that any institution, however great may be its antiquity, however transcendent may have been its uses in a remote past, can permanently justify its existence, unless it can be

shown to exercise a really beneficial influence over our
own society and our own age. It is equally true that no
institution which is exercising such a beneficial influence
should be condemned, because it can be shown from
history that under other conditions and in other times its
influence was rather for evil than for good.

These propositions may seem like truisms ; yet how
often do we hear a kind of reasoning that is inconsistent
with them ! How often, for example, in the discussions
on the Continent on the advantages and disadvantages of
monastic institutions has the chief stress of the argument
been laid upon the great benefits which those institutions
produced in ages that were utterly different from our
own,—in the dark period of the barbarian invasions, when
they were the only refuges of a pacific civilisation, the
only libraries, the only schools, the only centres of art,
the only refuge for gentle and intellectual natures ; the
chief barrier against violence and rapine; the chief
promoters of agriculture and industry ! How often in
discussions on the merits and demerits of an Established
Church in England have we heard arguments drawn from
the hostility which the Church of England showed
towards English liberty in the time of the Stuarts ;
although it is abundantly evident that the dangers of
a royal despotism, which were then so serious, have
utterly disappeared, and that the political action of the
Church of England at that period was mainly governed
by a doctrine of the Divine right of kings, and of the duty
of passive obedience, which is now as dead as the old
belief that the king's touch could cure scrofula ! How
often have the champions of modern democracy appealed
in support of their views to the glories of the democracies
of ancient Greece, without ever reminding their hearers

that these small municipal republics rested on the basis of slavery, and that the bulk of those who would exercise the chief controlling influence over affairs in a pure democracy of the modern type were absolutely excluded from political power! How often in discussions about the advantages and disadvantages of Home Rule in Ireland do we find arguments drawn from the merits or demerits of the Irish Parliament of the eighteenth century, with a complete forgetfulness of the fact that this Parliament consisted exclusively of a Protestant gentry; that it represented in the highest degree the property of the country, and the classes who are most closely attached to English rule; that it was constituted in such a manner that the English Government could exercise a complete control over its deliberations, and that for good or for ill it was utterly unlike any body that could now be constituted in Ireland!

Or again, to turn to another field : it is quite certain that every age has special dangers to guard against, and that as time moves on these dangers not only change, but are sometimes even reversed. There have been periods in English history when the great dangers to be encountered sprang from the excessive and encroaching power of a monarchy or of an aristocracy. The battle to be then fought was for the free exercise of religious worship and expression of religious opinion, for a free parliament, for a free press, for a free platform, for an independent jury-box. All the best patriotism, all the most heroic self-sacrifice of the nation, was thrown into defence of these causes ; and the wisest statesmen of the time made it the main object of their legislation to protect and consolidate them.

These things are now as valuable as they ever were,

but no reasonable man will maintain that they are in the smallest danger. The battles of the sixteenth and seventeenth centuries have been definitely won. A kind of language which at one period of English history implied the noblest heroism is now the idlest and cheapest of clap-trap. The sycophant and the self-seeker bow before quite other idols than of old. The dangers of the time come from other quarters ; other tendencies prevail, other tasks remain to be accomplished ; and a public man who in framing his course followed blindly in the steps of the heroes or reformers of the past would be like a mariner who set his sails to the winds of yesterday.

It is difficult, I think, to doubt that the judgments of all of us are more or less affected by causes of this kind. It is, I imagine, true of the great majority of educated men that their first political impression or bias is formed much less by the events of their own time than by childish recollections of the more dramatic conflicts of the past. We are Cavaliers or Roundheads before we are Conservatives or Liberals ; and although we gradually learn to realise how profoundly the condition of affairs and the balance of forces have altered, yet no wise man can doubt the power which the first bias of the imagination exercises in very many cases through a whole life. Language which grew out of bygone conflicts continues to be used long after those conflicts and their causes have ended; but that which was once a very genuine voice comes at last to be little more than an insincere echo.

The best corrective for this kind of evil is a really intelligent study of history. One of the first tasks that every sincere student should set before himself is to endeavour to understand what is the dominant idea or characteristic of the period with which he is occupied ;

what forces chiefly ruled it, what forces were then rising into a dangerous ascendancy, and what forces were on the decline; what illusions, what exaggerations, what false hopes and unworthy influences chiefly prevailed. It is only when studied in this spirit that the true significance of history is disclosed, and the same method which furnishes a key to the past forms also an admirable discipline for the judgment of the present. He who has learnt to understand the true character and tendencies of many succeeding ages is not likely to go very far wrong in estimating his own.

Another branch of history which I would especially commend to the attention of all political students is the history of Institutions. In the constantly fluctuating conditions of human life no institution ever remained for a long period unaltered. Sometimes with changed beliefs and changed conditions institutions lose all their original utility. They become simply useless, obstructive, and corrupt; and though by mere passive resistance they may continue to exist long after they have ceased to serve any good purpose, they will at last be undermined by their own abuses. Other institutions, on the other hand, show the true characteristic of vitality—the power of adapting themselves to changed conditions and new utilities. Few things in history are more interesting and more instructive than a careful study of these transformations. Sometimes the original objects almost wholly disappear, and utilities which were either never contemplated by the founders or were only regarded as of purely secondary importance take the first place on the scene. The old plan and symmetry almost disappear as the institution is modified now in this direction and now in that to meet some pressing want. The first architects, if they could rise from the dead, would scarcely recognise their creation—would perhaps look on it with horror. The indirect advantages of an institution are sometimes greater than its direct ones; and institutions are often more valuable on account of the evils they avert than on account of the positive advantages they produce. Not unfrequently in their later and transformed condition they exercise wider and greater influence than when they were originally established; for the strength derived from the long traditions of the past and from the habits that are formed around anything that is deeply rooted in the national life gives them a vastly increased importance.

There is probably no better test of the political genius of a nation than the power which it possesses of adapting old institutions to new wants; and it is, I think, in this skill and in this disposition that the political pre-eminence of the English people has been most conspicuously shown. It is difficult to overrate its importance. It is the institutions of a country that chiefly maintain the sense of its organic unity, its essential connection with its past. By their continuous existence they bind together as by a living chain the past with the present, the living with the dead.

Few greater calamities can befall a nation than to cut herself off, as France did in her great Revolution, from all vital connection with her own past. This is one of the chief lessons you will learn from Burke—the greatest and truest of all our political teachers. Bacon expressed in an admirable sentence the best spirit of English politics when he urged that 'men in their innovations should follow the example of Time itself, which indeed innovated greatly, but quietly, and by degrees scarcely to be perceived.'

There is a third department of history which appears to me especially valuable to political students. It is the history of those vast Revolutions for good or for ill which seem to have transformed the characters or permanently changed the fortunes of nations, either by a sudden and violent shock or by the slow process of gradual renovation. You will find on this subject, in our country, two great and opposite exaggerations. There is a school of writers, of which Buckle is an admirable representative, who are so struck by the long chain of causes, extending over many centuries, that preceded and prepared Revolutions, that they teach a kind of historic fatalism, reducing almost to nothing the action of Individualities ; and there is another school, which is specially represented by Carlyle, who reduce all history into biographies, into the action of a few great men upon their kind.

The one class of writers will tell you with great truth that the Roman Republic was not destroyed by Cæsar, but by the long train of influences that made the career of Cæsar a possibility. They will show how influences working through many generations had sapped the foundations of the Republic—how the beliefs and habits on which it once rested had passed away—how its institutions no longer corresponded with the prevailing wants and ideas—how a form of government which had proved excellently adapted for a restricted dominion failed when the Roman eagles flew triumphantly over the whole civilised world, and how in this manner the strongest tendencies of the time were preparing the downfall of the Republic, and the establishment of a great empire upon its ruins. They will show how the intellectual influences of the Renaissance, the invention of printing, and a crowd of other causes, many of them at first sight very remote from theological controversies, had in the sixteenth century so shaken the power of the Roman Catholic Church, that the way was prepared for the Reformation, and it became possible for Luther and Calvin to succeed, where Wyckliffe and Huss had failed. They will show how profoundly our theological beliefs are affected by our general conception of the system of the universe, and how inevitably, as Science changes the latter, the former will undergo a corresponding process of modification. Creeds that are no longer in harmony with the general spirit of the time may long continue, but a new spirit will be breathed into the old forms. Those portions which are most discordant with our fresh knowledge will be neglected or attenuated. Although they may not be openly discarded, they will cease to be realised or vitally operative.

In the sphere of politics a similar law prevails, and the fate of nations largely depends upon forces quite different from those on which the mere political historian concentrates his attention. The growth of military or industrial habits; the elevation or depression of different classes; the changes that take place in the distribution of wealth; inventions or discoveries that alter the course or character of industry or commerce, or reverse the relative advantages of different nations in the competitions of life; the increase and, still more, the diffusion of knowledge; the many influences that affect convictions, habits and ideals, that raise, or lower, or modify the moral tone and type—all these things concur in shaping the destinies of nations. Legislation is only really successful when it is in harmony with the general spirit of the age. Laws and statesmen for the most part indicate and ratify, but do not create. They are like the hands of the watch, which move obedient to the hidden machinery behind.

In all this kind of speculation there is, I believe, great truth, and it opens out fields of inquiry that are of the utmost interest and importance. I have, however, long thought that it has been pushed by some modern writers to extravagant exaggeration. As you well know, there is another aspect of history, which, long before Carlyle, was enforced by some of the ablest and most independent intellects of Christendom. Pascal tells us that if Cleopatra's nose had been shorter, the whole face of the world might have been changed, and Voltaire is never tired of dwelling on the small springs on which the greatest events of history turn. Frederick the Great, who was probably the keenest practical intellect of his age, constantly insisted on the same view. In the vast field of politics, he maintained, casual events which no human sagacity can predict play by far the largest part. We are in most cases groping our way blindly in the dark. Occasionally, when favourable circumstances occur, there is a gleam of light of which the skilful avail themselves. All the rest is uncertainty. The world is mainly governed by a multitude of secondary, obscure, or impenetrable causes. It is a game of chance in which the most skilful may lose like the most ignorant. ' The older one becomes the more clearly one sees that King Hazard fashions three-fourths of the events in this miserable world.'

My own view of this question is that though there are certain streams of tendency, though there is a certain steady and orderly evolution that it is impossible in the long run to resist, yet individual action and even mere accident have borne a very great part in modifying the direction of history. It is with History as with the general laws of Nature. We can none of us escape the all-pervading force of gravitation, or the influence of the climate under which we live, or the succession of the seasons, or the laws of growth and of decay ; yet man is not a mere passive weed drifting helplessly upon the sea of life, and human wisdom and human folly can do and have done much to modify the conditions of his being.

It is quite true that religions depend largely for their continued vitality upon the knowledge and intellectual atmosphere of their time ; but there are periods when the human mind is in such a state of pliancy that a small pressure can give it a bent which will last for generations. If Mohammed had been killed in one of the first skir-mishes of his career, I know no reason for believing that a great monotheistic religion would have arisen in Arabia, capable of moulding for more than twelve hundred years not only the beliefs, laws, and governments, but also the inmost moral and mental character of a vast section of the human race. Gibbon was probably right in his conjecture that if Charles Martel had been defeated at the famous battle near Tours, the creed of Islam would have overspread a great part of what is now Christian Europe, and in that case it might have ruled over it for centuries. No one can follow the history of the conver-sion of the barbarians to Christianity without perceiving how often a religion has been imposed in the first instance by the mere will of the ruler, which gradually took such root that it became far too strong for any political power to destroy. Persecution cannot annihilate a creed which is firmly established, or maintain a creed which has been thoroughly undermined, but there are intermediate stages in which its influence on national beliefs has been enormously great. Even at the Reformation, though more general causes were of capital importance, political events had a very large part in defining the frontier line between the rival creeds, and the divisions so created have for the most part endured.

In secular politics numerous instances of the same kind will occur to every thoughtful reader of history. If, as might easily have happened, Hannibal after the battle of Cannae had taken and burned Rome, and transferred the supremacy of the world to a maritime commercial State upon the Mediterranean; if, instead of the Regency, Louis XV. and Louis XVI., France had passed during the eighteenth century under sovereigns of the stamp of the elder branch of the House of Orange or of Henry IV., or of the Great Elector, or of Frederick the Great; if, at the French Revolution, the supreme military genius had been connected with the character of Washington rather than with the character of Napoleon—who can doubt that the course of European history would have been vastly changed? The causes that made constitutional liberty succeed in England, while it failed in other countries where its prospects seemed once at least as promising, are many and complex; but no careful student of English history will doubt the prominence among them of the accidental fact that James II., by embracing Catholicism, had thrown the Church feeling at a very critical moment into opposition to the monarchical feeling, and that in the last days of Anne, when the question of the succession was trembling most doubtfully in the balance, his son refused to conform to the Anglican creed.

Laws are no doubt in a great degree inoperative when they do not spring from and represent the opinion of the nation, but they have in their turn a great power of consolidating, deepening, and directing opinion. When some important progress has been attained, and with the support of public opinion has been embodied in a law, that law will do much to prevent the natural reflux of the wave. It becomes a kind of moral landmark, a powerful educating influence, and by giving what had been achieved the sanction of legality, it contributes largely to its permanence. Roman law undoubtedly played a great part in European history long after all the conditions in which it was first enacted had passed away, and the legislator who can determine in any country the system of national education, or the succession of property, will do much to influence the opinions and social types of many succeeding generations.

The point, however, on which I would here especially insist is that there has scarcely been a great revolution in the world which might not at some stage of its progress have been either averted, or materially modified, or at least greatly postponed, by wise statesmanship and timely compromise. Take, for example, the American Revolution, which destroyed the political unity of the English race. You will often hear this event treated as if it were simply due to the wanton tyranny of an English Government, which desired to reduce its colonies to servitude by taxing them without their consent. But if you will look closely into the history of that time—and there is no history which is more instructive—you will find that this is a gross misrepresentation. What happened was essentially this. England, under the guidance of the elder Pitt, had been waging a great and most successful war, which left her with an enormously extended Empire, but also with an addition of more than seventy millions to her

National Debt. That debt was now nearly one hundred and forty millions, and England was reeling under the taxation it required. The war had been waged largely in America, and its most brilliant result was the conquest of Canada, by which the old American colonies had benefited more than any other part of the Empire, for the expulsion of the French from North America put an end to the one great danger which hung over them. It was, however, extremely probable that if France ever regained her strength, one of her first objects would be to recover her dominion in America.

Under these circumstances the English Government concluded that it was impossible that England alone, overburdened as she was by taxation, could undertake the military defence of her greatly extended Empire. Their object, therefore, was to create subsidiary armies for its defence. Ireland already raised by the vote of the Irish Parliament, and out of exclusively Irish resources, an army consisting of from twelve to fifteen thousand men, most of whom were available for the general purposes of the Empire. In India, under a despotic system, a separate army was maintained for the protection of India. It was the strong belief of the English Government that a third army should be maintained in America for the defence of the American colonies and of the neighbouring islands, and that it was just and reasonable that America should bear some part of the expense of her own defence. She was charged with no part of the interest of the National Debt; she paid nothing towards the cost of the navy which protected her coast; she was the most lightly taxed and the most prosperous portion of the Empire; she was the part which had benefited most by the late war, and she was the part which was most likely to be

menaced if the war was renewed. Under these circumstances Grenville determined that a small army of
ten thousand men should be kept in America, under the
distinct promise that it was never to serve beyond that
country and the West Indian Isles, and he asked America
to contribute 100,000l. a year, or about a third part of
its expense.

But here the difficulty arose. The Irish army was
maintained by the vote of the Irish Parliament; but
there was no single parliament representing the American
colonies, and it soon became evident that it was impossible to induce thirteen State legislatures to agree
upon any scheme for supporting an army in America.
Under these circumstances Grenville in an ill-omened
moment resolved to revive a dormant power which
existed in the Constitution, and levy this new war-tax by
Imperial taxation. He at the same time guaranteed the
colonists that the proceeds of this tax should be expended
solely in America; he intimated to them in the clearest
way that if they would meet his wishes by themselves
providing the necessary sum, he would be abundantly
satisfied, and he delayed the enforcement of the measure
for a year in order to give them ample time for doing so.

Such and so small was the original cause of difference
between England and her colonies. Who can fail to see
that it was a difference abundantly susceptible of compromise, and that a wise and moderate statesmanship
might easily have averted the catastrophe? There are
few sadder and few more instructive pages in history than
those which show how mistake after mistake was committed, till the rift which was once so small widened and
deepened; till the two sections of the English race were
thrown into an irreconcilable antagonism, and the fair

vision of an United Empire in the East and in the West came for ever to an end.

Or glance for a moment at the French Revolution. It is a favourite task of historians to trace through the preceding generations the long train of causes that made the transformation of French institutions absolutely inevitable; but it is not so often remembered that when the States-General met in 1789 by far the larger part of the benefits of the Revolution could have been attained without difficulty, without convulsion, and by general consent. The nobles and clergy had pledged themselves to surrender their feudal privileges and their privileges in taxation; a reforming king was on the throne, and a reforming minister was at his side. If the spirit of moderation had then prevailed, the inevitable transformation might probably have been made without the effusion of a drop of blood. Jefferson was at this time the Minister of the United States in Paris. As an old republican he knew well the conditions of free governments, and among the politicians of his own country he represented the democratic section. I know few words in history more pathetic than those in which he described the situation. 'I was much acquainted,' he writes, 'with the leading patriots of the Assembly. Being from a country which had successfully passed through a similar reformation, they were disposed to my acquaintance, and had some confidence in me. I urged most strenuously an immediate compromise to secure what the Government were now ready to yield. . . . It was well understood that the King would grant at this time (1) freedom of the person by Habeas Corpus; (2) freedom of conscience; (3) freedom of the press; (4) trial by jury; (5) a representative legislature; (6) annual meetings; (7) the origination of laws ; (8) the exclusive right of taxation and appropriation; and (9) the responsibility of Ministers; and with the exercise of these powers they could obtain in future whatever might be further necessary to improve and preserve their constitution. They thought otherwise,' continued Jefferson; 'and events have proved their lamentable error ; for after thirty years of war, foreign and domestic, the loss of millions of lives, the prostration of private happiness, and the foreign subjugation of their own country for a time, they have obtained no more, nor even that securely.' [1]

Let me, in concluding these observations, sum up in a few words some other advantages which you may derive from history. It is, I think, one of the best schools for that kind of reasoning which is most useful in practical life. It teaches men to weigh conflicting probabilities, to estimate degrees of evidence, to form a sound judgment of the value of authorities. Reasoning is taught by actual practice much more than by any a priori methods. Many good judges—and I own I am inclined to agree with them—doubt much whether a study of formal logic ever yet made a good reasoner. Mathematics are no doubt invaluable in this respect, but they only deal with demonstrations ; and it has often been observed how many excellent mathematicians are somewhat peculiarly destitute of the power of measuring degrees of probability. But history is largely concerned with the kind of probabilities on which the conduct of life mainly depends. There is one hint about historical reasoning which I think may not be unworthy of your notice. When studying some great historical controversy, place yourselves by an effort of the imagination alternately on each side

[1] Jefferson's *Memoirs*, i. 80.

of the battle; try to realise as fully as you can the point of view of the best men on either side, and then draw up upon paper the arguments of each in the strongest form you can give them. You will find that few practices do more to elucidate the past, or form a better mental discipline.

History, again, greatly expands our horizon and enlarges our experience by bringing us in direct contact with men of many times and countries. It gives young men something of the experience of old men, and untravelled men something of the experience of travelled ones. A great source of error in our judgment of men is that we do not make sufficient allowance for the difference of types. The essentials of right and wrong no doubt continue the same, but if you look carefully into history you will find that the special stress which is attached to particular virtues is constantly changing. Sometimes it is the civic virtues, sometimes the religious virtues, sometimes the industrial virtues, sometimes the love of truth, sometimes the more amiable dispositions, that are most valued, and occupy the foremost place in the moral type. The men of each age must be judged by the ideal of their own age and country, and not by the ideal of ours. Men look at life in very different aspects, and they differ greatly in their ways of reasoning, in the qualities they admire, in the aims which they chiefly prize. In few things do they differ more than in their capacity for self-government; in the kinds of liberty they especially value; in their love or dislike of government guidance or control.

The power of realising and understanding types of character very different from our own is not, I think, an English quality, and a great many of our mistakes in

governing other nations come from this deficiency.
Some thirty or forty years ago especially it was the
custom of English statesmen to write and speak as if the
salvation of every nation depended mainly upon its
adoption of a miniature copy of the British Constitution.
Now, if there is a lesson which history teaches clearly,
it is that the same institutions are not fitted for all
nations, and that what in one nation may prove perfectly
successful, will in another be supremely disastrous. The
habits and traditions of a nation ; the peculiar bent of its
character and intellect; the degree in which self-control,
respect for law, the spirit of compromise, and disinterested
public spirit are diffused through the people ; the relations
of classes, and the divisions of property, are all considerations of capital importance. It is a great error, both
in history and in practical politics, to attach too much
value to a political machine. The essential consideration is by what men and in what spirit that machine
is likely to be worked. Few Constitutions contain more
theoretical anomalies, and even absurdities, than that
under which England has attained to such an unexampled
height of political prosperity ; while a servile imitation of
some of the most skilfully-devised Constitutions in
Europe has not saved some of the South American States
from long courses of anarchy, bankruptcy, and revolution.

These are some of the political lessons that may be
drawn from history. Permit me, in conclusion, to say
that its most precious lessons are moral ones. It expands
the range of our vision, and teaches us in judging the
true interests of nations to look beyond the immediate
future. Few good judges will deny that this habit is
now much wanted. The immensely increased prominence in political life of ephemeral influences, and

especially of the influence of a daily press ; the immense multiplication of elections, which intensifies party conflicts, all tend to concentrate our thoughts more and more upon an immediate issue. They narrow the range of our vision, and make us somewhat insensible to distant consequences and remote contingencies. It is not easy, in the heat and passion of modern political life, to look beyond a parliament or an election, beyond the interest of a party or the triumph of an hour. Yet nothing is more certain than that the ultimate, distant, and perhaps indirect consequences of political measures are often far more important than their immediate fruits, and that in the prosperity of nations a large amount of continuity in politics and the gradual formation of political habits are of transcendent importance. History is never more valuable than when it enables us, standing as on a height, to look beyond the smoke and turmoil of our petty quarrels, and to detect in the slow developments of the past the great permanent forces that are steadily bearing nations onwards to improvement or decay.

The strongest of these forces are the moral ones. Mistakes in statesmanship, military triumphs or disasters, no doubt affect materially the prosperity of nations, but their permanent political well-being is essentially the outcome of their moral state. Its foundation is laid in pure domestic life, in commercial integrity, in a high standard of moral worth and of public spirit ; in simple habits, in courage, uprightness, and self-sacrifice, in a certain soundness and moderation of judgment, which springs quite as much from character as from intellect. If you would form a wise judgment of the future of a nation, òbserve carefully whether these qualities are increasing or decaying. Observe especially what qualities count for most in public life. Is character becoming of greater or less importance? Are the men who obtain the highest posts in the nation men of whom in private life and irrespective of party competent judges speak with genuine respect? Are they men of sincere convictions, sound judgment, consistent lives, indisputable integrity, or are they men who have won their positions by the arts of a demagogue or an intriguer; men of nimble tongues and not earnest beliefs—skilful, above all things, in spreading their sails to each passing breeze of popularity? Such considerations as these are apt to be forgotten in the fierce excitement of a party contest; but if history has any meaning, it is such considerations that affect most vitally the permanent well-being of communities, and it is by observing this moral current that you can best cast the horoscope of a nation.

THE EMPIRE: ITS VALUE AND ITS GROWTH

I HAVE been asked on the present occasion to deliver a short address which might serve as an introduction to the course of lectures and conferences on the history and resources of the different portions of the Empire which are to take place in the Imperial Institute. In attempting to discharge this task my first reflection is one which the very existence of the Institute can hardly fail to suggest to anyone with any knowledge of recent history. It is the great revolution of opinion which has taken place in England within the last few years about the real value to her both of her colonies and of her Indian Empire. Not many years ago it was a popular doctrine among a large and important class of politicians that these vast dominions were not merely useless but detrimental to the mother-country, and that it should be the end of a wise policy to prepare and facilitate their disruption. Bentham, in a pamphlet called 'Emancipate your Colonies,' advocated a speedy and complete separation. James Mill, who held a high place among these politicians, wrote an article on Colonies for the 'Encyclopædia Britannica' which clearly expresses their view. Colonies, he contended, are very little calculated to yield any advantage whatever to the countries that hold them, and their chief influence is to produce and prolong bad government. Why, then, he asks, do European nations maintain them? The answer is very characteristic, both of the man and of his school. Something, he charitably admits, is due to mere ignorance, to mistaken views of utility; but the main cause is of another kind. He quotes the saying of Sancho Panza, who desired to possess an island in order that he might sell its inhabitants as slaves, and put the money in his pocket; and he maintains that the chief cause of our Colonial Empire is the selfish interest of the governing few who valued colonies because they gave them places and enabled them to multiply wars. In more moderate and decorous language, Goldwin Smith wrote a book, the object of which was to show how desirable it was that this Empire should be gradually but steadily reduced to the sweet simplicity of two islands. Similar views prevailed very generally in the Manchester school. Cobden frequently expressed them. The question of the colonies, he maintained, was mainly a question of pounds, shillings, and pence; he proved, as he imagined, by many figures that they were a very bad bargain; and he expressed his confident hope that one of the results of free trade would be 'gradually and imperceptibly to loosen the bands which unite our colonies to us.' About our Indian Empire he entertained much stronger opinions. He described it as a calamity and a curse to the people of England. He looked on it, in his own words, 'with an eye of despair,' and declared that it was destroying and demoralising the national character. It was the belief of his school of politicians that all the nations of the world would speedily follow the example of England and adopt a policy of perfect free trade; that when all men were able to sell their industries with equal facility in all countries, it would become a matter of little consequence to them under what flag they lived, and that this complete commercial assimilation would soon be followed by a general movement for disarming, which would put an end to all fear of future war.

Many politicians who certainly cannot be classified with the Manchester school held views tending in some degree in the same direction. Even Sir Cornewall Lewis in his treatise on the 'Government of Dependencies,' which was published in 1841, summed up the advantages and disadvantages of a great empire in a manner that gives the impression that in his own judgment the disadvantages on the whole predominated. In the Autobiography of that great writer and excellent public servant Sir Henry Taylor, who for many years exercised much influence in the Colonial Office, we have a curious picture of the opinions which were held on this subject about thirty years ago, both by Sir Henry Taylor himself and by Sir Frederick Rogers, who was at this time permanent Under-Secretary of State for the Colonies. They both agreed that all our North American colonies were a kind of *damnosa hereditas*, and that it was in a high degree desirable that they should be amicably separated from Great Britain. Sir Henry Taylor wrote his views on the subject with great frankness to the Duke of Newcastle, who was then Secretary of State. 'When your Grace and the Prince of Wales,' he said, 'were employing yourselves so successfully in conciliating the colonists, I thought that you were drawing closer ties which might better be slackened, if there were any chance of their slipping away altogether. I think that a policy which has regard to a not very far off future should prepare facilities and propensities for separation. . . . In my estimation the worst consequence of the late dispute with the United States has been that of involving this country and its North American provinces in closer relations and a common cause.'[1] 'I have always believed,' wrote Sir Frederick Rogers in 1885—' and the belief has so confirmed and consolidated itself, that I can hardly realise the possibility of anyone seriously thinking the contrary—that the destiny of our colonies is independence ; and that in this point of view the function of the Colonial Office is to secure that our connection while it lasts shall be as profitable to both parties, and our separation when it comes as amicable as possible.'

I do not believe that opinions of this kind, though they were held by a large and powerful section of English politicians, ever penetrated very deeply into the English nation. One of the causes of Mr. Cobden's ' despair ' was his conviction that the English people would never be persuaded to surrender India except at the close of a disastrous and exhausting war, and in his day the policy of national surrender was certainly not that of the statesmen who led either party in Parliament. No one would attribute it to Mr. Disraeli, in whose long political life the note of Imperialism was perhaps that which sounded with the clearest ring, and it was quite as repugnant to Lord Palmerston and Lord John Russell. In an admirable speech which was delivered in the beginning of 1850, Lord John Russell disclaimed all sympathy with it, and I can well remember the indignation with which in his latter days he was accustomed to speak of the views on the subject which were then frequently expressed. ' When I was young,' he once said to me, ' it was thought the mark of a wise statesman that he had turned a small kingdom into a great empire. In my old age it appears

[1] *Autobiography*, ii. pp. 234, 235.

to be thought the object of a statesman to turn a great empire into a small kingdom.'

I do not think that anyone who has watched the current of English opinion will doubt that the views of the Manchester school on this subject have within the last few years steadily lost ground, and that a far warmer and, in my opinion, nobler and more healthy feeling towards India and the colonies has grown up. The change may be attributed to many causes. In the first place, what Carlyle called 'The Calico Millennium' has not arrived. The nations have not adopted free trade, but nearly all of them, including unfortunately many of our own colonies, have raised tariff walls against our trade. The Reign of Peace has not come. National antipathies and jealousies play about as great a part in human affairs as they ever did, and there are certainly not less than three and a half millions, there are probably nearly four millions, of men under arms in what are called the peace establishments of Europe. It is beginning to be clearly seen that, with our vast, redundant, ever-growing population, with our enormous manufactures, and our utterly insufficient supply of home-grown food, it is a matter of life and death to the nation, and especially to its working classes, that there should be secure and extending fields open to our goods, and in the present condition of the world we must mainly look for these fields within our own Empire. The gigantic dimensions that Indian trade has assumed within the last few years, and the extraordinary commercial development of some other parts of our Empire, have pointed the moral, and it has been made still more apparent by the eagerness with which other Powers, and especially Germany, have flung themselves into the path of colonisation. In an age, too, when all the paths of professional and industrial life in our country are crowded to excess, the competitive system has combined with our new acquisitions of territory to throw open noble fields of employment, enterprise and ambition to poor and struggling talent, and India is proving a school of inestimable value for maintaining some of the best and most masculine qualities of our race. It is the great seed-plot of our military strength; and the problems of Indian administration are peculiarly fitted to form men of a kind that is much needed among us—men of strong purpose and firm will, and high ruling and organising powers, men accustomed to deal with facts rather than with words, and to estimate measures by their intrinsic value, and not merely by their party advantages, men skilful in judging human character under its many types and aspects and disguises.

If again we turn to our great self-governing colonies, we have learnt to feel how valuable it is, in an age in which international jealousies are so rife, that there should be vast and rapidly growing portions of the globe that are not only at peace with us, but at one with us; how unspeakably important it is to the future of the world that the English race, through the ages that are to come, should cling as closely as possible together. As a distinguished statesman who lately represented the United States in England [1] has admirably said, ' If it is not always true that trade follows flag, it is at least true that " heart follows flag," and the feeling that our fellow-subjects in distant parts of the Empire bear to us is very different from the feeling even of the most friendly foreign nation. Our great colonies have readily

[1] Mr. Bayard.

undertaken the responsibility of providing for their own
defence by land, and even in some degree by sea. If the
protection of their coasts in time of war might become a
great strain upon our navy, this disadvantage is largely
balanced by the importance of distant maritime possessions to every nation that desires to maintain an efficient
fleet ; by the immense advantage to a great commercial
Power of secure harbours and coaling stations scattered
over the world. It is not difficult to conceive circumstances in which the destruction of some of our main
industries, occurring, perhaps, in the midst of a great
war, might make it utterly impossible for our present
population to live upon British soil, and when the
possession of vast territories under the British flag, and
in the hands of the British race, might become a matter
of transcendent importance. Think for a moment of the
colossal, and indeed appalling, proportions which our
great towns are assuming ! Think of all the vice and
ignorance and disease, of all the sordid abject misery, of
all the lawless passions that are festering within them !
And then consider how precarious are many of the
conditions of our industrial prosperity, how grave and
how numerous are the dangers that threaten it both from
within and from without. Who can reflect seriously on
these things without feeling that the day may come—
perhaps at no distant date—when the question of emigration may overshadow all others ? To many of us, indeed,
it seems one of the greatest errors of modern English
statesmanship that when the great exodus from Ireland
took place after the famine, Government took no step to
aid it, or to direct it to quarters where it would have
been of real benefit to the Empire. Many good judges
think that the advantages of such interference in allaying

E

bitter feelings, softening a disastrous crisis, and permanently strengthening the Empire, might have been well purchased even if they cost as much as England has sometimes lost by one comparatively insignificant war or by one disastrous strike. In dealing with this question of emigration in the future, colonial assistance may be of supreme importance. And those who have understood the significance of that memorable incident in our recent history—the despatch of Australian troops to fight our battles in the Soudan—may perceive that there is at least a possibility of a still closer and more beneficent union between England and her colonies—a union that would vastly increase the strength of both, and by doing so become a great guarantee of peace in the world.

It would be a calumny to suppose that the change of feeling I have described was solely due to a calculation of interests. Patriotism cannot be reduced to a mere question of money, and a nation which has grown tired of the responsibilities of empire, and careless of the acquisitions of its past and of its greatness in the future, would indeed have entered into a period of inevitable decadence. Happily we have not yet come to this. I believe the overwhelming majority of the people of these islands are convinced that an England reduced to the limits which the Manchester school would assign to it would be an England shorn of the chief elements of its dignity in the world, and that no greater disgrace could befall them than to have sacrificed through indifference, or negligence, or faint-heartedness, an Empire which has been built up by so much genius and so much heroism in the past. Railways and telegraphs and newspapers have brought us into closer touch with our distant possessions, have enabled us to realise more vividly both their character and their greatness, and have thus extended the horizon of our sympathies and interests. The figures of illustrious colonial statesmen are becoming familiar to us. Men formed in Indian and colonial spheres are becoming more numerous and prominent in our own public life. The presence in England of a High Commissioner from Canada, and of Agents-General from our other colonies, constitutes a real though informal colonial representation, and on more than one recent occasion our foreign policy has been swayed by colonial pressure. These young democracies, with their vast undeveloped resources, their unwearied energies, their great social and industrial problems, are beginning to loom largely in the imaginations of Europe. They feel, we believe, a just pride in being members of a great and ancient Empire, and heirs to the glories of its past. We, in our turn, feel a no less just pride in our union with those coming nations which are still lit with the hues of sunrise and rich in the promise of the future.

It has been suggested to me that I should on the present occasion say something about the methods by which this great Empire was built up, but it is obvious that in a short address like the present it is only possible to touch on so large a subject in the most cursory manner. Much is due to our insular position and our command of the sea, which gave Englishmen, in the competition of nations, a peculiar power both of conquering and holding distant dependencies. Being precluded, perhaps quite as much by their position as by their desire, from throwing themselves, like most continental nations, into a long course of European aggression, they have largely employed their redundant energies in exploring, conquering, civilising, and governing distant and half-savage lands. They have found, like all other nations, that an Empire planted amid the shifting sands of half-civilised and anarchical races is compelled for its own security, and as a mere matter of police, to extend its borders. The chapter of accidents--which has played a larger part in most human affairs than many very philosophical enquirers are inclined to admit—has counted for something. But, in addition to these things, there are certain general characteristics of English policy which have contributed very largely to the success of the Empire.

It has been the habit of most nations to regulate colonial governments in all their details according to the best metropolitan ideas, and to surround them with a network of restrictions. England has in general pursued a different course. Partly on system, but partly also, I think, from neglect, she has always allowed an unusual latitude to local knowledge and to local wishes. She has endeavoured to secure, wherever her power extends, life and property, and contract and personal freedom, and, in these latter days, religious liberty; but for the rest she has meddled very little; she has allowed her settlements to develop much as they please, and has given, in practice if not in theory, the fullest powers to her governors. It is astonishing, in the history of the British Empire, how large a part of its greatness is due to the independent action of individual adventurers, or groups of emigrants, or commercial companies, almost wholly unassisted and uncontrolled by the Government at home. An Empire formed by such methods is not likely to exhibit much symmetry and unity of plan, but it is certain to be pervaded in an unusual degree, in all its parts, by a spirit of enterprise and self-reliance; it will probably be peculiarly fertile in men not only of energy but of resource, capable of dealing with strange conditions and unforeseen exigencies. England in the past periods of her history has, on the whole, been singularly successful in adapting her different administrations to widely different national circumstances and characters, and governments of the most various types have arisen under her rule. Nothing in the history of the world is more wonderful than that under the flag of these two little islands there should have grown up the greatest and most beneficent despotism in the world, comprising nearly two hundred and thirty millions of inhabitants under direct British rule, and more than fifty millions under British protectorates; while at the same time British colonies and settlements that are scattered throughout the globe number not less than fifty-six distinct subordinate governments.

This system would have been less successful if it had not been for two important facts. The original stuff of which our Colonial Empire was formed was singularly good. Some of the most important of our colonies were founded in the days of religious war, and the early settlers consisted largely of religious refugees—a class who are usually superior to the average of men in intellectual and industrial qualities, and are nearly always greatly superior to them in strength of conviction, and in those high moral qualities which play so great a part in the well-being of nations. Besides this, in those distant days, the difficulties of emigration were so great that they were rarely voluntarily encountered except by men of much more than average courage, enterprise and resource. These early adventurers were certainly often of no saintly type, but they were largely endowed with the robuster qualities that are most needed for grappling with new circumstances and carving out the empires of the future.

The second fact is the high standard of patriotism and honour which we may, I think, truly say has nearly always prevailed among English public servants. It is not an easy thing to secure honest and faithful administration in remote countries, far from the supervision and practical control of the central government. I think we may boast with truth that England has attained this end, not indeed perfectly, but at least to a greater degree than most other nations. The history of Indian and colonial governors has never been written as a whole, but it is well worthy of study. In the appointment of these men party has always counted for something, and family has counted for something; but they have never been the only considerations, and, on the whole, I believe it will be found, if we consider the three elements of character, capacity and experience, that our Indian and colonial governors represent a higher level of ruling qualities than has been attained by any line of hereditary sovereigns, or by any line of elected presidents. In the period of the foundation of our Indian Empire much was done that was violent and rapacious, but the best modern research seems to show that the picture which a few years ago was generally accepted had been greatly overcharged. The history of Warren Hastings and his companions has been recently studied with great knowledge and ability, and with the result that the more serious opinions on the subject have been considerably modified. Much exaggeration undoubtedly grew up in the last century, partly through ignorance of Oriental affairs, and partly also through the eloquence of Burke. There is no figure in English political history for which I at least entertain a greater reverence than Edmund Burke. I believe him to have been a man of transparent honesty, as well as of transcendent genius ; but his politics were too apt to be steeped in passion, and he was often carried away by the irresistible force of his own imagination and feelings. Misrepresentations were greatly consolidated by the Indian History of James Mill, which was for a long time the main, and indeed almost the only, source from which Englishmen obtained their knowledge of Indian history. It was written, as might be expected, with the strongest bias of hostility to the English in India, yet I suspect that many superficial readers imagined that a history which was so unquestionably dull must be at least impartial and philosophical. Unfortunately, Macaulay relied greatly on it, and, without having made any serious independent studies on the subject, he invested some of its misrepresentations with all the splendour of his eloquence. I believe all competent authorities are now agreed that his essay on Warren Hastings, though it is one of the most brilliant of his writings, is also one of the most seriously misleading.

I am not prepared to say that the reaction of opinion produced by the new school of Indian historians has not been sometimes carried too far, but these writers have certainly dispelled much exaggeration and some positive falsehood. They have shown that, although under circumstances of extreme difficulty and extraordinary temptation, some very bad things were done by Englishmen in India, these things were neither as numerous nor as grave as has been alleged.

On the whole, too, it may be truly said that English colonial policy in its broad lines has to a remarkable degree avoided grave errors. The chief exception is to be found in the series of mistakes which produced the American Revolution, and ended in the loss of our chief American colonies. Yet even in this instance it is, I believe, coming to be perceived that there is much more to be said for the English case than the historians of the last generation were apt to imagine. In imposing commercial restrictions on the colonies and endeavouring to secure for the mother-country the monopoly of their trade, we merely acted upon ideas that were then almost universally received, and our commercial code was on the whole less illiberal than that of other nations. Both Spain and France imposed restrictions on their colonies which were far more severe, and the English restrictions were at least mitigated by frequent partial relaxations and exceptions, by some important monopolies granted in favour of the colonies in the English market and by bounties encouraging several branches of colonial produce. It is at least certain that under the large measure of political liberty granted by the English Government to the English colonies their material prosperity, even in the worst period of commercial restriction, steadily and rapidly advanced. This has been clearly shown by more than one writer on our side of the Atlantic, but the subject has never been treated with more exhaustive knowledge and more perfect impartiality than by an American writer—Mr. George Beer—whose work on the Commercial Policy of England has recently been published by Columbia College, in New York. No one will now altogether defend Grenville's policy of taxing America by the Imperial Parliament, but it ought not to be forgotten that it was expressly provided that every farthing of this taxation was to be expended in America, and devoted to colonial defence. England had just terminated a great war, which, by expelling the French from Canada, had been of inestimable advantage to her colonies, but which had left the mother-country almost crushed by debt. All that Grenville desired was, that the American colonies should provide a portion of the cost of their own defence, as our great colonies are doing at the present time, and he only resorted to Imperial taxation because he despaired of achieving this end by any other means. The step which he took was no doubt a false one. As is so often the case in England, it was made worse by party changes and by party recriminations, and many later mistakes aggravated and embittered the original dispute; but I think an impartial reader of this melancholy chapter of English history will come to the conclusion that these mistakes were by no means all on one side.

It is a story which is certainly not without its lesson to our own time. It is very improbable that any future statesman will follow the example of George Grenville, and endeavour by Act of Parliament to impose taxation on a self-governing colony; but it would be a grave error to suppose that the danger of unwise parliamentary interference in Indian and colonial affairs has diminished. Great as are the advantages of telegraphs and newspapers in the government of the Empire, they are not without their drawbacks. Government by telegraph is a very dangerous thing, and there is, I fear, an increasing tendency to override local knowledge, and to apply English standards and methods of government to wholly un-English conditions. Ill-considered resolutions of the House of Commons, often passed in obedience to some popular fad, and without any real intention of carrying them into effect; language used in Parliament which is often due to no deeper motive than a desire to win the favour of some class of voters in an English constituency, may do as much as serious misgovernment to alienate great masses of British subjects beyond the sea. All really competent judges are agreed that one of the first conditions of successful government in India has been that Indian questions have for the most part been kept out of the range of English party politics, and that Indian government has been conducted on principles essentially different from democratic government at home.

On the whole, however, it is impossible to review the colonial history of England without being struck with the many serious dangers that might easily have shattered the Empire, which were averted by wise statesmanship and timely—or at least not fatally tardy—concession. There was the question of the criminal population which we once transported to Australia. In the early stage of the colony, when the population was very sparse and the need for labour very imperative, this was not regarded as in any degree a grievance; but the time came when it became a grievance of the gravest kind, and the Imperial power had at length the wisdom to abandon it. There was the question of the different and hostile religious bodies existing in different portions of the Empire, at a time when the monopoly of political power by the members of a single Established Church, the exclusive endowment of its clergy, and the maintenance of the purely Protestant character of the English Government were cherished as religious duties by politicians at home. Yet at this very time an established and endowed Roman Catholic Church was flourishing in Canada, and there were numerous examples throughout the British dominions of the concurrent endowment of different forms of religious belief by the State,[1] while in India it

---

[1] See the enumeration of these endowments in Gladstone's *State and Church*, Ch. IX.

abstained, with an extreme, and sometimes even an exaggerated, scrupulousness, from all measures that could by any possibility offend the native religious prejudices. There was the question of Slavery—though we were freed from the most difficult part of this problem by the secession of America. In addition, however, to its moral aspects, it affected most vitally the material prosperity of some of our richest colonies ; it raised the very dangerous constitutional question of the right of the Imperial Parliament to interfere with the internal affairs of a self-governing colony, and it brought the Home Government into more serious collision with the local Governments than any question since the American Revolution. Whatever may be thought of the wisdom of the measures by which we abolished slavery in our West Indian colonies, no one at least can deny the liberality of a Parliament which voted from Imperial resources twenty millions for the accomplishment of the work. There was the conflict of race and creed which between 1830 and 1840 had brought Canada to absolute rebellion, and threatened a complete alienation of Canadian feeling from the mother-country. This discontent was effectually allayed and dispelled by the union of Upper and Lower Canada under a system of constitutional government of the most liberal character, which gave the colonists on all subjects of internal legislation a legislative independence that was in practice almost complete. Considered as a measure of conciliation this has proved one of the most successful of the nineteenth century, and in spite of a few discordant notes it may be truly said that there are few greater contrasts in the present reign than are presented between Canadian feeling towards the mother-country when Queen Victoria ascended the throne and

Canadian feeling at the present hour. There was also the great and dangerous task to be accomplished of adapting the system of colonial government to the different stages of colonial development. There was a time when the colonies were so weak that they depended mainly on England for their protection; but, unlike some of the great colonising Powers of ancient and modern times, England never drew a direct tribute from her colonies, and, in spite of much unwise and some unjust legislation, I believe there was never a time when they were not on the whole benefited by the connection. Soon, however, the colonies grew to the strength and maturity of nationhood, and the mother-country speedily recognised the fact, and allowed no unworthy or ungenerous fears to restrain her from granting them the fullest powers, both of self-government and of federation. It is true that she still sends out a governor—usually drawn from the ranks of experienced and considerable English public men—to preside over colonial affairs. It is true that she retains a right of veto which is scarcely ever exercised except to prevent some intercolonial or international dispute, some act of violence, or some grave anomaly in the legislation of the Empire. It is true that colonial cases may be carried, on appeal, to an English tribunal, representing the very highest judicial capacity of the mother-country, and free from all possibility and suspicion of partiality; but I do not believe that any of these light ties are unpopular with any considerable section of the colonists. On the other hand, though it would be idle to suppose that our great colonies depend largely upon the mother-country, I believe that most colonists recognise that there is something in the weight and dignity attaching to fellow-membership and fellow-

citizenship in a great Empire—something in the protection
of the greatest navy in the world—something in the
improved credit which connection with a very rich centre
undoubtedly gives to colonial finance.

It is the custom of our friends and neighbours on the
Continent to bestow much scornful remark on the egotism
of English policy, which attends mainly to the interests
of the British Empire, and is not ready to make war for
an idea and in support of the interests of others. I think,
if it were necessary, we might fairly defend ourselves by
showing that in the past we have meddled with the
affairs of other nations quite as much as is reasonable.
For my own part, I confess that I distrust greatly these
explosions of military benevolence. They always begin
by killing a great many men. They usually end in ways
that are not those of a disinterested philanthropy. After
all, an egotism that mainly confines itself to the well-
being of about a fifth part of the globe cannot be said
to be of a very narrow type, and it is essentially by her
conduct to her own Empire that the part of England in
promoting the happiness of mankind must be ultimately
judged. It is indeed but too true that many of the
political causes which have played a great part on plat-
forms, in parties, and in Parliaments are of such a nature
that their full attainment would not bring relief to one
suffering human heart, or staunch one tear of pain, or
add in any appreciable degree to the real happiness of a
single home. But most assuredly Imperial questions are
not of this order. Remember what India had been for
countless ages before the establishment of British rule.
Think of its endless wars of race and creed, its savage
oppressions, its fierce anarchies, its barbarous customs;
and then consider what it is to have established for so

many years over the vast space from the Himalayas to
Cape Comorin a reign of perfect peace ; to have conferred
upon more than two hundred and fifty millions of the
human race perfect religious freedom, perfect security of
life, liberty, and property; to have planted in the midst
of these teeming multitudes a strong central government,
enlightened by the best knowledge of Western Europe,
and steadily occupied in preventing famine, alleviating
disease, extirpating savage customs, multiplying the
agencies of civilisation and progress. This is the true
meaning of that system of government on which Mr.
Cobden looked with ' an eye of despair.' What work of
human policy—I would even say what form of human
philanthropy—has ever contributed more largely to reduce
the great sum of human misery and to add to the possi-
bilities of human happiness ?

And if we turn to the other side of our Empire,
although it is quite true that our great free colonies are
fully capable of shaping their destinies for themselves,
may we not truly say that these noble flowers have
sprung from British and from Irish seeds ? May we not
say that the laws, the Constitutions, the habits of thought
and character that have so largely made them what they
are, are mainly of English origin ? May we not even
add that it is in no small part due to their place in
the British Empire that these vast sections of the globe,
with their diverse and sometimes jarring interests, have
remained at perfect peace with us and with each other,
and have escaped the curse of an exaggerated militarism,
which is fast eating like a canker into the prosperity of
the great nations of Europe ?

When responsible government was conceded by the
British Government to her more important colonies,

it was done in the fullest and largest measure. Although the mother-country remained burdened with the task of defending them she made no reservation securing for herself free trade with her colonies or even preferential treatment, and she surrendered unconditionally to the local legislatures the waste and unoccupied lands which had long been regarded in England as held in trust for the benefit of the Empire as a whole. The growing belief that the connection with the colonies was likely to be a very transitory one, and also the belief that free-trade doctrines were likely speedily to prevail, no doubt influenced English statesmen, and it is not probable that any of them foresaw that both Canada and Australia would speedily make use of their newly acquired power to impose heavy duties on English goods. The strongly protectionist character which the English colonies assumed at a time when England had committed herself to the most extreme free-trade policy tended no doubt to separation, and when the English Government adopted the policy of withdrawing its garrisons from the colonies, when the North American colonies, with the full assent of the mother-country, formed themselves into a great federation, and when a movement in the same direction sprang up in Australia, it was the opinion of some of the most sagacious statesmen and thinkers in England that the time of separation was very near.[1]

On the whole, however, these predictions have hitherto been falsified. The federation of North America and, at a later period, the federation of Australia have been followed by an increased and not a diminished disposition on the side of the colonists to draw closer the ties with the mother-country, while in England the popular

---

[1] See Cairnes' *Political Essays*, 49-50, 56.

imagination has been more and more impressed with
the growing magnitude and importance of her colonial
dominions. The tendency towards great political ag-
glomerations based upon an affinity of race, language and
creed, which has produced the Pan-Slavonic movement
and the Pan-Germanic movement, and which chiefly
made the unity of Italy, has not been without its influence
in the English-speaking world, and it is felt that a close
union between its several parts is essential if it is fully
to maintain its relative position under the new conditions
of the world. The English-speaking nations comprise
the most rapidly increasing, the most progressive, the
most happily situated nations of the earth, and if their
power and influence are not wasted by internal quarrels
their type of civilisation must one day become dominant
in the world.

Whether their harmony and unity are likely to be
attained is one of the great problems of the future, but
the ideal is one which every patriotic Englishman should
at least set before him. It is not one which can be
called an assured destiny, and to many the chances seem
on the whole against it. Unexpected collisions of interest
or passion or ambition may at any time mar the prospects, and in great democracies largely influenced by
demagogues and by an irresponsible and anonymous Press
there are always powerful agencies that do not make
for peace. Immediate party interests both at home
and in the colonies too frequently blind men to distant
and ulterior consequences, and the many ill-wishers
to the British Empire are sure to direct their policy
largely to its disruption. The natural bond of union
of a great Empire is economical unity, binding its several
parts together by a common system of free trade and
by a common commercial policy towards other Powers.

Unfortunately the profoundly different policy adopted on these matters in England and her colonies has made such a Union almost impracticable, and it is quite possible for the English colonies to be united by closer commercial ties with foreign countries than with the mother-country. The question of the common defence of the Empire and the question of the representation of the colonies in Imperial politics are also questions of great difficulty and of pressing importance.

Something has been done showing at least a disposition to meet them. The concession of preferential duties in favour of England by some of our most important colonies, the small subsidies made to the maintenance of the British navy, and the far more important military assistance given by the colonies to the mother-country in the Egyptian and the South African wars are indicative of the feeling of closer unity which has grown up between England and her colonies, and in addition to the appointment of Agents-General, the introduction of a few eminent colonial judges into the Judicial Committee of the Privy Council, which is the Supreme Court of Appeal of the Empire, has given the colonies some real representation in Imperial affairs. Much more, however, in this direction may be done. There have been several instances of eminent colonials obtaining seats in the English House of Commons to the great advantage of the Empire, but a regular representation of the colonies in this assembly may, I think, be dismissed as altogether impracticable. The mere distance is a sufficient objection, and at least nine-tenths of the business of the House of Commons deals with purely English questions depending for their wise solution on inherited English habits and on compromises with

F

existing institutions, and a large proportion of them are problems which have been already dealt with in the colonies on other grounds and without any of the complexities of an old country. What reason could there be for calling in the colonists to adjudicate, perhaps even to turn the balance, on questions relating to English education, English licensing laws, English taxation, English dispositions of property? The difficulty of distinguishing between Imperial and local questions would be insuperable. The division of the House into two categories of members with distinct spheres of voting power would prove unworkable, and the colonial representatives would during most of their time in Parliament have nothing to do. An increase in the number of peers drawn from the colonies would be less impracticable, but there would be much that is invidious in the choice ; much danger that the colonial peers living in England would get out of touch with the colonies and become an object of envy and jealousy ; and English lawyers do not think that a large infusion of colonial law peers would raise the competence of the Supreme Judicial Tribunal of the Empire, which represents at present the highest legal talent and attainments in England and deals mainly with English legal questions. A Consultative Council, however, consisting of the Agents-General and perhaps reinforced by additional colonial representatives and dealing exclusively with Imperial questions, does not seem wholly impracticable, and many competent judges believe that a supreme legal tribunal for dealing with inter-colonial and international conflicts might be constructed which would be both more efficient and more representative than any that now exists.

It is probable, however, that the true tie that must unite the different portions of the Empire must be mainly a moral one. In the conditions of modern life no power is likely to maintain long a vast, scattered, heterogeneous Empire if the central governing power within it has declined ; if through want of efficiency, or moral energy, or moral purity, it ceases to win the respect of its several parts. It is no less true that the cohesion can only be permanently maintained by the wide diffusion of a larger and Imperial patriotism, pervading the whole like a vital principle ; binding men by the ties of pride and of affection to the great Empire to which they belong, and subordinating to its maintenance local and party and class interests. If this spirit dies out, the movement of disintegration is sure to begin. No political machinery, no utilitarian calculation, will in the long run be powerful enough to arrest it.

What may be the future place of these islands in the government of the world no human being can foretell. Nations, as history but too plainly shows, have their periods of decay as well as their periods of growth. The balance of power in the world is constantly shifting. Maxims and influences very different from those which made England what she is are in the ascendant, and the clouds upon the horizon are neither few nor slight. But, whatever fate may be in store for these islands, and for the political unity we so justly prize, we may at least confidently predict that no revolution in human affairs can now destroy the future ascendancy of the English language and of the Imperial race. Whatever misfortunes, whatever humiliations the future may reserve to us, they cannot deprive England of the glory of having created this mighty Empire.

Not Heaven itself upon the Past has power.
But what has been, has been—and we have had our hour.

IRELAND IN THE LIGHT OF HISTORY

THE kind of interest which belongs to Irish history is curiously different from that which attaches to the history of England and to that of most of the great nations of the Continent. In very few histories do we find so little national unity or continuous progress, or such long spaces which are almost wholly occupied by perplexed, petty internal broils, often stained by atrocious crimes, but turning on no large issue and leading to no clear or stable results. Except during the great missionary period of the sixth and seventh centuries, and during a brief portion of the eighteenth century, we have little of the interest that arises from dramatic situations or shining characters, and in few countries has the highest intellect been, on the whole, so slightly connected with the administration of affairs. To a philosophical student of politics, however, Irish history possesses an interest of the highest order. It is an invaluable study of morbid anatomy. In very few histories can we trace so clearly the effects of political and social circumstances in forming national character ; the calamity of missed opportunities and of fluctuating and procrastinating policy ; the folly of attempting to govern by the same methods and institutions nations that are wholly different in their characters and their civilisation.

The idea which still floats vaguely in many minds that Ireland, before the arrival of the Normans, was a single and independent nation, is wholly false. Ireland was not a nation, but a collection of separate tribes and kingdoms, engaged in almost constant warfare. In this respect, however, she resembled many countries which have since attained the most perfect unity, and there can be little doubt that, if her development had been impeded by no extraneous influences, Ireland would have followed the same path as England or France. Much stress has been justly laid on the disorganising influence of a long succession of Danish invasions, though it must be remembered that Ireland owes to the Danes the foundation of some of her most important cities. Roman conquest, which introduced into most of Europe invaluable elements of order, organisation, and respect for law, never extended to Ireland. The Anglo-Norman invasion and conquest produced consequences which were almost wholly evil. If the invaders had been driven from the Irish shore, the natural course of development would, no doubt, have been in time continued. If the invaders had completely conquered Ireland, a fusion might have taken place as complete and as healthy as in England. Neither of these two events occurred. The English conquest was prolonged over nearly four hundred years. A hostile and separate power was planted in the centre of Ireland sufficiently powerful to prevent the formation of another civilisation, yet not sufficiently powerful to impose a civilisation of its own. Feudalism was introduced, but the keystone of the system, a strong resident sovereign, was wanting, and Ireland was soon torn by the wars of great Anglo-Norman nobles, who were, in fact, independent sovereigns, much like the old Irish kings. The Scotch invasion of the fourteenth century added enormously to the anarchy and confusion ; the English power as a

living reality contracted to the narrow limits of the pale ;
in outlying districts the Anglo-Norman assimilated
quickly with the Celtic element, while the English
legislators in Ireland, alarmed at the tendency, made it
the main object of their policy, in the words of Sir John
Davies, ' to make a perpetual separation and enmity
between the English and Irish, pretending no doubt that
the English should in the end root out the Irish.'

Such a state of things continued till the long and terrible
wars of Henry VIII. and Elizabeth broke the power of
the independent chiefs and of the Celtic clans, and gave
Ireland, for the first time, a political unity. It is one of
the great infelicities of Irish history that this result was
obtained at the very period of the Reformation. The conquerors adopted one religion, while the conquered retained
the other, and thus a new and most enduring barrier was
raised between the two nations in Ireland, and a pernicious
antagonism was established between law and religion.

Another influence not less powerful than religion had
at the same time come into play. It had become the
English policy to place great bodies of English and Scotch
settlers on the land that was confiscated in consequence
of rebellion, and under the impulse of the strong spirit of
adventure which grew up in the generation that followed
the Reformation, streams of English and Scotch adventurers poured over. The great settlement of Ulster under
James I. proved ultimately a success, and laid the foundation of the prosperity of that province. Other plantations
were in time absorbed and assimilated by the Celtic population ; but vast revolutions in the ownership of land,
accompanied by the subversion of the old tribal customs,
laid the foundation of an agrarian war which still continues.

Religious and agrarian causes combined with the civil war in England to produce the great rebellion of 1641 and the eleven years of ghastly, exterminating war which followed. Hardly any page in human history is more appalling. A full third of the population of Ireland perished. Thirty or forty thousand of the most energetic left the country and took service in foreign armies. Great tracts were left absolutely depopulated, and after the rearrangement of land, which was accomplished by the Act of Settlement, the immense preponderance of landed property remained in the hands of the Protestant nation.

New elements, however, of great energy had been planted in Ireland, and the field had been thrown open to their exertions. The excellence of Irish wool and the cheapness of Irish labour laid the foundation of a flourishing woollen manufacture, and with peace, mild administration, and much practical tolerance, the wounds of the country seemed gradually healing. The later Stuart reigns, which form a dark page in English history, were a period of considerable prosperity in Ireland, but that period was soon interrupted by the Revolution. There was no general or passionate rising in Ireland resembling that of 1641, but it was inevitable that the Irish Catholics should have adopted the side of the Catholic King, and it was equally inevitable that when a Catholic Parliament, consisting largely of sons of the men whose properties had recently been confiscated, had assembled at Dublin, its members should have made a desperate effort to reverse their fortunes and replace the land of the country mainly in Catholic hands. The battle of the Boyne shattered the Catholic hopes, and it was followed by a new confiscation, by a new emigration of the ablest and most energetic Catholics, by a long period of commercial restraints, penal laws, and complete Protestant ascendancy.

The commercial restraints formed part of a protective policy which was at that time general in Europe, and which was severely felt in the American colonies. Though it did not absolutely originate in, it was greatly intensified by, the Revolution, which gave the manufacturing and commercial classes a new power in English government. The linen manufacture was spared, but the total destruction by law of the flourishing woollen manufacture, followed by a number of restrictions imposed on other branches of industry, deprived Ireland of her most promising sources of wealth, drove great multitudes of energetic Protestants out of the country, and threw the people more and more upon the soil as almost their sole means of support.

The penal laws against the Catholics accompanied or closely followed the commercial restraints. The blame of them may be divided with some equality between the Government of England and the Parliament of Ireland. It was the Irish Parliament which enacted these laws, but an English Act first made the Irish Parliament exclusively Protestant, and the whole legislation was carried at a time when the Irish Parliament was completely dependent, and incompetent even to discuss any measure without the previous approbation of the English Government. In order to judge this legislation with equity, it must be remembered that in the beginning of the eighteenth century restrictive laws against Protestantism in Catholic countries, and against Catholicism in Protestant ones, almost universally prevailed. The laws against Irish Catholics were, on the whole, less stringent than those against Catholics in England. They were largely modelled after the French legislation against the Huguenots, but persecution in Ireland never approached in severity that of Louis XIV., and was absolutely insignificant compared with that which had extirpated Protestantism and Judaism from Spain. The code, however, was not mainly the product of religious feeling, but of policy, and in this respect it has been defended in its broad outlines, though not in all its details, by such Irishmen as Charlemont, Flood, and Parsons. They argued that at the close of a long period of savage civil war it was absolutely necessary for a small minority, who found themselves in possession of the government and land of the country, to deprive the conquered and hostile majority of every element of political and military strength. This was the real object of the code. It was a measure of self-defence justified by necessity and by the fact that it produced in Ireland for the space of about eighty years the most perfect tranquillity.

There is much truth in these considerations, but it is also true that the penal code produced more pernicious moral, social, and political effects than many sanguinary persecutions. In other countries disqualifying or persecuting laws were directed against small fractions of the nation. In Ireland they were directed against the bulk of the community. Being supported by little or no genuine religious fanaticism or proselytising ardour, they made few Protestants except in the upper orders, where many conformed in order to keep their land or to enter professions ; but they drove nearly all the best and most energetic Catholics to the Continent ; they discouraged industry ; closed the door of knowledge ; taught the people to look upon law as something hostile to religion ;

introduced division and immorality into families by the
rewards they offered to apostasy; and condemned the
whole country to poverty and impotence by fatally
depressing the great majority of its people. Under the
influence of the penal laws the Catholics inevitably
acquired the vices of serfs, and the Protestants the vices
of monopolists. A great portion of the code was pronounced, with good reason, to be flagrantly opposed to
the articles of the Treaty of Limerick, and it completed
the work of the confiscations by making the landlord
class in Ireland almost wholly Protestant, while the great
majority of the tenantry were Catholics.

There was a moment, however, in the beginning of
the century when the whole current of Irish history
might easily have changed. Scotland had suffered, like
Ireland, from the protective policy that followed the
Revolution, and her independent Parliament had re-
taliated by measures which threatened the speedy
separation of the two crowns, and soon led to a legislative Union. In Ireland such a Union was ardently
desired by enlightened Irishmen, and there is every
reason to believe that it could then have been carried
with universal consent. The Catholics were perfectly
passive, and would gladly have accepted a change which
withdrew them from the direct government of the
conquerors in a recent civil war. The Protestants had
as yet no distinctively national feeling, and a legislative
Union would have emancipated their industry and added
enormously to their security. Molyneux, the first great
champion of the legislative independence of Ireland,
emphatically declared that he and those who thought
with him would gladly have accepted the alternative of
a Union, and both the Irish Houses of Parliament voted

addresses in favour of such a measure. If it had been carried, Ireland would have been at least saved from the evils that rose from the commercial restrictions and from the extreme jobbing that grew up around the local legislature, and she would, perhaps, have been saved from some parts of the penal code. But the golden opportunity was lost. The English commercial classes dreaded Irish competition in their markets, and the petition of the Irish legislature was disregarded.

Nearly seventy years of quiet followed. The establishment of the Hanoverian dynasty, the Jacobite risings of 1715 and 1745, the different wars in which England was engaged, left Ireland absolutely undisturbed. The House of Commons then sat for a whole reign and met only every second year. It was completely subservient to the English Privy Council, and it consisted so largely of nomination boroughs that a few great nobles commanded a decisive preponderance, and they practically conducted the government and administered the patronage of Ireland. There was great jobbing and corruption, but taxation, on the whole, was exceedingly light, and there was no tendency to throw it unduly on the poor, or to create in Ireland any of the many feudal burdens that prevailed in France and Germany. The practical evil most felt was the system of tithes for the support of the Protestant establishment, and it was aggravated by a very unfair exemption of pasture land, and also by the prevailing system of farming out tithes to a class of men known as tithe proctors. In the country districts all power was concentrated in the hands of the landlords, who, with many faults and under many difficulties, at least succeeded in attaining a large measure of genuine popularity.

There was an Irish army of twelve thousand men, but the greater part of it was always sent abroad in time of war, and Ireland was then often left with not more than five thousand soldiers. No militia and no constabulary force existed, but when Whiteboy or other disturbances arose, the landlords put themselves at the head of their tenantry, and usually succeeded in suppressing them. Law was very little observed; industrial virtues were at the lowest ebb; there was abundance of drunkenness, idleness, turbulence, neglect of duty, extreme ignorance, and extreme poverty; but there was not much real oppression or religious bigotry, and there were no signs of political disturbance or conspiracy. After a few years the portions of the penal code which restricted the Catholic worship became a dead letter, and Catholic chapels were everywhere rising on the Protestant estates. The monopoly, however, of place and power continued, though the legal profession was full of professing converts. The theological temperature in both sects had greatly subsided. Land was usually let by the owner on long leases, and at very low rents, to tenants who almost invariably divided and sublet their tenancies.

At a later period of the century, when population pressed closely on subsistence, the system of middlemen produced a fierce competition which raised rent in the lower grades to an enormous height, but this evil was less felt with a scanty population, and the hierarchy of tenants at least saved the landlords from the dangerous isolation which their circumstances tended to produce. Arthur Young, who examined the condition of the country very carefully between 1776 and 1778, perceived great signs of growing prosperity, especially in the towns, and, although agriculture was far behind that of England, he found a considerable number of active, intelligent, and improving landlords. In the opinion of Young the rental of Ireland was unduly and unnaturally low, but he urged the landlords to exercise a more direct and controlling influence over their estates, and he recommended them, for this purpose, to give leases for shorter periods and gradually to abolish the system of middlemen and subletting.

In the north there was a powerful, intelligent Protestant community, with a strong leaning to republicanism. They were chiefly Presbyterians, and they resented bitterly the commercial restrictions and the obligation of paying tithes to an Episcopal church. The Irish Parliament was so constituted that they had no political power at all equivalent to their importance, and, like the Presbyterians in England, they were burdened by the Test Act, and their marriages were only valid if celebrated in the Established Church. The great power of the bishops, both in the Privy Council and in the House of Lords, formed a very serious obstacle to church reform. In all classes of Protestants, however, in the closing years of George II., there was a strong resentment at the political subjection of Ireland, and a determination to obtain, if possible, those constitutional rights which the Revolution of 1688 had secured for England.

It is impossible, within the narrow limits assigned to me, to give even a sketch of the successive stages by which the independence of the Irish Parliament was established. The movement began with the Octennial Act, limiting the duration of Parliament, and it came to full maturity during the war of the American Revolution. Among the Irish Catholics there appears to have been absolutely no sympathy with the American cause, but Ulster Protestantism was enthusiastically on

the side of America. Presbyterians from Ulster bore
a considerable part in the American armies, and under
the influence of American example public opinion in
Ireland rapidly advanced. The great Volunteer movement
of 1778 and the following years was originated by the
fact that the Government could supply no troops for the
defence of Ulster at a time when it was in imminent danger
of attack from France. The Protestant gentry called
their people to arms ; and a great Protestant force was
created, which not only secured the country against
foreign danger and maintained the most perfect internal
order, but also exercised a decisive influence over Irish
politics. Volunteer conventions were assembled which
represented both property and educated Protestant
opinion much more truly than the borough Parliament,
and which loudly demanded free trade and Parliamentary
independence. Grattan made himself the mouthpiece
of the popular feeling ; and the English Government and
Parliament yielded to the demand. The whole system
of commercial restraints, which prevented Ireland from
developing her resources and trading with foreign countries
and the British colonies, was abolished, leaving the
commercial intercourse between Great Britain and Ireland
to be regulated by special Acts. The power of the Privy
Council over legislation was abolished. The appellate
jurisdiction of the Irish House of Lords was restored,
and, above all, the sole competence of the King, Lords,
and Commons of Ireland to legislate for Ireland was
recognised. The Irish Parliament nearly at the same
time made great steps towards uniting the people by
relieving the Presbyterians from the Test Act and from
the restrictions on their marriages, and the Catholics
from those parts of the penal code which chiefly restrained

their worship, their education, and their industry. At the same time the Protestant monopoly of political power and of the higher offices remained.

Ireland thus found herself in possession of a Parliament which was, in name at least, perfectly independent. It was a purely Protestant Parliament, elected by Protestants, consisting mainly of landlords and great Protestant lawyers, and representing pre-eminently the property of the country. It was intensely and exclusively loyal, and always ready to adopt far more stringent coercive measures against anarchy and sedition than have ever been adopted by an Imperial Parliament. It included many men of great talents and great liberality, and through the county constituencies and the representatives of the chief towns educated public opinion was seriously felt within its walls; but the large majority of its members sat for nomination boroughs within the control of the Government, and places and pensions were inordinately multiplied for the purpose of securing a majority.

Could this constitution last? In framing the course of foreign and Imperial policy, in all questions of peace or war, of negotiations or alliances, the Irish Parliament had no voice. Yet it might in time of war, by withholding its concurrence, withdraw the whole weight of Ireland from the forces and fatally dislocate the policy of the Empire. It might pursue a commercial policy absolutely inconsistent with Imperial interests, and bring Ireland into intimate commercial connection with the enemies of England; and if English party spirit extended to Ireland and ran in opposite directions in the two legislatures, a collision was inevitable. The Lord Lieutenant and Chief Secretary, who administered the government of Ireland, were appointed by a British Ministry representing the dominant British party; the counsels of the Irish Government were framed in a British Cabinet; the royal consent was given to every Irish Bill under the Great Seal of Great Britain and upon the advice of a British Minister. If a machine so constituted could work as long as it was in the hands of a small and undoubtedly loyal and largely influenced class, could it work if Parliamentary reform made the Irish Parliament subject to the fierce and fluctuating tides of popular opinion? above all, if Catholic enfranchisement brought a vast, ignorant, and possibly seditious element into political life?

It was the recorded opinion of each successive Lord Lieutenant who administered the Irish Government after 1782 that it could not, and that it must sooner or later end either in a union or a separation. They said this, though they fully acknowledged the perfect loyalty hitherto shown by the Irish Parliament; the liberality with which it voted its supplies; the care with which it subordinated its particular measures to the general interests of the Empire. The failure—not solely or even mainly through Irish fault—of an attempt to establish a fixed commercial arrangement between England and Ireland, and a difference between the British and Irish Parliaments on the Imperial question of a regency, strengthened the opinion of the English Government, and for many years before the Union was enacted it was in contemplation. On the two great and pressing questions at issue this policy exercised a powerful influence. The Government obstinately resisted every serious attempt to reform the Parliament, lest they should lose that controlling power which they believed to be essential to the permanence of the connection. On the Catholic question their views were more fluctuating, but their dominant impression was that emancipation could only be safely conceded in an Imperial Parliament, and that it ought to be reserved as a boon which might one day make a legislative Union acceptable to the Irish people.

In Ireland, or at least in Protestant Ireland, the idea of a Union was now intensely unpopular, but the reformers in the Irish Parliament were seriously divided. Flood and Charlemont desired Parliamentary reform on a purely Protestant basis. They believed that this would include in political life the bulk of the property, loyalty, intelligence, and energy of the country, and that the Irish Catholics could not for a long period be safely admitted to political power. Grattan, on the other hand, believed that it was the first interest of Ireland to efface the political distinction between the two creeds and nations, and that an introduction of a certain proportion of Catholic gentry into the Irish Parliament would be in the highest degree beneficial. He, at the same time, always taught that Ireland was utterly unfit for democracy, and that under her peculiar conditions no policy could be more disastrous than one which would 'destroy the influence of landed property'; 'set population adrift from the influence of property'; subvert or weaken the guiding influence of the loyal and educated. When the United Irishmen proposed a Reform Bill which would have made the Irish Parliament a purely democratic body, Grattan denounced it with the greatest vehemence. 'This plan of personal representation,' he said, 'from a revolution of power, would speedily lead to a revolution of property, and become a plan of plunder as well as a scene of confusion. . . . Of such a representation the

G

first ordinance would be robbery, accompanied with the circumstance incidental to robbery, murder.' He believed, however, that with a substantial property qualification independent constituencies might be formed which would safely represent the best elements of both creeds.

The denial of parliamentary reform and Catholic emancipation, and the refusal of the Irish Parliament to deal with the still more pressing question of tithes, produced much disaffection; but still the country was steadily improving, and no serious danger was felt till the French Revolution burst upon Europe. In every country it stimulated the smouldering elements of disorder. In few countries was its influence more fatal than in Ireland. I have very lately described at length the terrible years of growing conspiracy, anarchy, and crime; of fluctuating policy, and savage repression, and revived religious animosity, and maddening panic, deliberately and malignantly fomented, that preceded and prepared the rebellion. It is sufficient here to say that in the beginning of 1798 three provinces were organised to assist a French invasion. But at the last moment the leaders were betrayed and arrested; the French did not arrive; the rebellion was almost confined to a few Leinster counties, and it broke out without leaders and without a plan. In most places the rebels proved to be wretched bands of marauders intent only on plunder, and, although they committed many murders, they were utterly incapable of meeting the loyalists in the field. But in Wexford, priests put themselves at the head of the movement and turned it into a religious war, deriving its main force from religious fanaticism, and waged with desperate courage and ferocity. The massacre of Protestants on Vinegar Hill, in Scullabogue Barn, and on Wexford Bridge, and the general

character the rebellion in Leinster assumed, at once and
for ever checked all that tendency to rebellion which had
so long existed among the Protestants of Ulster. Some
twenty thousand persons perished before the flame was
extinguished. The repression was as savage as the
rebellion, and it left Ireland torn by fiercer religious
animosities than at any period since the Restoration.

It will dispel many illusions if the reader will remember that the great Irish rebellion was directed mainly
against the Irish Parliament, and that it received its
death-blow from Irish loyalists acting under that Parliament before any assistance arrived from England. The
conspiracy began among Protestants and Deists, who
aimed at a union of sects for the purpose of obtaining
a democratic republic. It turned into a war which was
scarcely less essentially religious than the wars of the
Cevennes or of the Anabaptists. Yet two great Catholic
provinces remained quiet during the struggle, and a great
proportion of the loyalist force which crushed the rebellion consisted of Catholic militia.

The English Government thought that the time had
now come for carrying a legislative Union, and, in the
eyes of Lord Cornwallis at least, one of its chief recommendations was that it would take the government of
Ireland out of the hands of the triumphant party, and
would make Catholic emancipation a possibility. The
Catholic bishops were sounded and found to be very
favourable. They declared their full willingness to accept
an endowment for the priesthood and to give the English
Government a right of veto on episcopal appointments,
and they warmly, efficiently, and unanimously supported
the Union. The great majority of the Catholic landed
gentry and probably of the lower priests were on the same

side ; but in general the Catholic laity seem to have
shown little interest and to have taken little part in the
contest. In Dublin, Catholics as well as Protestants
were generally hostile, but Catholic Cork was decidedly
favourable, and an assurance that the Government desired
to carry emancipation in an Imperial Parliament proved
sufficient to prevent any serious Catholic opposition.
The United Irishmen seem to have witnessed rather with
pleasure than the reverse the dethronement of the body
which had defeated them, and the Presbyterians showed
scarcely any interest in the question.

Yet outside the ranks of the Catholic clergy the
measure found few active supporters, while the Protestants of the Established Church were in general
ardently and passionately hostile. The great majority
of the county members and the great preponderance of
petitions were against the Union, and the opposition to
it, which was led by Foster, Grattan, Parsons, and
Plunket, comprised nearly all the independent and un-
bribed talent in Parliament. The very eminent ability
of that small group of Protestant gentlemen never flashed
more brightly than in the closing scenes, and there was
a moment when the attitude of the Orangemen and the
yeomanry was so menacing that the Government were
seriously alarmed. But a lavish distribution of peerages
and places purchased a majority, and the troops stationed
in Ireland were too numerous for armed opposition to
be possible. In truth, however, no opposition beyond the
dimensions of a riot was to be feared. Outside Dublin,
Catholic, Presbyterian, and seditious Ireland remained
almost indifferent. Even before the measure had passed,
opposition speakers complained bitterly that they were
deserted by popular support ; and it is a memorable

fact that in the general election that followed the Union not a single Irish member of Parliament was defeated because he had voted for it.

Pitt intended the Union to be immediately followed by measures admitting the Catholics into the Imperial Parliament, paying the priests, and commuting the tithes. If these three measures, or even if the last two (which were, in truth, the most important), had been promptly carried, the Union might have become popular. The Catholic question had, of late, been greatly mismanaged. The chief men who directed the government in Ireland were bitterly opposed to any concession of political power to the Catholics, but the views of the English Ministers had been materially changed. They desired above all things to separate the Catholics from the United Irishmen, and in 1793 they forced upon their reluctant advisers in Ireland an Act which extended the suffrage to the vast ignorant Catholic masses, though it left the Catholic gentry still excluded from Parliament. Two years later Lord Fitzwilliam was sent over with instructions to postpone the question if possible, but with authority, as he believed, to carry emancipation if it could not be postponed, and he found the Irish Parliament perfectly prepared to pass it. But the opposition of the King and a question of patronage produced a fatal division and led to the recall of the Viceroy. The passions aroused by the rebellion greatly increased the difficulties of admitting Catholics to a separate Parliament, but there is clear evidence that at the time of the Union the Irish Protestants were in favour of their admission into the Imperial one. The dispositions of the King were well known, but it was believed that, if the scheme of Pitt was submitted to him as the matured policy of a united Cabinet, he must have yielded. It is well known how the plan was prematurely revealed; how Pitt resigned office when the King refused his consent; how the agitation of the question threw the King into an access of insanity; and how Pitt then promised that he would not again raise it during the reign. Pitt's conduct on this occasion is, and probably always will be, differently judged. There can be but one opinion of its calamitous effect upon Irish history.

Ninety years have passed since the Union, and the conditions of Ireland have completely changed. The whole system of religious disqualification and commercial disability has long since passed away. Every path has been thrown open, and English professions, as well as the great Colonial and Indian services, are crowded with Irishmen. The Established Church no longer exists. Representation has been placed on a broadly democratic basis, giving Ireland, however, an absurdly disproportioned weight in the representation of the kingdom, and its poorest and most backward districts an absurdly disproportioned weight in the representation of Ireland. Finally, an attempt has been made to put down agrarian agitation by legislation to which there is no real parallel in English history, and some parts of which would have been impossible under the Constitution of the United States. Landlords who possessed by the clearest title known to English law the most absolute ownership of their estates have been converted into mere rent-chargers. Tenants who entered upon their tenancies under formal written contracts for limited periods have been rooted for ever on the soil. Rents have been reduced by judicial sentence, with complete disregard both to previous contracts and to market value, and the legal owner has had no option of refusing the change and re-entering on the occupation of his land.   A scheme of purchase, too, based upon Imperial credit, has been established and will probably soon be largely extended, which is so extravagantly and almost grotesquely favorable to the tenant that it enables him by paying for the space of forty-nine years, instead of his reduced judicial rent, an annual sum which is considerably smaller, to purchase the freehold of his farm.   It is a simple and incontestable truth that neither in the United States, nor in England, nor in any portion of the Continent of Europe, is the agricultural tenant so favoured by law as in Ireland, or anything of the nature of landlord oppression made so impossible. But though agitation has diminished, it has not ceased, and the great body of the poorer Catholics still follow the banner of Home Rule.

About a third of the population of Ireland, on the other hand, regard Home Rule as the greatest catastrophe that could befall themselves, their country, or the Empire ; and it is worthy of notice that they include almost all the descendants of Grattan's Parliament, and of the volunteers and of those classes who in the eighteenth century sustained the spirit of nationality in Ireland.   Belfast and the surrounding counties, which alone in Ireland have attained the full height and vigour of English industrial civilisation ; almost all the Protestants, both Episcopalian and Nonconformist ; almost all the Catholic gentry ; the decided preponderance of Catholics in the lay professions, and a great and guiding section of the Catholic middle-class are on the same side.   Their conviction does not rest upon any abstract doctrine about the evil of federal governments or of local parliaments.   It rests upon their firm persuasion that in the existing conditions of Ireland no Parliament

could be established there which could be trusted to fulfil
the most elementary conditions of honest government—to
maintain law ; to protect property ; to observe or enforce
contracts; to secure the rights and liberties of individuals
and minorities ; to act loyally in times of difficulty and
danger in the interests of the Empire.

They know that the existing Home Rule movement has
grown up by the guidance and by the support of men who
are implacable enemies to the British Empire; that it has
been for years the steady object of its leaders to inspire
the Irish masses with feelings of hatred to that Empire,
contempt for contracts, defiance of law and of those who
administer it ; that, having signally failed in rousing the
agricultural population in a national struggle, those
leaders resolved to turn the movement into an organised
attack upon landed property ; that in the prosecution of
this enterprise they have been guilty, not only of measures
which are grossly and palpably dishonest, but also of an
amount of intimidation, of cruelty, of systematic disregard
for individual freedom scarcely paralleled in any country
during the present century ; and finally that, through
subscriptions which are not drawn from Ireland, political
agitation in Ireland has become a large and highly
lucrative trade—a trade which, like most others, will no
doubt continue as long as it pays.

The nature, methods, and objects of the organisation
which would probably exercise a dominant influence
over an Irish Parliament have been established by overwhelming evidence and beyond all reasonable doubt, after
a long, careful, and most impartial judicial investigation.
The report of the late Special Commissioners [1] and the
evidence on which it is founded have been published ;

---

[1] The Parnell Commission.—Ed.

and their conclusions have very recently been summed up in an admirable work by Professor Dicey, perhaps the ablest of living writers on political subjects. Readers may find in these works abundant evidence of the true character of the Irish Home Rule movement. If they read them with impartiality they will, I believe, have little difficulty in concluding that there have been few political movements in the nineteenth century which are less deserving of the respect or support of honest men.

FORMATIVE INFLUENCES

IT was about four years before the great upheaval of beliefs in England, which was partly caused and partly disclosed by the publication of the 'Essays and Reviews,' in 1860, that I entered Trinity College, Dublin. I had then a strong leaning toward theological studies and looked forward to a peaceful clerical life in a family living near Cork; and in addition to the ordinary university course, I went through that appointed for divinity students. I found my life at the university one of more than common intellectual activity, for although circumstances and temperament made me perhaps culpably indifferent to college ambitions and competitions, I soon threw myself with intense eagerness into a long course of private reading, chiefly relating to the formation and history of opinions. The great High Church wave which had a few years before been so powerful, had been broken when Newman and many other leaders of the party had passed to Catholicism. Darwin and Herbert Spencer had not yet risen above the horizon. Mill was in the zenith of his fame and influence. The intellectual atmosphere was much agitated by the recent discoveries of geology, by their manifest bearing on the Mosaic cosmogony and on the history of the Fall, and by the attempts of Hugh Miller, Hitchcock, and other writers to reconcile them with the received theology. In poetry, Tennyson and

Longfellow reigned, I think with an approach to equality which has not continued. In politics, the school of orthodox political economy was almost unchallenged. In spite of the protests of Carlyle, all sound Liberals in England then desired to restrict as much as possible the functions of government, and to enlarge as much as possible the sphere of individual liberty; and they regarded unrestrained competition and inviolable contracts as the chief conditions of material progress.

The first great intellectual influence which I experienced was, I believe, that of Bishop Butler, who was at that time probably studied more assiduously at Dublin than in any other university in the kingdom. There were few sermons in the college chapel in which some allusion to his writings might not be found, and few serious students whose modes of thought were not at least coloured by his influence. That influence now appears to me to have been not only various, but even in some measure contradictory. The 'Analogy' is perhaps the most original, if not the most powerful, book ever written in defence of the Christian creed; but it has probably been the parent of much modern Agnosticism, for its method is to parallel every difficulty in revealed religion by a corresponding difficulty in natural religion, and to argue that the two must stand or fall together. Butler's unrivalled sermons on human nature, on the other hand, have been essentially conservative and constructive, and their influence has been at least as strong on character as on belief. Their doctrine is that consciousness reveals in the inner principles of our being a moral hierarchy, 'a difference in nature and kind altogether distinct from strength'; and that among these principles conscience has, by the very structure of our nature, a recognised supremacy or guiding authority which clearly distinguishes it from all others.

'The principle of reflection or conscience being compared with the various appetites, affections, and passions in men, the former is manifestly supreme and chief, without regard to strength. . . . From its very nature it manifestly claims superiority over all others, so that you cannot form a notion of this faculty, conscience, without taking in judgment, direction, superintendency. To preside and govern, from the very economy and constitution of man, belongs to it. Had it strength as it has right, it would govern the world.'

It was a noble philosophy, well fitted to strengthen and elevate the character, and it has supported many amid the dissolution of positive beliefs. Utilitarian theories of morals move very smoothly as long as their only task is to define the course which it is in the interests of society that each man should pursue. They are less successful in furnishing any firm and adequate reason why a man should pursue that course when individual interests and individual passion are opposed to it. It is the merit of the schools of Kant and of Butler, that they raise the idea of duty above all the calculations of self-interest, and make it the supreme and guiding principle of life.

Among living men, the strongest intellectual influence at that time in Dublin was, I think, Whately, our archbishop, an original and powerful thinker who has scarcely obtained a place in the literary and intellectual history of his time commensurate with the wide and deep influence he undoubtedly exercised. For this there are many reasons. Unlike the High Church leaders who flourished with him at Oxford in the second quarter of the nineteenth century, he never identified himself with any organised party or school of thought, and he thus deprived himself of many echoes and of much support. It was, indeed, one of his first principles that there is no more fatal obstacle to the discovery of truth than the deflecting influence of party and system, and that the jealous maintenance of an independent judgment is the first element of intellectual honesty. Few considerable writers have appealed less to common passions or wide sympathies ; and the only passion—if it can be called so—that appears strongly in his writings, is the love of truth for its own sake, which is the rarest and highest of all. He was accustomed to speculate much upon that strange power of intellectual magnetism which enables some men to draw others to their views apart from any process of definite reasoning ; and he acknowledged with truth that he was wholly destitute of it; that he had never produced any effect which could not be clearly accounted for, or altered any judgment except by distinct reasons. As a writer, his style, though wholly without grace, was admirable in its lucidity. He had a singular felicity of illustration, and especially of metaphor, and a rare power of throwing his thoughts into terse and pithy sentences ; but his many books, though full of original thinking and in a high degree suggestive to other writers, had always a certain fragmentary and occasional character, which prevented them from taking a place in standard literature. He was conscious of it himself, and was accustomed to say that it was the mission of his life to make up cartridges for others to fire. The little volume of 'Miscellanies,' including his commonplace book and his notes for his books, which was published by his daughter, exhibits with great clearness the character of his mind. Though a very candid and, in

the best sense of the word, a very tolerant man, and an
excellent scholar, he had, I think, little power of reproducing the modes of thought of men whose mental
structure was widely different from his own, or of entering
into the intellectual conditions of other ages; but he
touched a large circle of subjects, social, political, and
even scientific, as well as moral and religious, with an
original and most independent judgment; and he raised
greatly the moral standard of love of truth and the
intellectual standard of severe reasoning wherever his
influence extended. He delighted in that fine saying of
Hobbes that, 'words are the counters of the wise man,
but the money of the fool'; he believed that most
controversies might be resolved into verbal ambiguities;
and his hatred of vagueness, grandiloquence, affected
obscurity, and rhetorical exaggeration exercised a very
useful influence over young men. He was also a most
attentive and sagacious observer of human nature, and few
modern writers have written so wisely on the diversities
and the management of character and on the science of
life. In this respect he had a strong affinity to Bacon—
the Bacon not of the 'Organon,' but of the 'Essays'—
and perhaps still more to Benjamin Franklin. In
theology he challenged the severest inquiry, and believed
that if honestly pursued it would lead only to orthodox
belief. 'A good man,' he once wrote, 'will indeed wish
to find the evidence of the Christian religion satisfactory;
but a wise man will not for that reason think it satisfactory, but will weigh the evidence the more carefully on
account of the importance of the question.'

His strongest antipathy was to the teaching of the
Oxford 'Tracts,' and he wrote about them with great
severity, but more from the moral than the intellectual

side. He believed the Tractarian doctrines of 'reserve'
and 'economy' to be essentially disingenuous ; he considered that there was good reason to conclude that
leading members of the Oxford school had remained in
the Church of England for a considerable time after they
had adopted the Roman theology, had used language
deliberately intended to mask their position, and had
employed their influence as English clergymen to sap
the English Church ; and he especially denounced as
the grossest dishonesty the attempt that was made in
Tract XC. to show that a man was justified in subscribing
to the Articles of the Church of England and at the
same time holding everything laid down by the Council
of Trent, 'though the Articles were expressly drawn up
to condemn the authoritative teaching of the Roman
Church, and after the Council of Trent had held 22
out of its whole number of 25 sessions.' The quibbling,
special-pleading, equivocating mind which is consciously
or half-consciously endeavouring by subtle distinctions to
maintain an untenable position, was of all things the
most abhorrent to him, and while the Evangelicals
denounced the Tractarians as leading men to Rome,
Whately, perhaps alone among his contemporaries,
steadily predicted that their teachings would be followed
by a great period of religious scepticism. This, he said,
would be the result of the discredit they were throwing
on the evidential school, of their habit of coupling
ecclesiastical with Scripture miracles, and of their
doctrine that it is the function of faith to supply the
missing links of imperfect evidence and to impart the
character of certainty to propositions which in reason
rest only on probabilities. He himself was of the school
of Grotius and Paley, and believed that simple historical

evidence established supernatural facts. This subject long held a foremost place in my thoughts and studies, and I afterward wrote much upon it in connection with the history of witchcraft and the miracles of the Saints.

I owed much to Whately, but I was studying concurrently with him teachers of very opposite schools, among others Coleridge, Newman, and Emerson in English; Pascal, Bossuet, Rousseau, and Voltaire in French. Locke's writings formed part of the college course, and I became very familiar with them, and fully shared Hallam's special admiration for the little treatise 'On the Conduct of the Understanding,' while Dugald Stewart, Mackintosh, and Mill opened out wide and various vistas in moral philosophy. The following passage from Coleridge, which I chose as the motto of almost my first published writing, exercised so great an influence over my later studies, and shows so happily the direction in which I was endeavoring to turn my mind, that I may be excused from quoting it at length:

' Let it be remembered by controversialists on all subjects, that every speculative error which boasts a multitude of advocates has its golden as well as its dark side; that there is always some truth connected with it, the exclusive attention to which has misled the understanding; some moral beauty which has given it charms for the heart. Let it be remembered that no assailant of an error can reasonably hope to be listened to by its advocates, who has not proved to them that he has seen the disputed subject in the same point of view and is capable of contemplating it with the same feelings as themselves; for why should we abandon a cause at the persuasion of one who is ignorant of the reasons which have attached us to it?'

Adopting an illustration which had been employed by
Bossuet for another purpose, I came to believe that
religious systems resemble those pictures occasionally
seen in the museums of the curious, which appear at first
to be mere incongruous assemblages of unconnected and
unmeaning figures, till they are regarded from one
particular point of view, when these figures immediately
mass themselves into a regular form, and the whole
picture assumes a coherent and symmetrical appearance.
To discover in each system this point of view; to cultivate
that peculiar form of imagination which makes it possible
to realise how different forms of opinions are held by
their more intelligent adherents, appeared to me the first
condition of understanding them.

In this method of inquiry I was, at a little later period,
much aided by the writings of Bayle, a great critic who
brought to the study of opinions an almost unrivalled
knowledge, and one of the keenest and most detached
of human intellects. Gradually, however, by a natural
and insensible process I passed into the habit of examining opinions mainly from an historical point of view—
investigating the circumstances under which they grow
up ; their relation to the general conditions of their time ;
the direction in which they naturally develop ; the part,
whether for good or ill, which during long spaces of time
they have played in the world. It was first of all in
connection with the Roman Catholic controversy, with
which we were much occupied in Ireland, that I learnt
to pursue this course. Of the enormous and essential
difference between matured Catholicism and the Christianity of the New Testament, I never doubted, and my
convictions were much deepened by long travels in Italy,
France, and Spain, during which I endeavoured to study

H

carefully Catholicism in its actual workings as a popular religion, and not as it appears clarified and rationalised in such books as the 'Exposition,' by Bossuet. I often asked myself, who could have imagined from a perusal of the New Testament that Christianity was intended to be a highly centralised monarchy, governed with supreme divine authority by the Bishop of Rome; that this bishop was to be connected, not with the great author of the Epistle to the Romans, but with St. Peter; that the figure which was to occupy the most prominent place in the devotions and imaginations of millions of Christian worshippers was to be the Virgin Mary, who is not so much as mentioned in the Epistles ; that in the immediate neighbourhood, and with the full sanction of the highest ecclesiastical authorities, graven images were to be employed in devotion as conspicuously as in a pagan temple, particular images being singled out from all others for particular devotion by special indulgences and by special miracles ? I soon convinced myself that popular Catholicism, as it exists in southern Europe and as it has existed through a long course of centuries, is as literally polytheistic and idolatrous as any form of paganism, though it has many beauties, and though much of its very mingled influence has been for good. In the teaching of my early youth, this transformation of Christianity was described as the great predicted apostasy, the mystery of iniquity, the work of Antichrist among mankind. Under the influence of the historic method it assumed a different aspect, and the mystery became very explicable. Hobbes had struck the keynote in a passage of profound truth as well as of admirable beauty :

    'If a man consider the original of this great ecclesiastical dominion, he will easily perceive that the Papacy is no other than the ghost of the deceased Roman Empire, sitting crowned upon the grave thereof.'

Few evolutions in history, indeed, can be more clearly traced than the successive stages through which Rome, by a gradual and very natural process, obtained the primacy of Christendom. In the condition of Europe, again, at the time of the downfall of the Roman Empire, the invasion, the triumph, and the rapid conversion of the barbarians, the chief causes of the materialising transformation which Christian ideas underwent appeared abundantly evident; and it became clear to me that some such transformation was inevitable, and essential to their enduring influence. Was it possible, I asked myself, that in ages of anarchy and convulsion, any religion resembling Protestant Christianity could have prevailed among great masses of wild and ignorant barbarians, with all the associations and mental habits of idolaters, at a time when neither rag paper nor printing was invented, and when a wide diffusion of the Bible was absolutely impossible? But such methods of reasoning could not stop there. I was naturally led to consider how different are the measures of probability, the predispositions toward the miraculous, the canons of evidence and proof, the standards and ideals of morals in different ages, and how largely these differences affect the whole question of evidence. I began to realise the existence of climates of opinion; to observe how particular forms of belief naturally grow and flourish in certain stages of intellectual development, and fade when these conditions have changed; how much that is called apostasy and imposture is in reality anachronism, the survival in one age of forms of belief that were the appropriate product of an earlier one.

A writer of extraordinary brilliancy and power was at this time exercising a great influence either of attraction or repulsion on all serious students of history. Those who are old enough to remember the appearance of the first volume of Buckle's ' History,' in 1857, and of the second volume, in 1861, will remember also how rapidly and how passionately it divided opinion. It was in truth a book in which extraordinary merits were balanced by extraordinary defects. On the special subject of the growth of religions, which most interested me, it was peculiarly deficient, for with all his great gifts Buckle was almost colour-blind to the devotional and reverential aspect of things, and he had little more power than Whately of projecting himself into the beliefs, ideals, and modes of thought of other men and ages. His unqualified, undiscriminating contempt for the ages of superstition is the more remarkable, because fifteen years before the appearance of his first volume, Comte, with whom Buckle had some affinity, and for whom he expressed great admiration, had ·been placing those ages on a pinnacle of extravagant eulogy. His doctrine that there is no real progress in moral ideas and no real history of morals, I have always believed to be profoundly untrue, and to have vitiated a large part of his conclusions ; and although he rendered valuable service in showing by ample illustrations that the capital changes in history are much less due to the great men who directly effected them than to the long train of intellectual, political, or industrial tendencies that had prepared them, he pushed this, like many of his other generalisations, to exaggeration and even to extravagance. Individuals, and even accidents, have had a great modifying and deflecting influence in history, and sometimes the part they have played can scarcely be over-estimated. If, as I have elsewhere said, a stray dart had struck down Mohammed in one of the early skirmishes of his career, there is no reason to believe that the world would have seen a great military and monotheistic religion arise in Arabia, powerful enough to sweep over a large part of three continents, and to mould during many centuries the lives and characters of about a fifth part of the human race. In one respect, too, Buckle was singularly unfortunate in the time in which he appeared. From the days of Bacon and Locke to the days of Condillac and Bentham, it had been the tendency of advanced liberal thinkers to aggrandise as much as possible the power of circumstances and experience over the individual, and to reduce to the narrowest limits every influence that is innate, transmitted, or hereditary. They represented man as essentially the creature of circumstances, and his mind as a sheet of blank paper on which education might write what it pleased. Buckle pushed this habit of thought so far that he even questioned the reality of such an evident and well-known fact as hereditary insanity. But only two years after the appearance of the first volume of the 'History of Civilisation,' Darwin published his 'Origin of Species,' which gradually effected a revolution in speculative philosophy almost as great as it effected in natural science ; and from that time the supreme importance of inborn and hereditary tendencies has become the very central fact in English philosophy. It must be added that Buckle had many of the distinctive faults of a young writer ; of a writer who had mixed little with men, and had formed his mind almost exclusively by solitary, unguided study. He had a very imperfect appreciation of the extreme complexity of social phenomena, an excessive tendency to sweeping generalisations, and an arrogance of assertion which provoked much hostility. His wide and multifarious knowledge was not always discriminating, and he sometimes mixed good and bad authorities with a strange indifference.

This is a long catalogue of defects, but in spite of them Buckle opened out wider horizons than any previous writer in the field of history. No other English historian had sketched his plan with so bold a hand, or had shown so clearly the transcendent importance of studying not merely the actions of soldiers, politicians, and diplomatists, but also those great connected evolutions of intellectual, social, and industrial life on which the type of each succeeding age mainly depends. To not a few of his contemporaries he imparted an altogether new interest in history, and his admirable literary talent, the vast range of topics which he illuminated with a fresh significance, and the noble enthusiasm for knowledge and for freedom that pervades his work, made its appearance an epoch in the lives of many who have passed far from its definite conclusions. The task which he had undertaken was almost too vast for the longest life, and when he died at Damascus, in 1862, he had not yet completed his fortieth year, and his judgment was probably still far from its full maturity. A few lines of Pliny which I wrote on the title-page of his history, will suffice to show the feelings with which I heard of his death :

‘Mihi autem videtur acerba semper et immatura mors eorum qui immortale aliquid parant. Nam qui voluptatibus dediti quasi in diem vivunt, vivendi causas quotidie finiunt; qui vero posteros cogitant et memoriam sui operibus extendunt, his nulla mors non repentina est, ut quæ semper inchoatum aliquid abrumpat.’

I do not purpose to pursue these recollections further. I had drifted far from my Cork living and very decisively into the ways of literature, and after I left the university I spent about four years on the Continent. I read much in foreign libraries, and I also derived great profit as well as keen pleasure from the study of Italian art, which throws an invaluable light on the branches of history I was then investigating. In its earlier phase especially, before the sense of beauty dominates over the idea, art represents with a singular fidelity not only, the religious beliefs of men, but also the far more delicate and evanescent shades of their realisations, ideals, and emotions.

The result of those years of study was my 'History of the Spirit of Rationalism in Europe,' which appeared in the early part of 1865. With many defects, it had at least the merit of describing with great sincerity the process by which the opinions of its author had been formed, and to this sincerity it probably owed no small part of its success.

CARLYLE'S MESSAGE TO HIS AGE.

WHEN Carlyle came to London in 1831, bringing with him the 'Sartor Resartus,' which is now perhaps the most famous of all his works, it is well known that he applied in turn to three of the principal publishers in London, and that each of them, after due deliberation, positively refused to print his manuscript. When at last, with great difficulty, he procured its admission into 'Fraser's Magazine,' Carlyle was accustomed to say that he only knew of two men who found anything to admire in it. One of them was the great American writer, Emerson, who afterwards superintended its publication in America. The other was a priest from Cork, who wrote to say that he wished to take in 'Fraser's Magazine' as long as anything by this writer appeared in it. On the other hand, several persons told Fraser that they would stop taking in the magazine if any more of such nonsense appeared in it. The editor wrote to Carlyle that the work had been received with 'unqualified disapprobation.' Five years elapsed before it was reprinted as a separate book, and in order that it should be reprinted it was found necessary for a number of Carlyle's private friends to club together and guarantee the publisher from loss by engaging to take three hundred copies. But when, a few years before his death, a cheap edition of Carlyle's works was published, 'Sartor Resartus' had acquired such a popularity that thirty thousand copies were almost immediately sold, and since his death it has been reprinted in a sixpenny form; it has penetrated far and wide through all classes, and it is now, I suppose, one of the most popular and most influential of the books that were published in England in the second quarter of the century.

Such a contrast between the first reception and the later judgment of a book is very remarkable, and it applies more or less to all Carlyle's earlier writings. It is a memorable fact in the literary history of the nineteenth century that one of the greatest and most industrious writers in England lived for many years in such poverty that he often thought of abandoning literature and emigrating to the colonies, and he would probably have done so if he had not found in public lecturing a means of supplying his frugal wants. The cause of this long-continued neglect is partly, no doubt, to be found in his style, for, like Browning, Carlyle wrote an English which was so contorted and sometimes so obscure that his readers had to be slowly educated into understanding, or at least enjoying, it. But there are other and deeper causes which I propose to devote the short time at my disposal to indicating.

It has been truly said that there are two great classes among writers. There are those who are echoes and there are those who are voices. There are some writers who represent faithfully and express strongly the dominant tendencies, opinions, habits, characteristics of their age, collecting as in a focus the half-formed thoughts that are prevailing around them, giving them an articulate voice, and by the force of their advocacy greatly strengthening them. There are others who either start new ways of thinking for which the public around them are still unprepared, or who throw themselves in opposition to the dominant tendencies of their times, pointing out the evils and dangers connected with them, and dwelling specially on neglected truths. It is not surprising that the first class are by far the most popular. The public is much like Narcissus in the fable, who fell in love with his own reflection in the water. All men like to find their own opinions expressed with a power and eloquence they cannot themselves attain, and most men dislike a writer who, in the first flush of a great enthusiasm, points out all that can be said on the other side. But when the first enthusiasm is over—when the prevailing tendency has fully triumphed and the evils and defects connected with it are disclosed—the words of this unpopular or neglected teacher will begin to gather weight. It will be found that although he may not have been wiser than those who advocated the other side, yet his words contained exactly that kind of truth which was most needed or most generally forgotten, and his reputation will steadily rise.

This appears to me to have been very much the position which Carlyle occupied towards the chief questions of his day, and it explains, I think, in a great degree the growth of his influence. It is remarkable, indeed, how many things there are in his writings which appeared paradoxes when he wrote, and which now seem almost truisms. Thus at a time when the political and intellectual ascendency of France over the Continent was at its height, Carlyle was one of the few men who clearly recognised the essential greatness that lay hid in Germany, and especially in Prussia—a greatness which after the wars of 1866 and 1870 became very evident to the world. He was one of the first men in England to recognise the importance of German literature, and especially the supreme greatness of Goethe. His translation of 'Wilhelm Meister' was published in 1824, and his noble essay on Goethe in 1832; but at first it seemed to find scarcely any echo. The editor for whom he wrote it reported that all the opinions he could gather about this essay were 'eminently unfavourable.' De Quincey, who of all English critics was believed to know Germany best, and Jeffrey, who exercised the greatest influence on English literary opinion, combined to depreciate or ridicule Goethe. But there is now no educated man who disputes that Carlyle in this matter was essentially right, and that his critics were wholly wrong. And to turn to subjects more directly connected with England, Carlyle wrote at a time when the whole school of what was called advanced thought rested upon the theory that the province of Government ought to be made as small as possible, and that all the relations of classes should be reduced to simple, temporary contracts founded on mutual interest. According to this theory, it was the one duty of Government to keep order. For the rest it should stand aside, and not attempt to meddle in social or industrial questions. The most complete liberty of thought and action should be established, and every-thing should be left to unrestricted competition—to the free play of unprivileged, untrammelled, unguided social forces. This was the theory which was called orthodox political economy—the *laisser-faire* system—the philo-sophy of competition or supply and demand, and it was incessantly denounced by Carlyle as Mammon worship, as 'devil take the hindmost,' as 'pure egoism'; 'the shabbiest gospel that had been taught among men.' He declared that in the long run no society could flourish, or even permanently cohere, if the only relation between man and man was a mere money tie. He maintained that what he called the condition of England question, or, in other words, the great mass of struggling, anarchical poverty that was growing up in the chief centres of population, was a question which imperiously demanded the most strenuous Government intervention—which was, in fact, far more important than any of the purely political questions. The whole system of factory legislation, the whole system of legislation about working men's dwellings, which has taken place in this century, has been a realisation of the ideas of Carlyle. When Carlyle first wrote, it was the received opinion that the education of the people was a matter in which the Government should in no degree interfere, and that it ought to be left altogether to individuals, or Churches, or societies. In his work on Chartism, which was published as early as 1834, Carlyle argued that the ' universal education of the people ' was an indispensable duty of the Government. It was not until about twenty years ago that this duty was fully recognised in England. In the same work he maintained that State-aided, State-organised, State-directed emigration must one day be undertaken on a large scale, as the only efficient agent in coping with the great masses of growing pauperism. In his ' Past and Present,' which was published in 1843, he threw out another idea which has proved very prolific, and which is probably destined to become still more so. It is that it may become both possible and needful for the master worker ' to grant his workers permanent interest in his enterprise and theirs.'

It is evident how much less strange those ideas appear now than they did when they were first put out some fifty years ago. One of the most remarkable changes that has taken place during the lives of men who are still of middle age has been in the opinion of advanced thinkers about the function of Government. In the early days of Carlyle the whole set, or lie, of opinion in England was towards cutting in all directions the bands of Government control, diminishing as much as possible the sphere of Government functions or interference. It was a revolt against the old Tory system of paternal Government, against the system of Guilds, against the State regulations which once prevailed in all departments of industrial life. In the present generation it is not too much to say that the current has been absolutely reversed. The constantly increasing tendency, whenever any abuse of any kind is discovered, is to call upon Parliament to make a law to remedy it. Every year the network of regulation is strengthened ; every year there is an increasing disposition to enlarge and multiply the functions, powers, and responsibilities of Government. I should not be dealing sincerely with you if I did not express my own opinion that this tendency carries with it dangers even more serious than those of the opposite exaggerations of a past century : dangers to character by sapping the spirit of self-reliance and independence ; dangers to liberty by accustoming men to the constant interference of authority, and abridging in innumerable ways the freedom of action and choice. I wish I could persuade those who form their estimate of the province of Government from Carlyle's ' Past and Present ' and ' Latter-day Pamphlets ' to study also the admirable little treatise of Herbert Spencer, called ' The Man and the State,' in which the opposite side is argued. What I have said however, is sufficient to show how remarkably Carlyle, in some of the parts of his teaching that were once the most unpopular, anticipated tendencies which only became very apparent in practical politics when he was an old man or after his death.

The main and fundamental part of his teaching is the supreme sanctity of work; the duty imposed on every human being, be he rich or be he poor, to find a life-purpose and to follow it out strenuously and honestly. 'All true work,' he said, 'is religion'; and the essence of every sound religion is, 'Know thy work and do it.' In his conception of life all true dignity and nobility grows out of the honest discharge of practical duty. He had always a strong sympathy with the feudal system which annexed indissolubly the idea of public function with the possession of property. The great landlord who is wisely governing large districts and using all his influence to diffuse order, comfort, education, and civilisation among his tenantry; the captain of industry who is faithfully and honestly organising the labour of thousands, and regarding his task as a moral duty; the rich man who, with all the means of enjoyment at his feet, devotes his energies ' to make some nook of God's creation a little fruitfuller, better, more worthy of God—to make some human hearts a little wiser, manfuller, happier, more blessed,' always received his admiration and applause. No one, on the other hand, spoke with more contempt of a governing class which had ceased to govern; of titles which had lost their original meaning, and no longer implied or expressed duties performed; of wealth that was employed solely or mainly in selfish enjoyment or in idle show. It was Carlyle's deep conviction that the best test of the moral worth of every nation, class, and individual, is to be found in their standard of work and in their dislike to a useless and idle life. As is well known, he had no sympathy with the prevailing political ideas. He believed that men were not only not equal, but were profoundly unequal; that it was the first interest of society that the wisest men should be selected as its leaders, and that the popular methods of finding the wisest were by no means those which were most likely to succeed. 'No British man,' he complained, 'can attain to be a statesman or chief of workers till he has first proved himself a chief of talkers.' 'The two greatest nations in the world, the English and American, are all going to wind and tongue.' He believed much more than his contemporaries did that there was need and room in our modern English life for strong Government organisation, guidance, discipline, reverence, obedience, and control. 'Wise command, wise obedience,' he wrote in one of his 'Latter-day Pamphlets,' 'the capability of these two is the best measure of culture and human virtue in every man.'

There is another class of workers to which he himself belonged—the men who are the teachers of mankind. He taught them by his example as well as by his precepts. Whatever else may be said about Carlyle, no one can question that he took his literary vocation most seriously. He was for a long time a very poor man, but he never sought wealth by advocating popular opinions, by pandering to common prejudices, or by veiling most unpalatable beliefs. In the vast mass of literature which he has bequeathed to us there is no scamped work, and every competent judge has recognised the untiring and conscientious accuracy with which he verified and sifted the minutest fact. His standard of truthfulness was extremely

high, and one of his great quarrels with his age was that
it was an age of half-beliefs and insincere professions.
He maintained that religious beliefs which had once been
living realities had too often degenerated into mere for-
mulas, untruly professed or mechanically repeated with
the lips only, and without any genuine or heartfelt conviction. He often repeated a saying of Coleridge : ' They
do not believe—they only believe that they believe.' He
used to speak of men who ' played false with their intellects ' ; or, in other words, turned away their minds from
unwelcome truths and by allowing their wishes or interests
to sway their judgments, persuaded or half-persuaded
themselves to believe whatever they wished. A firm
grasp of facts, he maintained, was the first characteristic
of an honest mind ; the main element in all honest,
intellectual work. His own special talent was the gift
of insight, the power of looking into the heart of things,
piercing to essential facts, discerning the real characters
of men, their true measure of genuine, solid worth.
Creeds, professions, opinions, circumstances, all these are
the externals or clothes of men. It is necessary to look
behind them and beyond them if we would reach the
genuine human heart. One of the reasons why he
detested what he called stump oratory was because he
believed it to be a great school of insincerity. Its end
was not truth, but plausibility. It was the effort of interested men to throw opinions into such forms as might
most captivate uninstructed men ; to keep back every
unpopular side ; to magnify everything in them that was
seductive. He once said to me that two great curses
seemed to him eating away the heart and worth of the
English people. One was drink. The other was stump
oratory, which accustomed men to say without shame

what they did not in their hearts believe to be true, and
accustomed their hearers to accept such a proceeding
as perfectly natural. And the same strong passion for
veracity he carried into his judgment of other forms of
work. Rightly or wrongly, he believed that the standard
of conscientious work had been lowered in England
through the feverish competition of modern times, and
under the system of what he called ' cheap and nasty '; that
English work had lost something of its old solidity and
worth, and was now made rather to captivate than to
wear. Carlyle saw in this much more than an industrial
change. He maintained that the love and pride of
thorough work had long been a pre-eminently English
quality, that it was the very tap-root of the moral worth of
the English character, and that anything that tended to
weaken it was a grave moral evil.

It is worth while trying to understand what truth
underlay those parts of his teaching which seem most
repulsive. The worship of force, which is so apparent
in many of his writings, is a striking example. He
was often accused of teaching that might is right. He
always answered that he had not done so—that what he
taught was that right is might; that by the providential
constitution of the Universe truth in the long run is sure
to be stronger than falsehood ; that good will prevail over
evil, and that right and might, though they differ widely
in short periods of time, would in long spaces prove to be
identical. Nothing, he was accustomed to say, seemed
weaker than the Christian religion when the disciples
assembled in the upper room; yet it was in truth the
strongest thing in the world, and it accordingly prevailed.
It was one of his favourite sayings ' that the soul of
the Universe is just,' and he believed therefore that the

I

ultimate fate of nations, whether it be good or bad, was very much what they deserved.   It is curious to observe the analogy between this teaching and the doctrine of the survival of the fittest, which a very different teacher— Charles Darwin—has made so conspicuous.

He scandalised—and I think with a good deal of reason—most of his contemporaries by the ridicule which he threw upon the career of Howard, and upon the great movement for prison reform which was so actively pursued in his time.   Much of what he wrote on this subject is, to me at least, very repulsive ; but you will generally find in the most extravagant utterances of Carlyle that there is some true meaning at bottom.   He maintained that the passion for reforming and improving prisons and prison-life had been carried in England to such a point that the lot of a convicted criminal was often much better than that of an honest and struggling artisan.   He believed that a just and wise distribution of compassion is a most important element of national well-being, and that the English people are very apt to be indifferent to great masses of unobtrusive, struggling, honourable, unsensational poverty at their very doors, while they fall into paroxysms of emotion about the actors in some sensational crime, about some seductive murderess, about the wrongs of some far-off and often half-savage race.   ' In one of these Lancashire weavers dying with hunger there is more thought and heart, a greater arithmetical amount of misery and desperation, than in whole gangs of Quashees.'   He maintained, too, that a strain of sentiment about criminals was very prevalent in his day, which tended seriously to obliterate or diminish the real difference between right and wrong.   He hated with an intense hatred that whole system of philosophy which denied that there was a deep, essential, fundamental difference between right and wrong, and turned the whole matter into a mere calculation of interests. He was accustomed to say that one of the chief merits of Chris-tianity was that it taught that right and wrong were as far apart as Heaven and Hell, and that no greater calamity can befall a nation than a weakening of the righteous hatred of evil.

The parts of Carlyle's teaching on which I have dwelt to-day will be chiefly found in his 'Past and Present,' his ' Heroes and Hero Worship,' his 'Latter-day Pamphlets,' his ' Chartism,' and in the two admirable essays called ' Signs of the Times ' and ' Characteristics.' In my own opinion, though Carlyle teaches much, his writings are most valuable as a moral force. Very few great writers have maintained more steadily that the moral element is the deepest and most important part of our being, deeper and stronger than all intellectual considerations. In his writings, amid much that has imperishable value, there is, I think, much that is exaggerated, much that is one-sided, much that is unwise. But no one can be imbued with his teaching without finding it a great moral tonic, and deriving from it a nobler, braver, and more unworldly conception of human life.

ISRAEL AMONG THE NATIONS[1]

AMONG the strange and unforeseen developments that have characterised the fourth quarter of the nineteenth century, few are likely to be regarded by the future historian with a deeper or more melancholy interest than the anti-Semite movement, which has swept with such a portentous rapidity over a great part of Europe. It has produced in Russia by far the most serious religious persecution of the century. It has raged fiercely in Roumania, the other great centre of the Oriental Jews. In enlightened Germany it has become a considerable parliamentary force. In Austria it counts among its adherents men of the highest social station. Even France, which from the days of the Revolution has been specially distinguished for its liberality to the Jews, has not escaped the contagion. General Boulanger found the anti-Jewish sentiment sufficiently powerful to make an appeal to it one of the articles of his programme, and the extraordinary popularity of the writings of Drumont shows that Boulanger had not altogether miscalculated its force.

It is this movement which has been the occasion of the very valuable work of M. Anatole Leroy-Beaulieu on 'Israel among the Nations.' The author, who is universally recognised as one of the greatest of living political writers, has special qualifications for his task. With an

[1] Mr. Lecky had made various notes with the intention of bringing this essay up to date, but failing health prevented him from accomplishing it.—ED.

exceedingly wide knowledge of the literature relating to his subject he combines much personal knowledge of the Jews in Palestine and in many other countries, and especially in those countries where the persecution has most furiously raged.

That persecution, he justly says, unites in different degrees three of the most powerful elements that can move mankind—the spirit of religious intolerance; the spirit of exclusive nationality; and the jealousy which springs from trade or mercantile competition. Of these elements M. Leroy-Beaulieu considers the first to be on the whole the weakest. In that hideous Russian Perse-cution which 'the New Exodus' of Frederic has made familiar to the English reader, the religious element certainly occupies a very leading place. Pobedonosteff, who shared with his master the chief guilt and infamy of this atrocious crime, belonged to the same type as the Torquemadas of the past, and the spirit that animated him has entered largely into the anti-Semite movement in other lands. The 'Gloria' of Galdos, perhaps the most powerful religious novel of our time, describes the conflict in modern Spain of the fanaticism of Catholicism with the fanaticism of Judaism. Even the old calumny that the Jews are accustomed at Easter to murder Christian children in order to mix their blood with the passover bread, is still living in many parts of Europe. M. Leroy-Beaulieu has collected much curious evidence on the sub-ject. It is a calumny which appears first to have become popular about 1100 A.D. It is embodied in a well-known tale of Chaucer. It is the subject of one of the great frescoes that were painted around the Cathedral of Toledo to commemorate the expulsion of the Jews from Spain. Two Popes of the thirteenth century, to their great honour, declared its falsehood, and by the order of Benedict XIV. Ganganelli wrote a full memoir examining and refuting it. But in spite of all condemnations, in spite of many exposures in the law courts, it is still a popular belief in Russia, Poland, Roumania, Hungary, and Bohemia, and even within the last ten years it has been the direct cause of many outrages against the Jews.

Another element to which M. Leroy-Beaulieu attaches considerable importance is the Kultur Kampf in Germany. When the German Government was engaged in its fierce struggle with the Catholics, these endeavoured to effect a diversion and to avenge themselves on papers, which were largely in the hands of Jews, by raising a new cry. They declared that a Kultur Kampf was indeed needed, but that it should be directed against the alien people who were undermining the moral foundations of Christian societies; who were the implacable enemies of the Christian creed and of Christian ideals. The cry was soon taken up by a large body of Evangelical Protestants. The ' Germania ' and the ' Civiltà Cattolica,' which were the chief organs of Ultramontanism in Germany and Italy, and the ' Kreuz Zeitung,' which represented the strictest forms of German Protestantism, agreed in fomenting it.

Still more powerful, in the opinion of our author, has been the spirit of intense and exclusive nationality which has in the present generation arisen in so many countries and which seeks to expel all alien or heterogeneous elements, and to mould the whole national being into a single definite type. The movement has been still further strengthened by the greater keenness of trade competition. In the midst of many idle, drunken, and ignorant populations the shrewd, thrifty, and sober Jew stands conspicuous as the most successful trader. His rare power of judging, influencing, and managing men, his fertility of resource, his indomitable perseverance and industry, continually force him into the foremost rank, and he is prominent in occupations which excite much animosity. The tax-gatherer, the agent, the middleman, and the moneylender are very commonly of Jewish race, and great Jewish capitalists largely control the money markets of Europe at a time when capital is the special object of socialistic attacks.

The most valuable portion of this work is, I think, that examining the part which the Jewish race is now playing in the world, and tracing the action of historical causes on the formation of their character. On the old problem of the continued existence of the race through so many ages M. Leroy-Beaulieu has much to say. He reminds us that in the East the idea of nationality is habitually absorbed in the idea of religion, and that there are many examples of the long survival of peoples or tribes which have lost their political individuality. He instances the Copts of Egypt, the Maronites and Druses of Lebanon, the Parsees of India, the Armenians and Greeks of Asia as displaying, though in a less degree, the same phenomenon as the Jews. He attributes the long continuance of the Jews as a separate people mainly to two causes. One of them is Christian hatred, which compelled the Jews for many centuries to remain a separate people, unmixed with surrounding nations ; living in a separate quarter ; marrying among themselves ; strengthened and disciplined in the struggle of life by enormous difficulties and by the constant elimination through persecution of the weaker elements. The other is the very elaborate Jewish ritual extending to all departments of life, which has stamped upon them an intensely distinctive character.

The force of these causes is undoubted, but they are not, I think, the only elements to be considered. M. Leroy-Beaulieu appears to me to have somewhat underrated the physiological force and tenacity of the Jewish race-type. Following the line of reasoning of a remarkable essay of Renan, he shows very clearly that the modern Jews are far from being pure Semites. He proves from Josephus and from other sources that there was a considerable period, both before and after the Christian era, when great numbers of Greeks, Latins, and Egyptians adopted the Jewish faith ; that much alien blood afterward poured into the race through conversions among the barbarians and through the circumcision of the slaves of Jewish masters, and that there is even reason to believe that, in some periods of history, marriages with Christians were not infrequent. It is probable, however, that most alien elements that were introduced into the race sooner or later mingled with the old stock, and no fact is more clearly shown than the extraordinary power of the Jewish type to survive and dominate in a mixed race. A single instance of a marriage with a Jewess will be sufficient to perpetuate it in a family for many generations. In this fact the Jews possess an element of stability which is wholly independent of all considerations of creed and ritual. Few things are more curious than the effect of persecution on the Jewish element in Spain and Portugal. Tens of thousands of Jews in those countries were burned at the stake or driven into exile, but great numbers also conformed. They mixed in a few generations with the old Christian population, and Spain and Portugal, M. Leroy-Beaulieu truly says, are now among the countries in which the Jewish blood is most evidently and most widely diffused.

Another consideration, which M. Leroy-Beaulieu has omitted to mention, but which appears to me to have much weight, is the condemnation of lending money at interest by the Church. This condemnation, which lasted many centuries, had two important consequences. One of them was that the Jews became almost the only moneylenders in Europe. The trade was deemed sinful for a Christian, but it was found to be a very necessary one; and the Jews (as some Catholic theologians observed) being already damned, were allowed to practise it. The other consequence was that on account of the stigma which the Church attached to moneylending, the amount of money to be lent was greatly diminished, or in other words, the rate of interest was enormously and artificially raised. At a time, therefore, when Catholic intolerance made it impossible for the Jews to mingle with and be absorbed in surrounding nations they acquired one of the greatest elements of power and stability that a race can possess—a monopoly of the most lucrative trade in the world.

The physical characteristics of the race are very remarkable and they are especially displayed among the Eastern Jews, who still maintain scrupulously amid poverty and persecution the religious observances of their ancestors. It is now clearly shown that the Levitical code was in a high degree hygienic, and even anticipates some of the discoveries of modern physiology. Prescriptions about forbidden kinds of food and about the mode of cooking food, which only excited the ridicule of Voltaire, have a real hygienic value in the eyes of Claude Bernard and of Pasteur. The Jews have never adopted the

Catholic notions about the sanctity of celibacy and virginity, but they lay great stress on the purity of marriage. Although they live chiefly in towns, illegitimate births are proportionately rarer among them than among either Protestants or Catholics. They have been as a rule singularly free from the kinds of vice that do most to enfeeble and corrode a race. They are distinguished for their domestic virtues, especially for care of their children, and they are nearly everywhere less addicted than Christian nations to intoxicating drinks. These things help to explain the curious fact that in nearly all countries the average duration of life is considerably longer among Jews than among Christians. This superiority is general, but, as M. Leroy-Beaulieu observes, it tends to diminish in Western countries where Jews, being freed from disabilities, are more assimilated to the surrounding populations. They now usually marry later than Christians; they have on the whole fewer children, but a proportionately larger number of Jewish than of Christian infants attain adult age. M. Leroy-Beaulieu mentions two curious facts which are less easy to explain. Still-born births are very rare among Jews, and there is among them a wholly abnormal preponderance of male births over female ones.

It might be supposed from these facts that the Jews were a robust race, but no one who has come much in contact with them will share this delusion. Nothing is more conspicuous among them than their unhealthy colouring, their frail, bent, and feeble bodies. They develop early, but they have very little of the spring and buoyancy of youth and they have everywhere a low average of physical strength. Malformations and deformities are common among them; their nervous organisation is extremely sensitive, and though they are as a race distinguished for their sound, clear, and practical judgment, they are very liable to insanity and to other nervous and brain disorders. Physical beauty as well as physical strength is much rarer among them than among Christians.

The causes of this inferiority may be easily explained. Life pursued during many generations in the crowded Ghetto ; the sordid habits that grow out of extreme poverty and out of the assumption of the appearance of poverty, which is natural in a persecuted and plundered race, go far to explain it ; but there is another and, I think, a more important cause which M. Leroy-Beaulieu has rather strangely neglected. Physical strength and beauty can be maintained at a high level in crowded town populations only by a constant influx from the country. The pure air and the healthy labour of the fields are their main source. This great school of health the Jews have never known. For many centuries it would have been impossible for them to have lived in peace as farmers or agricultural labourers among a Christian peasantry, and if they ever possessed any aptitude or taste for agricultural pursuits they have long since wholly lost it.

Their moral like their physical characteristics present strange contrasts. No natural want of moral elevation or tenderness or grace can be ascribed to the nation that has produced both the Old Testament and the Gospels, and has most largely shaped and inspired the moral life of the civilised world. In Christian times no race has maintained its faith with a more devoted courage, and it has encountered and survived persecutions before which the persecutions of other creeds dwindle almost into insignificance. M. Leroy-Beaulieu quotes the statement of the grand Rabbi Lehmann, that it is a clearly attested fact that in two months of the year 1096 twelve thousand Jews, whose names have been preserved, were massacred in the towns of the Rhine alone, because they refused to accept a Christian baptism. The Spanish Jews who perished by one of the most excruciating deaths rather than forswear their faith may be numbered by thousands, and those who preferred exile and spoliation to apostasy, by hundreds of thousands. Even in our own sceptical and materialising age the conduct of the Russian Jews under the recent savage persecution shows that the old spirit is not extinct. In the face of the long and splendid roll of Jewish heroism, it is idle to dwell on the fact that in each great persecution some Jews have yielded to the fear of death and consented to perform the rites of a faith which they inwardly abhorred, or on the fact that a few Rabbis have under such circumstances justified these feigned conversions.

Prolonged persecution, however, has had a profound influence on their character, and its influence in some respects has been very pernicious. Hatred naturally provokes hatred, and violent oppression against which there is no redress is naturally encountered by subterfuge and fraud. A race who were for centuries playing their part in life against overwhelming obstacles learned to avail themselves of every advantage. Adulation, servility, falsehood, and deception became common among them. They became at once hard, wily, and rapacious, and ready instruments in ignoble and oppressive callings. Shut out from open paths and honourable ambitions they haunted the obscurer byways of industry; they were to be found in many occupations which sharpen the intellect but blunt the moral sense, and they threw themselves passionately into the acquisition of wealth and of secret power. Exposed for generations, even in lands where they were not more seriously persecuted, to constant insult and contempt, they often lost their self-respect and learned to acquiesce tamely in what another race would resent. Slavish conditions produced, as they always do, slavish characteristics, and, as is always the case, those characteristics did not at once disappear when the conditions that produced them had altered.

M. Leroy-Beaulieu has dwelt with much force on this subject, and he ascribes considerable weight to the fact that the Jews have been wholly outside the system of feudalism and chivalry in which the modern conception of honour was chiefly formed. Perhaps the Jew might retort with some justice, that he has had at least the compensating moral advantage of having derived no part of his notions of right and wrong from a Church in which such an institution as the Spanish Inquisition was deemed a holy thing.

Defects of another kind have contributed largely to his unpopularity. Great as is the power of assimilation which the Jewish race possesses, the charm and grace of manner seem to have been among the qualities they most slowly and most imperfectly acquire. It is natural that men who have been excluded from honours but not from wealth should value money and the ostentatious display of riches more than their neighbours. In the professions in which the Jews chiefly excel, men rise most rapidly from low origin and culture to conspicuous wealth. Direct money-making has some tendency to materialise and lower the character, and Jews have been for generations prominent in occupations which do much to impair those delicacies of feeling on which the charm of manner largely depends. Besides this, as M. Leroy-Beaulieu truly remarks, though the oldest of the cultured races they are a race of *parvenus* in the good society of Europe. In nearly all countries they have till very recently been excluded from the kind of society and from the kind of education in which the best manners are formed. The exaggerations of bad taste ; the love of the loud, the gaudy, the ostentatious, and the meretricious ; the awkwardness of men who are ill at ease in an unaccustomed sphere, who have not yet mastered the happy mean between arrogance and obsequiousness and who are therefore somewhat prone to both extremes, still frequently characterise them. Few persons who know Germany will doubt that the tone of manners of the German Jews has contributed quite as much as any other cause to their unpopularity.

It is probable that these defects will gradually diminish, and it would be a grave error to regard the Jewish race as wholly devoted to material ends. The multitude of their martyrs is a sufficient answer to the charge, and no people cherish more strongly the ideals of their past and have more of the pride both of race and of creed. They have at all times, as M. Leroy-Beaulieu observes, been distinguished for their reverence for learning, and it is an undoubted fact that Jewish families and families mixed with Jewish blood have produced an amount and variety of ability that far exceed the average of men. The ability goes rather with the race than with the religion. Spinosa, Heine, Ricardo, and Disraeli — to quote but a few of the most illustrious names—were not believers in the synagogue. Some of the forms in which the Jews have most excelled are such as might have been expected from their past. It is natural that the descendants of the most nomadic and cosmopolitan of races should have been great masters of language and in the foremost rank of philologists, and it is not surprising that the descendants of the chief moneylenders and calculators of the world should have produced great financiers, and have shown a very eminent aptitude for mathematics. Medicine more than most professions depends on individual ability, and has been exercised independently of the favour of Churches and Governments, and in medicine the Jews were for a long period pre-eminent. Their marked taste and turn for music may appear more surprising. It is universally recognised and is sufficiently evident to anyone who will look at the faces of the chief orchestras of Europe. Besides a crowd of lesser names they have produced among composers Mendelssohn, Meyerbeer, and Halévy, and among contemporary performers Rubinstein, Joachim, Hermann Levy, and Lucca. A Jewess is the most popular tragic actress on the contemporary stage, and another Jewess was probably the greatest tragic actress of the century. M. Leroy-Beaulieu notices that in painting and sculpture the Jews have been less conspicuous, and he attributes this to their horror of idolatry. I should rather ascribe it to the fact that European art in its best period was mainly devoted to depicting Christian subjects for Christian churches. At all events several considerable Jewish names may be cited in contemporary art, and the Dutch painter who bears the name of Israels is perhaps the greatest living master of the pathetic in painting. In Western Europe, wherever public life has been opened to them, Jews have thrown themselves into almost all the great movements of their time and have distinguished themselves in nearly all. Crémieux, who was a leading figure in the French

Republic of 1848, was a Jew both by birth and by creed. David Manin and Léon Gambetta had Jewish blood in their veins. Lassalle and Marx, the chief names in German socialism, as well as great numbers of their followers belong to the same race, and more than one English example of political eminence will occur to the reader. In both German and Dutch literature Jewish names are frequent and they are nearly everywhere prominent in journalism. In the army they have been much less distinguished. Many Jews no doubt serve in the great continental armies with honour, but the Jew is naturally a pacific being, hating violence and recoiling with a peculiar horror from blood. The beneficence of the Jew was for a long time very naturally confined to his own race, but since the hand of persecution has been withdrawn, and wherever the Jews have been suffered to mingle freely with the Christian population, it has taken a wider range and Jewish names are conspicuous in some of the best forms of unsectarian philanthropy.

It is the evident tendency of modern political life to split up into a number of distinct groups representing distinct interests or forms of thought. We find a Catholic party, a Nonconformist party, a Labour party, a Socialist party, a Temperance party, and many others. But in spite of the crusade that has arisen in so many countries against the Jews, we nowhere find a distinct and clearly defined Jewish party. The tendency of the race is rather to throw themselves ardently into existing movements, and their power of assimilation is one of their most remarkable gifts. As M. Leroy-Beaulieu shows by many illustrations, they are apt in most Western nations even to exaggerate the national characteristics, though they usually combine with them a certain flexibility of adaptation and a certain cosmopolitanism of view which is essentially their own.

It was inevitable that with such tendencies the old rigidity of creed should be impaired and that the observances which completely severed the Jew from other people should be discarded. There can be little doubt that the dissolution of old beliefs which has been such a marked and ominous characteristic of the latter half of the nineteenth century has been even more common among the Western Jews than in Christian nations, and it appears to have spread quite as rapidly among the women as among the men. Many Jews have passed into complete religious indifference—into absolute and often very cynical negation. They have become, as Sheridan wittily said, like the blank page between the Old and the New Testament. Others have taken refuge in a kind of highly rationalised Judaism little different from pure Theism. Some of the most independent, scientific, and trenchant criticism of the Old Testament writings has proceeded from members of the race which was once distinguished for the most complete and superstitious worship of the letter of the law. Spinoza in his ' Tractatus Theologico-Politicus ' led the way in this path, and in our own day I need only mention the writings of Salvador, Kalisch, and Darmesteter and the remarkable Hibbert Lectures of Mr. Montefiore.

This movement, however, is chiefly confined to the Western Jews. The Oriental Jews have retained in a far greater measure their old creed and ritual, their old fanaticism and aspirations. To them Palestine is still the land of promise, and they still dream that it is destined to become once more a Jewish State. Few persons who consider the conditions of the East and the

K

power of the Jewish race will pronounce the realisation of this dream to be impossible or even in a very high degree improbable. Perhaps the most formidable obstacle is the poverty of the land and the total absence among the Jews of agricultural tastes and aptitudes. One thing, however, may be safely predicted. If Palestine is ever again to become a Jewish land, this will be effected only through the wealth and energy of the Western Jews, and it is not those Jews who are likely to inhabit it.

MADAME DE STAËL

AMONG the many important works which have lately been published on the Continent, reconstructing the history of France during the struggle of the Revolution and during the periods that immediately preceded and followed it, scarcely any have been so comprehensive, and not many have been so valuable, as ' The History of the Life and Times of Madame de Staël,' by Lady Blenner-hassett. The author—a Bavarian lady who was an intimate friend and favourite pupil of Dr. Döllinger—has brought to her task a knowledge, which is scarcely rivalled in its completeness, of the French, German, English, and Italian literatures relating to the period ; and she has produced a work of which it is in one sense the merit, but in another the defect, that it sweeps over a far wider field than might be expected from its title. It is seldom, I think, a judicious thing to confuse the provinces of history and biography by turning the life of an individual into an elaborate history of his time ; and in the few cases in which this method has been successfully pursued, the biographer has selected as his subject some man like Cromwell, or Frederick the Great, or Napoleon, who was indisputably the chief mover of his age. When figures of less prominence are chosen, both the history and the biography are apt to suffer. The true perspective, or relative magnitude, of events is impaired, and the book is almost sure to lose something of its artistic charm and of

its popularity. Mr. Masson, as it seems to me, committed
a mistake of this kind in his 'Life of Milton,' when he
grouped around the great Puritan poet—who, however
illustrious, was certainly not the central figure of his
time—a full and valuable history of the Commonwealth,
and of large sections of the reigns of Charles I. and
Charles II.

In like manner, a great part of the work of Lady
Blennerhassett is not biography, but history, and history
of a very high order. Madame de Staël was so closely
connected in her own person, and still more through her
father, with the early events of the French Revolution,
that we accept with gratitude the admirable sketch of
that period which Lady Blennerhassett has given us ; but
we should scarcely expect to find in a work primarily
devoted to Madame de Staël full and masterly accounts
of the Ministry of Turgot, of the rise and teaching of
the Economists, of the rival influence of the writings
of Montesquieu and Rousseau on the French political
character, of the effect of English influence and American
example in preparing the Revolution, and of the part
played by Germans and Swedes in French politics. At
the same time, the pictures of the social and intellectual
life prevailing in the different countries with which
Madame de Staël was connected, and the full accounts
given of a crowd of persons with whom she came into
casual contact, though in themselves both interesting and
valuable, often tend to divert the reader from the main
subject of the book. In truth, Lady Blennerhassett has
not been able to resist the temptation of a very full mind
to pour out all its knowledge, and, while possessing many
rare and brilliant literary gifts, she appears to me to want
that restraining sense of literary perspective which gives

biography its true proportion and symmetry. This defect has, I fear, diminished the popularity of a most valuable book. In the original German, and in an excellent French translation which was revised by the author and which I especially commend to my readers, the work consists of three very substantial volumes.[1] A hasty reader will readily conclude that, in this short and crowded life, such a space is far more than should be allotted to a long-vanished figure which, though interesting and brilliant, was not of the first magnitude. But if he has the courage to persevere, he will soon discover that few modern books have lighted up in so many directions the political, social, moral, and intellectual history of a momentous period, and have exhibited at once so many kinds of talent and so wide a range of sympathies and knowledge. The complete competence, the firm, sober, and—if I may use the expression— masculine judgment with which Lady Blennerhassett has grasped the great political problems of the period of the Revolution, is not less conspicuous than the truly feminine delicacy of observation and touch with which she has delineated social life in many different countries, and painted the finer shades of many widely dissimilar characters.

Anne Louise Germaine Necker was born in Paris on April 22, 1766. Her father was at that time known only as a Swiss banker of high character and reputation, who had amassed a vast fortune and had come to Paris for his private affairs; but about two years after the birth of his daughter he was appointed to represent the interests of Geneva at Paris, and when she was ten years old he rose, for the first time, to a leading place in the Ministry of

[1] There is also an English, and somewhat abridged, translation.

France. Her mother had been the Mademoiselle Curchod whose charms and accomplishments had captivated Gibbon when he was a young man at Lausanne. Every reader of his autobiography will remember the famous passage in which he describes his engagement, the opposition of his father, and the resignation with which he 'sighed as a lover, but obeyed as a son.' M. d'Haussonville has published from the archives at Coppet some melancholy letters which show clearly that Gibbon exhibited more heartlessness and inflicted more suffering than might be gathered from his own stately narrative. But no lasting scar remained. After a few years of poverty and hardship, during which she was obliged to earn a livelihood as a schoolmistress, Mademoiselle Curchod found in Necker a husband who realised her fondest wishes ; and when, soon after, she became the centre of a brilliant salon at Paris, her former lover, then in the zenith of his fame, was often among her guests. Madame Necker did not always abstain from slightly veiled allusions to the past, but it is pleasant to see that a warm and solid friendship seems to have grown up between Gibbon and both his host and hostess. A pretty anecdote is related of how, on one occasion, after he had left the house, they agreed in expressing the deep regret with which they looked forward to his approaching departure for England ; when their little daughter, who was then just ten years old, gravely offered to prevent the catastrophe by marrying the illustrious, but by no means prepossessing, historian.

It was a saying of Talleyrand that he who had not lived before 1789 had never known the full charm of life. Germaine Necker grew up in the last bright flush of a society which had, perhaps, as many fascinations as any that the world has known. Her mother, however, though she occupied a prominent position in this brilliant world, was never altogether of it. She shared fully, indeed, its intellectual tastes, and had herself won some small place in literature. She threw herself ardently into its philanthropic movements, and especially into that for the reform of the hospitals. She formed a warm and true friendship with Buffon and Thomas. She corresponded with Voltaire, and attracted to her house most of the best writers of the age. But to the last she remained eminently and characteristically Swiss, and she never acquired the light touch, or the easy, pliant grace, of the true Parisian. She was a little cold, a little prim, a little pedantic, a little self-conscious. Neither her reserved manners nor her strong domestic tastes, nor the vein of Puritanism that ran through her opinions, harmonised with the lax and sceptical society around her, and it was no sacrifice to her to exchange the splendours and the gaieties of Paris for her peaceful retreat on the Lake of Geneva.

In this, as in most respects, her daughter was very different. In her the Swiss element had altogether disappeared, and, as is often the case with the eminent child of eminent parents, her character shot out in directions wholly unlike both that of her father and that of her mother. She was not beautiful, though her dark and eminently lustrous eyes, beaming with intelligence, and her rich brown tint, gave some charm to her large and rather coarse features ; while her massive shoulders, arms, and breast, her full lips and the firm grasp of her vigorous hand, indicated a strong, frank, ruling, and passionate nature, overflowing with life and with many forms of energy. Her education was somewhat fitfully conducted, but she threw herself eagerly into literary enthusiasms. At fifteen we find her annotating Montesquieu. Raynal and Richardson were among her idols, but, like most of the more ardent spirits of her generation, her ideas and character were moulded chiefly by the genius of Rousseau. Her first work of importance was an exposition of his doctrines, and his influence left deep traces on both ' Corinne ' and ' Delphine.' Her strong sane judgment, however, her genuine humanity, and the moderating influence of her father, saved her from being swept away, like Madame Roland and most of the disciples of Rousseau, by the sanguinary torrent of revolutionary enthusiasm ; and in times of wild passion and exaggeration she usually exhibited a singular soundness and sobriety of political judgment. She was sometimes mistaken, but on the whole it may well be doubted whether there is any other French writer or politician of the period of the Revolution whose contemporary judgments of men and events have been more frequently ratified by posterity.

In this respect she was not of the school of Rousseau. In another and less admirable way she was curiously untouched by his spirit, for few superior intellects have been so openly, so utterly, insensible to the charms of nature. She once spoke of ' the infernal peace ' of her Swiss home, and she candidly acknowledged that if it were not for respect for the opinions of others she would not open her window to look for the first time on the Bay of Naples, though she would gladly travel five hundred leagues to make the acquaintance of a man of talent. On the borders of the Lake of Geneva, with one of the fairest scenes on earth expanding before her, she was incessantly pining for ' le ruisseau de la Rue du

Bac'—for the interest and the excitement of a society which had become the passion of her life.

Her gifts of conversation were very wonderful, and she had a wide range of sympathies, keen insight into character, and great power of describing it by a few vivid words. She had, however, no reticence or reserve, she made many enemies by her unbounded frankness, and she often fatigued or overwhelmed by her exuberant animal spirits and by the torrent of her words. At the same time, unlike most great talkers, she possessed to a very eminent degree the gifts of learning from others, of grasping the characteristic features of their teaching, of awakening sympathies, of dispelling bashfulness, and of kindling latent intellect into a flame. Few women combined so remarkably a sound and moderate judgment with extreme vividness and impetuosity of emotion. She admired deeply, and she generally admired wisely; her first judgments and impulses were almost always generous; and, although she was subject to violent gusts of passion, she could be very patient with those she loved. Through her whole life she was the warmest and most self-sacrificing of friends, and her few antipathies were singularly devoid of rancour. One of those who knew her best pronounced her to be 'absolutely incapable of hatred.'

She soon became the most attractive figure in the salon of Madame Necker, and as the health of her mother declined she became its central figure. Her rare accomplishments and her position as a great heiress naturally would have drawn many suitors around her, but in that age the determined Protestantism of her family was a formidable barrier. It appears from something that she wrote late in life to a German correspondent that, when a mere girl, she had come under the spell of Louis de Narbonne, who asked her hand, and with whom, in after years, she had relations which caused much scandal and which greatly coloured her political life. The story that her parents at one time contemplated a marriage between her and William Pitt, on the occasion of his visit to France in 1783, was discredited by Lord Stanhope ; but M. d'Haussonville pronounces it to be quite true, though there is no clear evidence that Pitt was apprised of the wish of the Neckers. She was then only seventeen, and her vehement protest against an English marriage nipped the project in the bud. In 1786, however, a marriage was negotiated for her with the Swedish ambassador, the Baron de Staël, who was at that time a special favourite of Gustavus III. It was a marriage into which but little affection entered, and twelve years later it ended in a separation. There was afterward, it is true, a partial reconciliation, and she was present with her husband when he died, in 1802, on the way from Paris to Coppet.

Her marriage gave her an independent position, and she mixed much in the politics of the early days of the Revolution. She corresponded regularly with the Swedish King, and formed intimate friendships with great numbers of the guiding politicians. The proudest moment of her life was in August 1788, when, amid a transport of transient enthusiasm and extravagant hopefulness, her father was for the second time called to the helm. Her devotion to him amounted almost to adoration, and she would never acknowledge, what the rest of the world soon perceived, that, though excellently adapted to be Minister in quiet, regular times, he had neither the daring nor the insight, nor the commanding power, that was needed to guide the bark of State through the fierce storms of the Revolution. She fully shared the enthusiasm with which the opening of the States General was received. She mentions that on that occasion she was watching the procession from a window with Madame de Montmorin, wife of the Minister of Foreign Affairs, and that as she expressed her delight, her companion said: 'You are wrong in rejoicing; great calamities will follow from this to France and to us.' The words were truly prophetic. Madame de Montmorin perished on the scaffold with one of her sons; the other was drowned. Her husband was murdered in prison during the massacre of the second of September. Her eldest daughter died in the prison hospital. Her youngest daughter withered away when not yet thirty, broken-hearted by the calamities of her family.

Madame de Staël, too, soon discovered that no millennium was at hand. She was an eye-witness of the terrible scenes of the fifth and sixth of October, when Versailles was invaded by a half-famished mob, when the guards were cut down and beheaded, and when the royal family were brought captive to Paris. She clearly saw that all power was passing from the Government to the clubs, and that the mob violence which reigned was either instigated or deliberately connived at by the very men whose first duty was to repress it. 'These gentlemen,' she once said, 'are like the rainbow; they always appear when the storm is over.' Under her influence the Swedish Embassy became the chief centre in which the 'Constitutional Party' was organised. Narbonne and Talleyrand were then completely devoted to her. Ségur, Choiseul, the Prince de Broglie, and other members of the party were constantly at her house; and at what were called her 'coalition dinners' she brought them in contact with leading men of other groups. She had a conspicuous talent for inspiring, encouraging, conciliating, and organising a party ; and for some months she exercised a very real political influence. Her aim was a constitutional monarchy of the English type; but she came gradually to believe that a republic, or at least a change of Sovereigns, had become inevitable. She never wavered in her devotion to liberty, order, and justice; but on minor questions she always exhibited a spirit of compromise which was very rare in her age and in her country. ' The true line of conduct in politics,' she once said, ' is always to be ready to rally to the least obnoxious party among your adversaries, even though it is far from representing exactly your own point of view.' At the end of 1791 she had a moment of delicious triumph, when her favourite Narbonne became Minister of War. Marie Antoinette, who disliked her, clearly recognised her hand. ' Count Louis de Narbonne,' she wrote to Fersen, ' has been Minister of War since yesterday. What a glory for Madame de Staël and what a pleasure for her to have the whole army at her disposal ! '

The triumphs of Madame de Staël, however, were very fleeting. Her father had fallen irretrievably, and in September 1790 he passed almost unnoticed out of the country where, but little more than a year before, he had been welcomed with such enthusiasm. The Ministry of Narbonne, to which she had attached her most ardent hopes, ended in four months, and before its conclusion her husband, whose views on French politics had been for some time diverging from those of his Sovereign, was recalled. He was not, however, replaced, and Madame de Staël remained alone in Paris till September 1792. Her position there was an extremely dangerous one. She had long been an object of incessant abuse in the

Royalist press, and now the red waves of Jacobinism were
rising higher and higher, surging fiercely around those to
whom she was most attached. Nothing in her life is so
admirable as the courage with which, in this period of
the Revolution, she devoted herself to saving the lives of
the proscribed. Her purse was always open, and she
often risked not only her fortune, but her life. The
royal family had always disliked her ; but she was filled
with horror at the fate that was impending over them,
and she herself organised a plan for their escape, in
which, if it had been accepted, she would have borne a
leading part, at the imminent risk of her head ; and she
afterward wrote an earnest and eloquent pamphlet in the
hope of saving the life of the Queen. Sometimes by
interceding with those in power, sometimes by concealing
fugitives in the Swedish Embassy, very often by large and
timely gifts of money, she saved many. Her own life, at
the time of the September massacres, was in extreme
danger, and she at last fled to Switzerland. Coppet then
became a great centre of refugees, and many of them
owed their lives to her help. Among others, Narbonne
appears to have owed his escape, in part at least, to her
assistance, and she chiefly managed the escape of his
daughter. She was for a long time completely under his
charm ; but he is said to have been irritated by her often
tactless impetuosity, and especially by the manner in
which public opinion regarded him as her creature, and
he seems to have treated her with much ingratitude.
There was no violent breach, but there was a separation,
and a wound which was long and bitterly felt. Many
years later, Madame de Staël, when praising the Prince
de Ligne, said of him : ' He had the manners of
Monsieur de Narbonne—and a heart.'

A short visit to England, in 1793, the death of her
mother in May 1794, and the publication of her first
purely political work, ' Reflections on Peace, addressed to
Mr. Pitt and to the French,' were the chief events of her
life during the next few months. In this work she dwelt
with much force on the absurdity of supposing that any
foreign intervention could restore what the Revolution
had destroyed, and she predicted that the inevitable effect
of the prolongation or extension of the war would be to
strengthen that militant Jacobinism which was now the
greatest danger to Europe. In this year, too, she first
came in contact with Benjamin Constant, and her
acquaintance soon developed into a connection which
gave her a new and powerful instrument, for acting on
French politics, but which also brought with it much
suffering, many reproaches, and long and lasting discredit. In May 1795 we find her again in Paris, with
her husband, who had once more been sent on a mission
to France ; again eagerly engaged in French politics ;
again largely occupied in defending the interests of her
proscribed friends. Among others, Talleyrand appears to
have owed his recall to her influence. As usual, she
excited many antipathies, she was denounced in the
Convention by Legendre for her political intrigues and
especially for her efforts in favour of the emigrants, and
she was obliged to leave Paris for about eighteen months.
Her pen was at this time very active, and to this period
belong her ' Essay on Novels ' and her ' Treatise on the
Passions.'

The star of Bonaparte was now rapidly rising, and it
profoundly affected the last years of her life. The pages
in her ' Considerations on the French Revolution ' in
which she describes her first interview with him, after

the peace of Campo Formio, are among the most graphic she ever wrote, though something of the shadow of the picture was, no doubt, drawn from later experience and antipathy. She was at first dazzled; she was at all times profoundly impressed by his genius, but she soon came to perceive that his nature was wholly unlike that of other men. She had seen, she said, men worthy of all respect, and she had seen men noted for their ferocity; but the impression produced on her by Bonaparte was generically different from that produced by either of these classes. She found that such epithets as 'good,' 'violent,' 'gentle,' and 'cruel' could not be applied to him in their ordinary senses. He was in truth a being who stood self-centred, and apart from the sympathies, passions, and enthusiasms of his kind, habitually regarding men, not as fellow-creatures, but as mere counters in a game; a will of colossal strength; an intellect of clear, cold, transcendent power, solely governed by the imperturbable calculation of the strictest egotism, and never drawn aside by love or hatred, by pity or religion, or by attachment to any cause. It was impossible, she found, to exaggerate his contempt for human nature and his disbelief in the reality of human virtue. A perfectly honest man was the only kind of man he never could understand. Such a man perplexed and baffled his calculations, acting on them as the sign of the cross acts on the machinations of a demon. The superiority which so clearly shone in his conversation was not that of a mind cultivated by study and by society; it was the supreme insight into the circumstances of life possessed by a mighty hunter of men. There was something in him, she said, like a cold and trenchant sword, which at the same moment could wound and chill.

Such was the estimate she formed of the man who, nearly at the same time, was presented by Talleyrand to the Directory as 'the pacificator of Europe,' as a hero ' who despised luxury and pomp—the wretched ambition of common souls—and who loved the poems of Ossian, especially because they detach men from the earth'! That two such different natures should come into collision was very natural. Bonaparte always hated superior women, and especially women who meddled in politics. He well knew that the circle of Madame de Staël was the centre of ideas about freedom and constitutional government irreconcilably opposed to his ambition, and that the world of good society and good taste, of independent thought and independent characters, in which she played so great a part, remained unsubdued and undazzled by his power. Benjamin Constant had been placed in 'the Tribunate,' and in the beginning of 1800 he made a speech there, indicating a desire to establish in that body an opposition like the opposition in the English Parliament. Bonaparte was furious at his attitude, and at once ascribed it to the inspiration of Madame de Staël. A year later the last work of her father appeared, and it contained an earnest warning against growing despotism in France and a strong argument for the establishment of a republican constitution. The sayings of Madame de Staël that were repeated from lip to lip, and the atmosphere of thought that grew up around her, irritated and disquieted Bonaparte. ' She is moving the minds of men,' he said, ' in a direction that does not suit me.' ' They pretend that she does not speak of politics or of me, but somehow it always happens that those who have been with her become less attached to me.' Soon her salon was emptied by an emphatic intimation that those who entered it would incur the displeasure of the First Consul. Official scribes were busily employed in depreciating her, and these measures were speedily followed by the long exile which darkened the later years of her life. It is impossible for me in this article to relate, even in outline, the story of this exile, and of her travels in England, Italy, Austria, Russia, and, above all, in Germany. Madame de Staël has herself described this period of her life in her 'Ten Years of Exile,' and all the details have been collected by Lady Blennerhassett with an industry that leaves nothing to be desired. A woman of a more heroic type would have borne with less repining an exclusion from Paris life which was mitigated by wealth, and fame, and abundant occupation, and a family that adored her, and troops of admiring friends. A woman who was less essentially noble would have assuredly accepted the overtures that were more than once made to her, and would have purchased her peace with Napoleon by burning a few grains of literary incense on his altar. But though, in a life of more than common vicissitude and temptation, Madame de Staël was betrayed into great weaknesses and into some serious faults, she never lost her sense of the dignity and integrity of literature, and her works are singularly free from unworthy flattery as well as from unworthy resentments and jealousies. The homage which Napoleon desired was never received, and in her great work on Italy and her still greater one on Germany there was no trace of his victories, influence, or animosities. 'In France,' he once said, 'there is a small literature and a great literature ; the small literature is on my side, but the great literature is not for me.'

The disfavour which thrust Madame de Staël out

of political influence, and then drove her into exile, proved a blessing in disguise, for it turned her mind decisively from political intrigues to those forms of literature in which she was most fitted to excel. Her treatise on 'Literature,' which was published in 1800, was conceived upon a scale too large for her own knowledge, and though she herself attributed to it the great and general favour that she enjoyed for a time in Paris society, it has not taken an enduring place in French literature. 'Delphine,' the most personal, and also the most censured, of her novels, had a still wider success, and made a deeper and more lasting impression. It appeared in 1802, and it was followed by a long interval, during which she appears to have published nothing except a short but admirable notice of her father, who died in the spring of 1804 ; but in 1807 'Corinne' burst upon the world, and at once obtained a European fame equalled by that of no French novel since 'La Nouvelle Héloise.' In this great work of imagination she embodied, in a highly poetic form, the impressions she had derived from her journeys in England and Italy, and its immense and instantaneous success placed her on the very pinnacle of fame. It is worthy of notice that a bitter attack upon 'Corinne' appeared in 'Le Moniteur,' based chiefly upon the fact that its hero was an Englishman ; and there is good reason to believe that this attack was from the pen of Napoleon himself.

A book of larger scope and of more serious influence soon followed. Germany at this time presented the singular spectacle of a people who had been reduced to the lowest depths of political depression, but who, at the same time, could boast of a contemporary literature that was the first in the world. In France a translation

of ' Werther ' had attained great popularity ; some of the
plays of Schiller, the idylls of Gessner, and a few other
German works were well known ; but scarcely any
Frenchman had a conception of the magnitude and
importance of the intellectual activity which was growing
up beyond the Rhine, or of the vast place which Goethe,
Schiller, and Kant were destined to take in European
thought. It was one of the chief pleasures and occupations of Madame de Staël, during her exile, to explore
this almost unknown field. It would scarcely have been
thought that she was well fitted for the task. She learned
the language late in life, and her characteristically French
mind seemed very little in harmony with either the
strength or the weakness of the Teutonic intellect. There
was nothing very profound, or very subtle, or very
poetical in her nature, and she had all that instinctive
dislike to the vague, the disproportioned, the exaggerated,
and the ambiguous, to fantastic and far-fetched conjecture,
and to imposing edifices of speculation based upon scanty
or shadowy materials, that pre-eminently distinguishes
the best French thought. Very wisely, however, she
placed herself in direct communication with the great
writers of Germany, and a wholly new world of thought
and sentiment gradually opened upon her mind. It is
not too much to say that it was her pen that first
revealed to the Latin world the intellectual greatness of
Germany. In England, Coleridge had already laboured
in the same field, and his admirable translation of
' Wallenstein ' had appeared as early as 1800 ; but it had
been completely still-born, and in England also it was
reserved for the great Frenchwoman to give the first considerable impulse to the study of German literature. For
the history, the merits, and the defects of her work on

Germany, I cannot do better than to refer to the admirable pages which Lady Blennerhassett has devoted to the subject. With the doubtful exception of 'Le Génie du Christianisme,' it was by far the most important French work which appeared during the reign of Napoleon. It is a characteristic fact that the whole of the first edition was confiscated by order of his Government. Happily the manuscript was saved, and about three years later it was printed in England.

After some discreditable scenes, on which a recently published correspondence has thrown a painful though somewhat doubtful light, the connection of Madame de Staël with Benjamin Constant was broken. The two continued occasionally to correspond, and as late as 1815 we find her lending him a large sum of money ; but their relations were never again what they had been, and on the side of Constant there appears to have been a large amount of positive malevolence. 'O Benjamin,' she wrote to him in one of her later letters, 'you have destroyed my life ! For ten years not a day has passed that my heart has not suffered for you—and yet I loved you so much !' A strong affection, such as she had not found in her marriage with the Baron de Staël, was an imperious necessity of her existence, and after her breach with Constant she soon found an object in a young officer from Geneva named Rocca, who had returned to his native town badly wounded after brilliant service in Spain. When they first met, in 1810, Madame de Staël was forty-four and Rocca about twenty-three; but a genuine and honourable affection seems to have grown up on both sides, and in the following year they were married. Madame de Staël, however, either clinging to her name or dreading the ridicule of such a strangely assorted marriage, insisted

upon its concealment, and Rocca generally passed in
society as her lover. A child was born in 1812, but it
was only after the death of Madame de Staël that the
legitimacy of the connection was established. It proved
much more productive of happiness than might have been
expected, and greatly brightened her closing years.
Nearly at the same time an important change passed over
her religious views, and the vague deism of her youth
deepened into a positive, definite, and earnest Christianity,
but without mysticism and without intolerance. Some
beautiful lines that are cited by Lady Blennerhassett very
faithfully express the spirit of her belief : ' Il faut avoir
soin, si l'on peut, que le déclin de cette vie soit la jeunesse
de l'autre. Se désintéresser de soi, sans cesser de
s'intéresser aux autres, met quelque chose de divin dans
l'âme.'

She lived to see the downfall of perhaps the only man
she really hated, his return from Elba, his final defeat at
Waterloo, and the restoration of the Bourbons. But,
though she detested Napoleon and his system, these
things gave her no pleasure. The spectacle of an invaded
and a dismembered France aroused her strongest feelings
of patriotism, and she loved liberty too truly and too
ardently to rejoice in the influences that triumphed in
1815. Her last years were chiefly spent in the com-
position of her ' Considerations on the French Revolution,'
in which she sums up the convictions of her life. It is
one of her most valuable and most lasting books. The
disproportioned prominence which is naturally assigned
in it to Necker, and the manifest personal element in
her antipathy to Napoleon, impair its weight, indeed, as
a history ; but few writers have criticised with more
justice the successive stages of the Revolution, and few

books of its generation are so rich in political wisdom.
The concluding chapters, in which, in a strain of noble
eloquence, she pleads the cause of moderate and constitutional freedom, show how steadily and how strongly,
in an age of many disenchantments, she clung to the
belief of her youth.

The ' Considerations on the French Revolution ' had
a vast and an immediate success, and in a few days sixty
thousand copies were sold. Madame de Staël, however,
did not live to witness her triumph. In February
1817 she was struck down by a paralytic illness, and on
July 14, after a long period of complete prostration, she
passed away tranquilly in her sleep. It was a peaceful
ending to an agitated and chequered career. She had
enjoyed much and suffered much. She had committed
grave faults, and had met with her full share of disappointment and ingratitude ; but few women have left
such an enduring monument behind them, or have
touched human life on so many sides and with so many
sympathies.

THE PRIVATE CORRESPONDENCE OF SIR ROBERT PEEL

THERE is probably no other English public man of the present century whose career has attracted in so large a measure the interest both of politicians and of men of letters as Sir Robert Peel. In addition to a crowd of industrious but not very distinguished compilers, it has been discussed with great skill by Guizot, by Lord Dalling, by Mr. Goldwin Smith, and by Mr. Spencer Walpole; and in that great literature of monographs which has grown up with such remarkable rapidity in England within the last decade, no less than three have been devoted to the life of Peel. The interest that attaches to him is, indeed, of a very peculiar character. He was almost wholly destitute of the power of imagination that is so conspicuous in the careers or speeches of Chatham and Burke, of Canning and Beaconsfield. Except during a few years that followed the Reform Bill of 1832, he never exhibited the spectacle of a leader struggling successfully against enormous odds. He was not one of those statesmen who see further than their contemporaries, and who, after years of failure and struggle, are proved by their ultimate triumph to have most truly read the tendencies of their age. Though he was three times Prime Minister of England, and though he was for a time deemed the most brilliant of party leaders, he left the great and powerful party which trusted him almost hopelessly shattered. Twice in his life he carried measures of transcendent importance which he had not only persistently opposed, but had been specially placed in power for the purpose of resisting. The most striking incidents in his career are incidents of failure rather than of success, and history has pronounced that, on the most important questions of his time, he was disastrously wrong. The long delay in the inevitable emancipation of the Catholics, which was largely due to him, and the circumstances under which he ultimately carried the measure, produced evils that are in full activity at the present hour. His persistent opposition to parliamentary reform contributed to bring England to the very verge of revolution; though when the Reform Bill had been carried he nobly retrieved his error by the frankness with which he accepted, and the skill with which he used, the new conditions of English politics. His abolition of the Corn Laws at the head of a Government which had been pledged to maintain them gave a great shock to public confidence, and for a long period most seriously dislocated the machinery of party government. But, in spite of all this, there are few statesmen who have carried so large a number of measures of great and acknowledged importance, who have impressed so deeply the sense of their superiority on the minds of their contemporaries, or who were followed to the grave by a more widespread and genuine regret.

It is this contrast between the leading incidents of Peel's life and the impression which he made on the world that constitutes the great interest of his career. The explanation is not difficult to discover. It is the common story of extraordinary qualities balanced by striking defects. He was not a great statesman, but he was a supremely great administrator, a supremely great master of parliamentary management and of parliamentary legislation. He had little prescience; he often grossly misread the signs of the times, or only recognised them when it was too late; but when he was once convinced, he acted on his conviction with frankness and courage, and when a thing had to be done, no one could do it like him. As Disraeli said: 'In the course of time the method which was natural to Sir Robert Peel matured into a habit of such expertness that no one in the despatch of affairs ever adapted the means more fitly to the end.'[1] In the words of Sir Cornewall Lewis: 'For concocting, producing, explaining, and defending measures, he had no equal, or anything like an equal.'[2]

In the interesting volumes which were published by Lord Mahon and Mr. Cardwell in 1856 we have Peel's own explanation of his conduct relating to the removal of the Catholic disabilities in 1829, and to the repeal of the Corn Laws in 1846; but the publication of his confidential correspondence has been long delayed, and the volume before us only carries the work down to 1827. It has been edited by Mr. Parker with great care and accuracy, and with undeviating good sense and good taste, and it throws much curious light upon a corner of history which has been but little explored.

Peel started in life with great advantages. The eldest son of a very wealthy manufacturer who had long occupied a respectable place in Parliament, and who was closely attached to the dominant party in the State, he was from his earliest youth destined by his father to be a statesman. Under such circumstances he was certain

---

[1] *Life of Lord George Bentinck*, p. 304.   [2] Lewis's *Letters*, p. 226.

in the pre-Reform period to have not only all the advantages which the best school and university education could give, but also the still greater advantages of an early introduction into both parliamentary and official life; provided always that no aberration of character, or taste, or imagination, or opinion drew him aside from the plain path that lay before him. He grew up in an atmosphere of the best middle-class virtues. Decorum, good sense, industry, strict morality; a sober religious orthodoxy; much simplicity of life, preserved in the midst of great wealth; ideals which, if not very lofty, were at least eminently practical and perfectly honourable, prevailed around him, and their influence imbued his whole nature. He accepted cordially the destiny that was before him, and threw himself into it with untiring industry. His opinions changed during his life much more than his character, and the shy, sensitive, industrious, somewhat self-conscious, somewhat awkward Harrow boy, prefigured very faithfully the future statesman. He is described as wandering when a schoolboy by himself among the hedges, knocking down birds with stones, a practice in which he was very skilful, and which eventually developed into a strong passion for shooting. He was quiet, good-natured, studious, scarcely ever in scrapes, and it was not until the last year of his school life that he threw himself with any keenness into the amusements of his comrades. He had good natural abilities; but probably the one point in which he greatly exceeded the average of intelligent boys was his memory, which was of extraordinary retentiveness, and which he carefully cultivated. During a few months which elapsed between leaving Harrow and going to Oxford he constantly attended the House of Commons, under the

Gallery; and he also attended some natural history lectures at the Royal Institution. His Oxford career was very successful. He is said to have worked before his degree examination for no less than eighteen hours, through the day and night. He gained a double-first, and in the first class of mathematics he stood alone. Such a success at once stamped him as a youth of extraordinary promise, and the impression it made was especially great because, the examination system having been very recently reorganised, he was the first Oxford man who had attained it.

He was brought into Parliament in April 1809, almost immediately after he came of age, for the borough of Cashel. No special significance attaches to the fact of his having entered Parliament for an Irish constituency, for his father had simply bought the seat, and the young member appears to have never gone over to his constituents or held any communication with them.

'When I sat for Cashel,' he afterwards wrote, 'and was not in office, having made those sacrifices which could then legally be made, but now cannot, I did not consider myself at all pledged to the support of Government.'[1] Perceval, who represented in its extreme form the Tory reaction that followed the Revolution, was then Prime Minister, and Peel at once took his place among his followers. He first spoke in seconding the Address in 1810, and in the partial judgment of his father his speech was considered, 'by men the best qualified to form a correct opinion of public speaking, the best first speech since that of Mr. Pitt.'[2]

It was not, perhaps, an unmixed advantage to Peel

---

[1] *Private Correspondence of Sir R. Peel*, 1788-1827. Ed. by C. S. Parker, M.P., 1891, p. 24.   [2] *Ibid.* p. 27.

that while he was still a mere boy his father had somewhat ostentatiously destined him to be one day a Tory
statesman. Such an education could hardly fail to
strengthen the self-consciousness which was never
wanting in Peel's character, and to give a decided bias
to his judgment. At the same time, the distinctive
merits of his career would have probably never been fully
developed without the early administrative training which
his opinions made possible for him, and there is nothing
in his early history to give the least countenance to the
belief that his adherence to the extreme type of Tory
politics imposed the slightest strain upon his judgment.
His immediate interests and his sentiments appear at this
time to have perfectly concurred. He came into Parliament with the party which was dominant, and with
the section of the party which was most poor in able men.
Had he adopted on the Catholic question the liberal
opinions of Canning and Castlereagh, he must have held
a position altogether subordinate to them ; and the same
causes that in the preceding Ministry had raised Perceval
to be leader of the House of Commons over the heads of
Castlereagh and Canning, marked out for Peel the future
leadership of the party of resistance to concession. It has
been said, on the authority of Sir Lawrence Peel, that
his first appointment was that of private secretary to
Lord Liverpool, but Mr. Parker has found no trace of
this in the papers either of Peel or of Lord Liverpool.
In 1810, however, when he was but just twenty-two, he
entered administrative life as Under-Secretary of State
for War and the Colonies, and he held that place till
August 1812, when he obtained the far more important
post of Chief Secretary for Ireland, and became for the
next six years virtual governor of that country.

It was a post requiring not only great administrative skill, but also great gifts of original statesmanship. During the last five years of the eighteenth century, and especially during the rebellion of 1798, religious passions in Ireland, which had for more than a generation been steadily subsiding, had been kindled into a flame, and the urgent necessity of settling the Catholic question had begun to press with irresistible force on the minds of the more intelligent statesmen. Pitt had intended to complete the Union by measures for admitting Catholics into Parliament, for commuting tithes, and for paying the Catholic clergy. Through the instrumentality of Lord Castlereagh assurances of the disposition of the Cabinet had been conveyed to the Catholic bishops and the leading Catholic laymen in 1799, which were sufficient to secure their active support for the Union and to prevent any serious opposition among the Catholic laity. The bishops met the wishes of the English Government by drawing up a series of resolutions, in which they declared their readiness to accept with gratitude an endowment for the priesthood, to confer upon the English Government a power of veto over the appointment of Catholic bishops which would prevent the introduction into that body of any disloyal men, and to certify to the Government the nomination of all Catholic parish priests, as well as the fact that they had taken the oath of allegiance. But the King had not been informed of the negotiations that had taken place, and it is well known how his uncompromising opposition produced the resignation of Pitt in 1801, how the agitation caused by the question threw the King into a temporary fit of insanity, and how Pitt at once promised that he would not move the question again during the reign. In the spring of

1804 Pitt resumed office, on the express understanding
that he would not permit Catholic Emancipation ; when
the question was introduced in 1805 by Lord Grenville in
the Lords, and by Fox in the Commons, it was defeated
in both Houses by immense majorities, and Pitt declared
that though he was still of opinion that there was no
danger in the concession, yet, as long as the circumstances
which prevented him from bringing it forward continued,
he would be no party to agitating the question.

In 1806 Pitt died, and Fox and Grenville were themselves in power, but the Catholics were again disap-
pointed. The prejudice of the King, the feeling of the
country, the recent vote of the House of Commons, the
presence of Lord Sidmouth in the Ministry, proved
insuperable obstacles, and Fox could only urge the
Catholic leaders to postpone the question. Fox died in
September 1806, and the Government presided over by
Lord Grenville met a new Parliament in the following
December. Grenville had been Pitt's colleague during
the negotiations with the Catholics that preceded the
Union ; he had strongly urged upon Pitt the necessity of
resigning in 1801, and he never forgave him for having
so lightly abandoned the cause. Grenville did not
attempt to carry emancipation, but he resolved to take
at least one serious step in the direction of concession, by
throwing open to the Catholics all the posts in the army
and navy. An Irish Act of 1793 had enabled them to
hold in Ireland commissions in the army, and to attain
any rank except commander-in-chief, master-general of
the ordnance, and general of the staff ; but if the regiments
in which they served were sent to England, they were
disqualified by law from remaining in the service. The
original Bill of Grenville's Government was intended to

remove this anomaly, and assimilate the law in the two
countries; but in the course of the discussions it was
agreed that the Catholics should be freed from the
exceptions to which they were subjected by the Irish Act,
that all posts in the army and navy should be thrown
open to men of all religious persuasions, subject only to
the obligation of taking an oath which was prescribed,
and that Catholic soldiers should be guaranteed by law
the free exercise of their religion. The King had been
informed of this, and was understood to have given a
distinct, though a reluctant, assent; but a strong Protestant party, headed by Perceval, fiercely opposed it.
The King withdrew his assent from the added clauses,
and expressed his disapprobation of the whole measure.
At last, after much discussion, the Ministers agreed for
the present to withdraw their Bill, reserving to themselves by a Cabinet minute, which was submitted to the
King, the right to renew it, or to propose any other
measure on the subject which they desired. But the
King was determined to push his victory to the end. He
demanded from his Ministers a promise in writing that
they would never again propose to him any measure
connected with Catholic emancipation, and as the
Ministers refused to give this unconstitutional pledge, the
King dismissed them from office, and called the Duke of
Portland to the head of affairs.

It was the second time that the King had broken up a
Ministry on the Catholic question, and his conduct was
especially significant, as his refusal to grant military
promotion to Catholics was announced in the midst of
a great war, and at a time when thousands of Catholics
were fighting in his armies. It at once appeared that
there were two entirely distinct schools of Tories. Pitt,

to the very close of his life, had declared that his opinions
on the Catholic question were unchanged, though he
would not force them against the inclination of the King ;
and his views were adopted by Canning, Castlereagh, and
Wellesley. Perceval, on the other hand, emphatically
declared that he 'could not conceive a time or any change
of circumstances which could render further concession to
the Catholics consistent with the safety of the State.'[1]
With the exception of Eldon, scarcely any man of real
ability adopted this view until Peel entered Parliament as
the follower of Perceval. It is sufficiently evident from
this fact how little truth there is in the theory that
attributes Peel's early Toryism to a blind admiration
for Pitt.

The party of the King triumphed. Parliament was
dissolved on the 'No Popery' cry, and on the first great
party division that followed the election the Ministers in
the House of Commons had a majority of 195. Canning
and Castlereagh, though they had no sympathy with that
cry, availed themselves of the current that ran so strongly
against the Whigs. In the Ministry of the Duke of
Portland they held the seals for the Foreign and War
Departments, but the leadership of the Commons and the
virtual leadership of the Ministry was given to Perceval,
who, though entirely without brilliant parts, exhibited
unexpected talents, both as a practical debater and as a
manager of men, and who had the advantage of representing fully the dominant party. Several circumstances,
however, other than a conviction of the danger of the
Catholic claims, contributed to the triumph of the
anti-Catholic party. The Whigs, already broken by
their policy towards France in the first stages of the

[1] *Hansard*, First Ser. xxi. 663.

Revolution and of the war, had become still more unpopular through their opposition to the seizure of the Danish fleet and to the Peninsular War. They were divided among themselves, for there was little sympathy between the more aristocratic Whigs, who were represented by Grenville and Lord Howick, and the more Radical party of Sir F. Burdett and Whitbread. A strong personal as well as political dislike already existed between Howick and Canning, and prevented their hearty co-operation on the one great question on which they were agreed. Above all, there was a general conviction among statesmen that the King's mind was trembling on the verge of insanity, and that a renewal of the Catholic complications of 1801 would produce a catastrophe.

The question was debated in both the Lords and Commons in 1808. In the former it was lost by a majority of 87, and in the latter by a majority of 153. Grattan on this occasion introduced the Catholic petition in a speech of consummate power; but both Castlereagh and Canning opposed the reception of the petition, on the ground that the time was unsuited for the agitation of the question; and the spirit of the ruling part of the Ministry was sufficiently shown by the reduction of the Maynooth grant from 13,000*l.* to 9,250*l.* When the Portland Government was broken up in September 1809 by the quarrel, duel, and resignation of Canning and Castlereagh, Perceval became the head of the new Ministry, Lord Wellesley occupying the place of Canning, and Lord Hawkesbury that of Castlereagh; and an intensely anti-Catholic ministry continued to the death of Perceval. In 1809 the Catholic question was not introduced into Parliament. In the spring of 1810 it was introduced into both Houses, but was defeated by

M

majorities of 86 and 104 ; but in October 1810 an event occurred which profoundly changed the aspect of affairs. The King's insanity broke out anew in a form which gave little hope of recovery, and the Prince of Wales was appointed Regent. For a year the regency was subject to restrictions similar to those which had been adopted in 1788, but on February 1, 1812, these restrictions were to cease, and the Regent was to enter into full fruition of the royal power.

The hopes of the Catholics were now raised to the highest point. With the confirmed insanity of George III. the most serious of all the obstacles to their claims was removed. During the year of the restricted regency, while there was still some chance of the recovery of the King, the Prince of Wales declined to remove the existing Ministry from office, though even this decision was not taken without some hesitation and some negotiations with the Whigs. The Catholics, however, fully expected that the royal influence would now be exerted in their favour, and that the Whig Ministry would speedily come. The Prince of Wales had long been in close connection with the Whigs. As early as 1797 he had expressed a desire to go over to Ireland as Lord-Lieutenant, carrying with him a policy of conciliation to the Catholics. In 1805, when Fox and Grenville had introduced the Catholic question into the Imperial Parliament, the Prince, while stating that considerations of obvious delicacy prevented him from taking an immediate and open part in its favour, had given the Whig leaders the fullest authority to assure the Catholics of Ireland that he would never forsake their interests, the 'most distinct and authentic pledge' of his wish to relieve them from the disabilities of which they complained, and to exert himself in their favour as soon as he was constitutionally able to do so. It is easy therefore to imagine the consternation and the indignation with which, in 1812, the Catholics found that the Prince Regent had changed his principles and his policy; that, after a short and perhaps insincere negotiation with the Whigs, he had resolved to maintain in power a Ministry which was constructed for the main purpose of maintaining the Catholic disabilities; and that his own opinions were rapidly verging towards this policy.

The situation in Ireland was becoming very dangerous. For some years after the Union a great apathy prevailed, and there is no reasonable doubt that, if events in England had been favourable, Catholic emancipation would have met with no serious opposition in Ireland, and could have been carried with every reasonable limitation and safeguard. The most competent English officials calculated that at least sixty-four of the hundred Irish representatives would vote for it, and that a decided preponderance of Irish Protestant opinion was in its favour. On the other hand, the Catholic bishops and aristocracy had fully accepted the policy of an endowment for the priests and a veto on the appointment of bishops, and the most Conservative elements in the Catholic body still exercised an ascendancy over their coreligionists. The question of the veto had been mentioned in the Commons, by Sir J. Hippisley, in 1805, and in 1808 Grattan and Ponsonby formally announced, on the authority of the Catholic bishops, their readiness to accept it. A letter from Bishop Milner was read to the House, which very clearly stated their position:

'The Catholic prelates of Ireland,' he wrote, 'are willing to give a direct negative power to his Majesty's

Government with respect to the nomination of their titular bishoprics, in such manner that when they have among themselves resolved who is the fittest person for the vacant see, they will transmit his name to his Majesty's Ministers ; and if the latter should object to that name, they will transmit another and another, until a name is presented to which no objection is made ; and (which is never likely to be the case) should the Pope refuse to give those essentially necessary spiritual powers, of which he is the depository, to the person so presented by the Catholic bishops and so approved by the Government, they will continue to propose names till one occurs which is agreeable to both parties—namely, the Crown and Apostolic See.'

The prelates also engaged to nominate no persons who had not previously taken the oath of allegiance.[1] But a democratic party had now arisen among the Catholics, which utterly repudiated the restrictions of the veto, which sought emancipation by violent and democratic agitation, and which was rapidly drawing the most dangerous elements in the country into its channel. The bishops, pushed on by the strong force that was behind them, speedily retraced their steps and passed resolutions against the restrictions they had accepted, and there were evident signs that the Catholic body was passing away from the guidance of Grattan and of the gentry. This was not surprising in a country where many elements of anarchy subsisted ; and the democratic party had already found in O'Connell a leader of consummate skill, and of untiring industry, energy, and ambition. But the chief cause of the great change that was passing over the Irish Catholics was to be found

---

[1] Butler's *Hist. Memoirs*, ii. 177.

in the disappointment of their hopes in 1801, in 1804, in 1806, and 1812 ; in the desertion of their cause by Pitt ; in the proved impotence of the Whigs ; in the failure of ' the securities ' even to mitigate the hostility of Perceval and his followers ; in the profound consternation and exasperation that were produced by the attitude of the Regent. The formation of the General Committee of Catholic Delegates was speedily followed by its suppression under the Convention Act. But the influence of O'Connell was rapidly growing ; there were already ominous signs of a possible agitation for the repeal of the Union, and the indignation of the Catholics was significantly shown by the famous 'witchery resolutions,' which were unanimously carried by the aggregate meeting of the Catholics in the June of 1812, reflecting on the influence which Lady Hertford was believed to exercise over the Prince. After calling for the ' total and unqualified repeal of the penal laws which aggrieve the Catholics,' they proceeded to use the following language : ' That from authentic documents now before us we hear, with deep disappointment and anguish, how cruelly the promised boon of Catholic freedom has been interrupted by the fatal witchery of an unworthy secret influence. . . . To this impure source we trace but too distinctly our baffled hopes and protracted servitude.' Such language was not calculated to conciliate the Prince, and he was only confirmed in his hostility to the Catholics. As early as September 1813 the Duke of Richmond wrote to Peel : ' I was delighted to find H.R.H. as steady a Protestant as the Attorney-General.'

The commencement, however, of what was virtually a new reign had given a new activity to the question. It was brought forward in different forms in the first months

of 1812 by Lord Wellesley and Lord Donoughmore in
one House, and by Lord Morpeth and Grattan in the
other; and although it was still defeated, the diminished
majorities, the evident signs of an increased Catholic
party in the country, and the language of some of the
most distinguished men in Parliament, clearly indicated
the progress of the measure. Canning especially now
strenuously urged that the time had come when the
Catholic question must be fully dealt with. The
assassination of Perceval on May 11, 1812, again
changed the situation and led to a long series of feeble
and abortive negotiations. An attempt was made to
continue the existing Ministry under the lead of Lord
Liverpool, with the addition of Canning and Lord
Wellesley; but these statesmen declined the offer, on the
ground that the other Ministers refused to carry Catholic
emancipation, and Lord Wellesley on the additional
ground of their languor in prosecuting the Spanish war.
The Regent then authorised Lord Wellesley to construct
a Ministry, with the assistance of Canning, and an offer
was made to Lords Grey and Grenville to join it,
promising an immediate consideration of the Catholic
claims with a view to a conciliatory settlement; while,
on the other hand, attempts were made to retain the
services of the leading members of Perceval's Ministry.
But the Whig leaders refused to take part in a coalition
Ministry, in which they would probably be outvoted, and
the former Cabinet was reconstructed, under the leadership of Lord Liverpool, but on the principle of leaving
the Catholic question an open one. Liverpool himself
was opposed to concession, but his opposition was by no
means of the unqualified kind which had been shown by
Perceval; and a large proportion of his colleagues,

including Castlereagh, who led the House of Commons, were in favour of Catholic emancipation. If Canning had consented to join the Ministry, Lord Wellesley would probably have been Lord-Lieutenant in Ireland, and under these circumstances the Catholic side could scarcely have failed to acquire a decisive preponderance. If, on the other hand, Castlereagh had followed the example of Canning, and refused to take part in a Ministry which declined to settle the Catholic question, or if the Whigs had consented to co-operate with Canning, the settlement of this great question could scarcely have been deferred. Unfortunately, none of these things happened. Castlereagh remained the leader of the House. Canning refused to follow his leadership, and two years later accepted the embassy to Lisbon. The Whig leaders stood aloof from all Ministerial combinations. The Duke of Richmond, who was violently anti-Catholic, continued to be Lord-Lieutenant of Ireland; the post of Chief Secretary was given to Peel, and Ireland was destined to undergo fifteen more years of demoralising and disorganising agitation before the Catholic question was settled.

Canning, however, as an independent member, brought forward a resolution pledging the House to an early consideration of the laws affecting his Majesty's Roman Catholic subjects, with a view to their final conciliatory adjustment, and the conditions of the question had so profoundly changed that it was carried by a majority of 129 ; while a similar motion by Lord Wellesley in the House of Lords was met by the previous question, which was carried by a majority of only one.

Peel, though he had come into Parliament as a special follower of Perceval, had not yet pledged himself decisively against the Catholics. He had voted silently against Canning's motion in June, and although he had spoken against a previous motion of Grattan, he had done so mainly on the ground that the time was not opportune, and had expressly guarded himself against giving any positive pledge. He was now, however, obliged to take a more prominent part, and for the next six years he was the chief support of the anti-Catholic party in Parliament. His part was a very difficult one, for he had to encounter Grattan, Plunket, Canning, and the Whig leaders, and he had scarcely any real supporters. Saurin, the Attorney-General, it is true, was strongly opposed to all concession. He was a lawyer of high character and attainments, of Huguenot descent and strong Huguenot principles, and he had borne a distinguished part in opposition to the Union; but Saurin refused to go to London. Bushe, who was Solicitor-General, leaned to the Catholic side; and, to the great indignation and consternation of the Government, Wellesley Pole, who had preceded Peel as Chief Secretary and who was the brother of Lord Wellesley, now pronounced himself strongly in Parliament in favour of the Catholics. This speech was entirely unexpected, for Pole had hitherto been regarded as a staunch adherent of the Protestant party, and as late as the last day of 1811 he had sent a memorandum on the Catholic question to the Secretary of State in England, which was intended to be laid before the Cabinet, and which maintained the impossibility of safely satisfying the Catholic claims, and the expediency of the Prince Regent's taking a decided part against them. A general election had taken place in September, and it is evident from the letters of Lord Liverpool and Peel that they at this time looked upon Canning and his followers with even more hostility than the regular Opposition.

In the new Parliament the Catholic question at once assumed a great prominence. A motion for the immediate consideration of the laws affecting the Catholics was introduced by Grattan, supported by Castlereagh, opposed by Peel, and ultimately carried by a majority of 40. A resolution of Grattan's for removing laws imposing civil and military disabilities on the Catholics, with such regulations and exceptions as might provide for the security of the Protestant succession and of the Established Church, was next introduced. Peel opposed it bitterly, but was beaten by a majority of 67.

'We were terribly beaten,' he wrote to his Under-Secretary, 'but we are sad cowards, I am afraid ; at least, we are shamefully used. Poor Duigenan could not get a hearing, and the general impression seemed against the Protestants. We will fight them out, however, to the last. I am sure it is better than to give way.' 'Your defence of the Protestant cause,' wrote Saurin, 'was not only by far the ablest and best, but the only one which did not seem to strengthen the cause of the adversary by some concession of principle. I really fear the Protestant cause is lost in the Commons. There can be no rally now but on the securities.' [1]

Grattan at once brought in a Bill in accordance with the terms of the Resolution that had been carried ; but the Protestant party now rallied around a motion of Sir John Hippisley, for a committee to inquire into the state and tenets of the Roman Catholics, and the laws affecting them. Canning pointed out with great force that a committee of inquiry was exactly what the

[1] *Peel Correspondence*, p. 80.

Protestant party had for so many years strenuously
resisted; but, as Peel wrote to the Duke of Richmond,
there was no inconsistency in their conduct : 'When the
question was whether we should consider the claims of
the Catholics and the laws affecting them, or should
resist their claims, we voted for resistance without
inquiry; the question now is, whether we shall consider
or concede, and we prefer inquiry to concession.' [1]

The motion for delay, however, was defeated by 187
to 235, and the second reading of Grattan's Bill was
carried by 245 to 203.   But a sudden change now
occurred in the prospects of the cause.   Canning and
Castlereagh, with the full assent of Grattan, introduced
clauses for the securities which had been before intimated, giving the Crown a control over the nomination
of the Catholic bishops.   But the bishops unanimously
condemned the proposal, and the large majority of the
Catholic Board supported them.   It became evident that
the Bill before Parliament would fail to satisfy the
Catholics, and after a long discussion the clause admitting Catholics to Parliament was rejected by 251
to 247.

Peel had triumphed.   The profound division which
had broken out among the supporters of Catholic
emancipation threw back for many years a cause which
had been almost gained, though in 1817 an Act was
passed without opposition throwing open to the Catholics
the military and naval positions which Grenville had
vainly attempted to open in 1807.   Few things could
have been eventually more disastrous both to Ireland and
to the Empire than the defeat of the influence represented
by Grattan and by the Catholic gentry, and the growing

[1] *Peel Correspondence*, p. 83.

ascendancy of O'Connell and the democratic and sacerdotal party in Irish popular politics. Grattan had long
predicted that, if concession was not speedily and wisely
made, population in Ireland would drift away from the
guiding and moderating influence of property; that
seditious and anarchical men would gain an ascendancy
which would make the whole problem of Irish Government incalculably difficult; that a priesthood unconnected
with the English Government would lead to a 'Catholic
laity discorporated from the people of England.' In the
Irish Parliament the strong bias of Conservatism in his
policy had been repeatedly displayed, and it was equally
apparent in the Imperial Parliament. In 1807 he had
supported the Insurrection Act, in opposition to many of
his friends, on the ground that there was a real and
dangerous French party in Ireland, which the common
law was insufficient to suppress. In 1814 he expressed
his full approval of the proclamation suppressing the
Catholic Board. He steadily and earnestly maintained
that, although it was vitally necessary that Catholic
emancipation should be speedily carried, it should be
accompanied by measures for securing, as far as possible,
the loyalty of the higher Catholic clergy, and uniting
them in interest and sentiment with the British Government. He looked with bitter hostility on the rise and
policy of O'Connell. He accused him of 'setting afloat
the bad passions of the people,' making grievances
instruments of power without any honest wish to redress
them, treating politics as a trade to serve a desperate and
interested purpose.

But the influence of Grattan was now manifestly
declining, and Peel watched the decline with a short-
sighted and not very generous pleasure. In Parliament,

though numbers were against the Catholics, the overwhelming preponderance of ability was still in favour of
the principle of emancipation, and it was in leading the
anti-Catholic party that Peel chiefly acquired his almost
unrivalled parliamentary skill. He had, indeed, all the
qualities of a great debater : courage, fluency, self-
possession, complete command of every subject he
treated, unfailing lucidity both in statement and reasoning ; admirable skill in marshalling and disentangling
great masses of facts, in meeting, evading, or retorting
arguments, and detecting the weak points of the case of
an opponent, in veiling, by plausible language, extreme
or unpalatable views, in extricating himself by subtle
distinctions and qualifications from embarrassing situations. He can scarcely, it is true, be called a great
orator. His style was formal, cumbrous, extremely
verbose, without sparkle and without fire. He had little
or no power of moving the passions, nothing of the
flexibility that can adapt itself to very different audiences,
nothing of the philosophic insight that can impart a
perennial interest to transient discussions. But few men
have ever understood the House of Commons like him, or
have possessed in so high a degree the qualities that are
most fitted to command and influence it. The great
mass of anti-Catholic sentiment in the country rallied
around him as its most powerful champion, and in 1817
he attained one of the chief objects of his ambition in
being elected member for Oxford University. It is well
known that his older and more brilliant rival had long
aspired to this honour. It was mainly through the
Catholic question that Canning missed and Peel won the
prize.

The nickname ' Orange Peel,' which was given to him

in Ireland, was not wholly deserved. His letters abundantly show that he had no sympathy with the ribbons, the anniversaries, the party tunes, the insulting processions and insulting language of the Orangemen ; and, although he believed that in Ireland anti-Catholicism and loyalty were very closely connected, he viewed with much dislike the growth of any political confederacies unconnected with the Government. Declamation and boastfulness and needless provocation were, indeed, wholly alien to his nature ; and even when defending extreme causes he rarely or never used the language of a fanatic. He resisted Catholic concession mainly on the ground that the admission of the Catholics to political power would prove incompatible with the existence of the Established Church in Ireland, with the security of property in a country where property was mainly in Protestant hands, and ultimately with the connection between the two countries. His arguments were not based on religion, but on political expediency ; but it was an expediency which he believed to be permanent.

'I see,' he wrote to the Duke of Richmond, 'one of the papers reports me as having said that I was not an advocate for perpetual exclusion. It might be inferred that I objected only to the time of discussing the question. That is not the case. . . . There are certain anomalies in the system which I would wish to remove, but the main principles of it I would retain untouched. . . . At no time, and under no circumstances, so long as the Catholic admits the supremacy in spirituals of a foreign earthly potentate, and will not tell us what supremacy in spirituals means—so long as he will not give us voluntarily the security which every despotic Sovereign

in Europe has by the concession of the Pope himself—
will I consent to admit them.' [1]

The letters before us show clearly that his political
sympathy was with Saurin, with Duigenan, with Lord
Eldon, and even with Lord Norbury. O'Connell early
perceived in Peel his most dangerous opponent, and a
strong personal enmity, which was as much due to profound differences of character as to differences of policy,
grew up between them. A scurrilous attack of O'Connell
on Peel in 1815 was followed by a challenge, and a duel
was prevented only by the arrest of O'Connell. The
antipathy between the two men was never mitigated.
O'Connell said of Peel that ' his smile was like the silver
plate on a coffin.' Peel, in his confidential letters,
expressed the utmost dislike and contempt for the
character of O'Connell, and when he was at length
compelled by the Clare election to concede Catholic
emancipation, his feeling towards him was significantly
and characteristically shown. He enumerated in a
brilliant passage the men to whom the triumph of
Catholic emancipation was really due. He spoke of
Fox and Grattan, of Plunket and of Canning, but he
made no mention of O'Connell.

The administrative side of Peel's Chief Secretaryship
is much more creditable to him than the political side.
The vivid picture which his letters present of the manner
in which Ireland was governed more than fifteen years
after the Union will probably strike the reader with some
surprise, when he remembers that the Union had extinguished about seventy small boroughs, and had at
the same time greatly diminished the importance of the
Irish representatives, and therefore the necessities for

[1] *Peel Correspondence*, p. 76.

corruption. Peel noticed that while 'the pension list of Great Britain was limited to 90,000*l.* per annum, the pension list of Ireland may amount to 80,000*l.* a year; and he found almost all Irish patronage still employed for political purposes, and almost every office honeycombed with abuses and peculations. A few extracts will give the reader some notion of the nature and extent of the evil, and of the efforts of Peel to reduce it :—

'How is it possible,' he wrote, 'to propose that a shilling should be granted to a general officer on the staff in Ireland when sixpence is granted in England? This is called a modification in official phrase, but it ought to be called doubling the allowance. Set your face steadily against all increase of salary, all extra allowances, all plausible claims for additional emolument. Economy must be the order of the day—rigid economy.'[1] 'When English members hear that the sheriff appoints the grand jury, that the grand jury tax the county, that the sheriff has a considerable influence at elections, and that the sheriff is appointed openly on the recommendation of the member supporting the Government, they are startled not a little. . . . I know that this is a most convenient patronage to the Government, but I know also that I cannot hint in the House of Commons at such a source of patronage, and I confess I have great doubts on the legitimacy of it. . . . After Lord Redesdale's declaration . . . that the mode of appointing sheriffs "poisons the sources of justice," and witnessing the general feeling among the English against making the nomination of a most important officer in the execution of justice dependent on the will of the county member, I thought it highly expedient to give a positive assurance

[1] *Peel Correspondence*, pp. 217, 218.

that the Government would revert to the ancient and legal practice of appointing sheriffs in Ireland. . . . With a pure Bench—and time will, I hope, purify it—the change would be an essential change for the better.'[1] 'Foster says that the abuses discovered in the office [of Clerk of the Pleas] are enormous, that the amount of fees exacted from suitors is not less than 30,000*l*. per annum, of which the principal clerk did not receive more than one-third. A Mr. Pollock, the first deputy, is in receipt of 8,000*l*. or 9,000*l*. a year as his own share of the profits ; other deputies and persons unnecessarily employed have profits amounting to 1,200*l*. or 1,400*l*. a year each. Foster thinks that every possible difficulty will be thrown in the way of an early decision in the Irish Courts. . . . In the meantime, the Chief Baron is receiving the enormous profits arising from these enormous abuses.'[2]

The practice of buying and selling public offices, and the practice of dividing the salaries of a single office between a principal and deputies, still continued ; but Peel did his utmost to eradicate them. If it were permitted in one case, he said, ' every officer in every department who purchased on corrupt terms and is now living may claim a right to sell the office so purchased.'

' With respect to a payment out of the salary to R., I can have no scruple in giving you my opinion that it would not be right. I have never been, and cannot conscientiously be, a party to an arrangement of that kind, because I think this is quite clear, that if the salary of the office is disproportionate to the labour of it, and can bear to be taxed to the amount of 200*l*., the public should benefit, and the emoluments of the office be reduced.'[3]

[1] *Peel Correspondence*, pp. 222–224.   [2] *Ibid.* p. 212.   [3] *Ibid.* p. 284.

One of Peel's first tasks was to conduct a general election, and he had ample opportunities of judging how these things were managed in Ireland. A law known as Curwen's Act had been recently passed, condemning to a heavy fine in the event of failure, and to the loss of his seat in the event of success, any person giving, or promising to give, or consenting to give either money or office for a seat in Parliament. The law was not a little embarrassing to Peel, as his own seat of Cashel had been purchased, and he thought it safer to transfer himself to the English seat of Chippenham, where his return was managed by his father without any intervention on his own part. At the same time, the elections in Ireland went on much as if Curwen's Act had never passed.

'I am placed in a delicate situation enough here,' he wrote to his friend Croker : 'bound to secure the Government interests, if possible, from dilapidation, but still more bound to faint with horror at the mention of money transactions, to threaten the unfortunate culprits with impeachment if they hint at an impure return, and yet to prevent those strongholds, Cashel, Mallow, and Tralee, from surrendering to the enemies who besiege them.'

Croker himself furnished an admirable illustration of the manner in which these principles were carried out. 'I find the borough ' [Down], he writes, ' extremely well disposed to me. Of the respectable and steady people I have a decided majority, not less than twenty ; but there are sixty-two persons who are extremely doubtful. . . . I have the greatest repugnance to bribery, . ., . but my agent informs me that many voters will require money. . . . The return absolutely depends upon pounds sterling. The best computation which my agents

can make is that a sum of 2,000l. will be necessary. The
natural expenses will be 500l. These, I think, I am
bound to make good. But with regard to the money for
votes, that I expect from Government.'

Peel replied that he could not answer for the Government in England, and that the Irish Government
possessed no funds for this purpose ; he would himself
have been ready to send Croker ' 1,000l. as a private
concern between ourselves with no reference whatever
to Government'; but he had it not. 'If you think
proper,' he added, 'to take the chance whether it [the
Government] will assist you, you can promise.' For
about six years Peel was constantly receiving from Croker
requests for places, in order to discharge ' debts of
gratitude ' incurred at this election ; and in 1816 we
find the Government very nearly beaten in the House of
Commons in an attempt to raise Croker's own salary.

'Could you tell me,' writes Lord Palmerston to Peel,
' whether you think there is any probability of a contest
for the county of Sligo at the next election ? I could
at the present moment make from 280 to 290 voters
by giving leases to tenants who are now holding at will.
If there is any chance of their being of use next year,
I will do so forthwith, and register them in time. If
not, I should perhaps postpone giving twenty-one years'
leases till matters look a little more propitious to the
payment of rents.'

' Lord Lorton wrote yesterday to his agent to make
all the freeholders he can on his small Queen's County
property. He says he is sorry he can't make more than
twenty, but that those shall go against Pole.'

A few illustrations of the minor details of patronage
may be added. One gentleman called upon Peel about

an election in Clare, but 'said that he would make no promise of his interest unless he received a pledge from me that his two brothers should be provided for—one in the Church, and the other advanced in the profession of the law.'

Lord C. 'wanted, long since, to make terms with me for his support in Cork, . . . and wished to be one of a committee for superintending the patronage of the county.'

'When G. wants a baronetcy, he is very rich; and when he wants a place, he is very poor. I think we may fairly turn the tables on him, and when he asks to be a baronet, make his poverty the objection, and his wealth when he asks for an office.'

'Pole is constantly pressing K., of the Navigation Board, for promotion. . . . I am told he entirely neglects his duty. Pole readily admits his hopeless stupidity and unfitness for office.'

'I do not think your son,' Peel wrote to his Under-Secretary, 'can make a more inefficient member of the Board of Stamps than Mr. T. has done. I am perfectly ready, therefore, to acquiesce in the exchange.' 'I make a great sacrifice,' he wrote to Lord Whitworth, 'when I say that I doubt whether O.'s habits would qualify him for such practical duties as the Collector of Belfast at least ought to perform. Belfast is so flourishing a town, and contributes so much to the revenue, that I fear the Collectorship of it is too prominent a situation to place in it a young man. . . . we must admit to be a ruined man by gambling. Considering how careless he has been of his own money, perhaps some office not connected with the collection of the public money . . . would be more suited to him. . . . What do you

think of the following arrangement? Make J. collector
for this very bad and very good reason, that he is the
most inefficient Commissioner, and therefore the public
service will suffer least from his appointment. Make
Colonel H. a Commissioner. He will be about as inefficient
as J. Make R. M. junior, the most inefficient of the
three, Surveyor of Lands, *vice* H., which (though he
will lose 200*l.* a year) will greatly oblige his father, the
member; and, lastly, fulfil your good intentions towards
O. by making him a Commissioner of Accounts, *vice* M.'

Many other characteristic pictures pass before us.
There were officers of the revenue who were recommended to 'the marked favour' of the Government
because they had shown what Peel somewhat rashly
called 'the common honesty' of refusing bribes.
There was an official who scandalously connived at an
abuse of justice by which innocent women were condemned to transportation, though taking measures that
the Government should indirectly hear of the transaction.
There were shameful abuses in the sale of the office of
gaoler, shameful frauds in the collection of taxes, in the
Customs, in the barrack charges.

' My most decided opinion,' Peel wrote about one of
these culprits, ' is in favour of his dismissal. I am quite
tired of, and disgusted with, the shameful corruptions
which every Irish inquiry brings to light.' [1]

Much trouble was given by newspapers which were
subsidised by the Government, and at the same time
conducted in a manner which no honest Government
could approve of.[2] Another evil is disclosed in the following very creditable letter written by Peel to one of his
successors :

---

[1] *Peel Correspondence*, p. 282.   [2] *Ibid.* pp. 114-116, 211, 218.

'I found in Ireland that every official man, not content with the favour of Government to himself, thought he had a right to quarter his family on the patronage of Government. I took the course that you have done in order to enable me to resist with effect such extravagant pretensions. I determined never to gratify any private wish of my own by the smallest Irish appointment. There is nothing half so disgusting as the personal monopoly of honours and offices by those to whom the distribution of them is entrusted.'[1]

In the Irish Pension List there had been enormous abuses, but Peel took credit for having effectually stopped them. 'No member of Parliament,' he wrote, 'has benefited by it. No vote has been influenced by it. . . . I do not think there are any three years in the whole period of the Irish history during which so honest a use has been made of it.'[2]

As might have been expected, blunders arising from extreme inefficiency were very numerous. In one case, by negligent drafting, the Insurrection Bill was made to extend to three instead of two years, while a simple mistake in one of the Revenue Bills was believed to have cost the Revenue not less than 40,000*l*.[3]

In all this dreary field the great administrative ability of Peel and the essential integrity of his character produced much real improvement, though it is very possible to exaggerate his merits. No one who has read the Hardwicke and Colchester papers will question that some of his predecessors, and especially the Chancellor, Lord Redesdale, had laboured with at least equal earnestness to purify Irish administration; and the energy with

---

[1] *Peel Correspondence*, p. 60.
[2] *Ibid.* p. 275.   [3] *Ibid.* p. 96.

which Lord Redesdale, though out of office, still recurred
to the subject, was extremely displeasing to Peel.[1] His
own patronage, as we have already seen, was by no means
ideal, and he was very anxious to stifle parliamentary
inquiries.

' I believe,' he wrote, ' an honest, despotic government
would be by far the fittest government for Ireland ' ; but
as this could not be attained he wished no essential
alteration. 'I think the present system on which the
government of Ireland is conducted is the best, but I am
terribly afraid that Englishmen, who know nothing of
Ireland, would not concur with me if they inquired into
detail. It is very difficult to manage even the most
limited inquiry. How could we prevent the introduction of
tithes, magistracy, the Catholic question itself ? ' [2]

Whatever might be the case in the future, he believed that in the present it was impossible for the Irish
Government to receive adequate support unless it made
up its mind to purchase it. ' It would be good policy,'
he says in one of his letters, 'to direct the channel of
patronage as plentifully as we can towards those who
are adhering to us on these pressing questions of army
establishments and property tax.' He refused in very
lofty tones applications for peerages as rewards for
political support ; but the merit of this refusal belongs
mainly to Lord Liverpool, who, at the beginning of the
Chief Secretaryship, took on this subject a very firm
and honourable line, both in England and Ireland, and
maintained it at the sacrifice of many votes. For Irish
honours unaccompanied by endowments there appear to
have been few applicants. Peel disliked the bestowal of
ecclesiastical dignities as rewards for political services ;

[1] *Peel Correspondence*, p. 211.   [2] *Ibid.* pp. 215, 219, 220.

but if he did not practise it quite as much as his predecessors, this appears to have been much more due to nature than to policy.

'There is nothing so extraordinary,' he wrote, 'in natural history as the longevity of all bishops, priests, and deacons in Ireland. During the last five years there has been literally no Church preferment to dispose of, to the infinite disappointment of many expectants.'

In the higher legal appointments, however, while insisting that 'attachment to the Government on principle' was very material, Peel cordially agreed with Saurin that it was vitally necessary to select men 'for character, and not for politics or connection'; and he added, that those were not likely to be the least fit for high office who were too proud to solicit it. 'It is a species of pride which occasions very little practical inconvenience in Ireland.'

His letters show clearly the terrible evils of Irish life. He speaks of 'the enormous and overgrown population,' with no employment except agriculture; of a poverty so extreme that in many districts widespread starvation was averted only by prompt Government intervention; of 'that infernal curse, the forty shilling freeholds'; of the evil system of employing the military in distraining for rent and in the collection of tithes; of juries, through fear or sympathy, acquitting prisoners in the face of the clearest evidence; of the gross perjury in the law courts; of the almost universal disaffection of the lower orders, fostered by a seditious press; of the growing spirit of animosity in the north of Ireland between the lower orders of Protestants and Catholics, which was breaking out in constant riots, and had already cost many lives. This last evil, it might be truly said, was very largely due to the policy of his own party, who had protracted through

so many years the Catholic question, which ought to
have been settled at the Union.   There was extreme and
chronic ignorance, poverty, and anarchy ; the payment of
tithes was constantly resisted ; and a failure of the potato
crop, and a sudden and terrible fall in the price of agricultural products after the peace, added enormously to
the difficulties of the situation.   It is remarkable, indeed,
that there appears to have been in 1816 and 1817 less
disturbance of the public peace in Ireland than in
England ; Peel found it even possible to reduce the
military establishments, and in Dublin extreme distress
was borne with remarkable patience ; but in many parts
of the country crimes of combination were frequent, and
almost incredibly savage.   Peel mentions one case of a
family of eight persons who were deliberately burnt in
their house by a party of armed men, because the owner
of the house had prosecuted to conviction three men, on
a capital charge, at the Louth assizes.   In another case
a farmer, who had shot two men who attacked his house,
was himself shot dead on a Sunday morning, after Mass,
at the chapel door, in the presence of hundreds of men,
not one of whom attempted to arrest the culprit.

These things filled Peel with a not unnatural horror,
and his letters showed clearly his intense dislike both
of the Irish character and of the Irish religion.[1]   By far
the most valuable contribution he made to the improvement of Ireland during his Chief Secretaryship was the
formation, in 1814, of an efficient police force, which has
ever since been popularly associated with his name, and
which was the nucleus from which the present admirable
constabulary force was developed in 1822 and in 1835.
'We ought to be crucified,' he wrote, 'if we make the

[1] *Peel Correspondence*, pp. 207, 231, 235, 236.

measure a job, and select our constables from the servants of our parliamentary friends.' He attempted also, though without much success, to institute a system of popular education on a perfectly unsectarian basis, and with Catholics among the commissioners.[1] He appears to have met with little encouragement, and at least one Catholic bishop lost no time in cursing ' these nefarious deistical schools '; but some schools were established, and Peel has the merit of being one of the earliest advocates of a general system of unsectarian national education for Ireland, which many years after was accomplished. His measures for the relief of distress appear to have been skilful and judicious, supporting and stimulating, but not superseding private benevolence.[2] For the rest, he relied chiefly on Insurrection Acts strengthening the Executive and giving a greater efficiency to the administration of justice, and on strong protective legislation encouraging the corn and the manufactures of Ireland.

' I have always,' he wrote, ' been, and always shall be, as strong an advocate for giving that preference to the productions of Ireland, natural or artificial, which will best promote the industry of the people, as I am for instructing the lower orders.'[3]

To the tithe system he would do nothing, and this is one of the fatal blots on his reputation as a statesman. There was no single source of crime, agitation, and disaffection in Ireland which was so prolific as this, and there was no subject on which the wisest statesmen had been more agreed than on the supreme importance of meeting this evil by a judicious system of commutation.

[1] *Peel Correspondence*, pp. 87-92.
[2] *Ibid.* pp. 244, 265. [3] *Ibid.* pp. 167, 233.

Pitt had clearly expressed his opinion of the necessity of such a commutation to the Duke of Rutland as early as 1786, and it was one of the measures which he intended to have followed the Union. Grattan had brought schemes of commutation in three successive years before the Irish Parliament. Lord Loughborough, who was the chief cause of the failure of Catholic emancipation after the Union, had himself drawn up a Tithe Commutation Bill. Lord Redesdale, who represented the extreme Toryism of the ministry of Addington, strongly urged the absolute necessity of speedy legislation on the subject. The Duke of Bedford, in 1807, dwelt on the importance of commuting tithes into a land-tax, and ultimately into land. Parnell and Grattan had brought the subject before the Imperial Parliament in 1810, and it was again and again insisted on by the Whig writers, and nowhere more strongly than in Sydney Smith's admirable letters to Peter Plymley and in some of the pages of the 'Edinburgh Review.' But nothing was done till the evil had become intolerable, and had brought the country to a state of anarchy and demoralisation that can scarcely be exaggerated. The connection of Peel with the question of Irish tithes is a very remarkable one. The Tithe Commutation Act, which was carried by a Whig Government in 1838, is one of the few instances of perfectly successful legislation in Irish history, and it is well known that the chief credit of this measure does not belong to the Ministers who carried it. It was the very measure which Sir Robert Peel had introduced in 1835, which the Whig party when in opposition defeated by connecting it with the Appropriation clause, and which the Whig party when in power were compelled to carry without that clause. But if the

chief credit of the final settlement of this momentous
question justly belongs to Peel, it must not be forgotten
that in the eleven years during which, as Chief Secretary
or as Home Secretary, he was directly responsible for the
government of Ireland, he had allowed this monster curse
to grow and strengthen without making any serious effort
to mitigate it.

Peel was Chief Secretary during the concluding part
of the viceroyalty of the Duke of Richmond, during the
whole of that of Lord Whitworth, and during part of
that of Lord Talbot. He had grown very tired of his
position, but agreed to postpone his departure till after
a general election, and he at last left Ireland, as he
says, with ' undiminished and unqualified satisfaction,' in
August 1818. He remained out of office until January
1822; but the interval was not spent in idleness, and
in 1819 he took the leading part in the great Act for
resuming cash payments, which, as it has been truly said,
attaches to his name ' the same meed of praise which he
had quoted as inscribed on the tomb of Queen Elizabeth :
" Moneta in justum valorem redacta." ' It is one of his
greatest legislative achievements; it is also the first of
that series of recantations which forms one of the most
distinctive features of his career, for it was based upon
the policy which Horner had advocated in 1811, and
against which Peel had then voted. He still took, on the
Catholic question, the leading part in opposition to
emancipation, declaring his determination to offer ' a most
sincere and uncompromising,' though he now feared
unavailing, resistance to Catholic concession. The
last time the question was brought forward, by Grattan,
was in 1819, and he was defeated by a majority of only
two. In 1821, after the death of Grattan, and in a new

Parliament, Plunket carried a Bill for Catholic emancipation successfully through all its stages in the House of
Commons, though it was afterwards rejected in the
Lords. In the ensuing session a similar fate befel a Bill
of Canning's to relieve Catholic peers of their disabilities.
Some considerable change, however, was introduced into
the spirit of the Irish Government by the appointment of
Lord Wellesley, who was in favour of the Catholics, to
the viceroyalty. One of its most important results was
the removal of Saurin from the office of Attorney-General
and the appointment of Plunket in his place. Lord
Wellesley described this measure to Lady Blessington
as the removal of 'an old Orangeman' who, though
'Attorney-General by title, had really been Lord-
Lieutenant for fifteen years'; but it is evident from
the letters of Peel that his warm sympathies, both
personal and political, were with Saurin.

The accession of George IV. to the throne in the
beginning of 1820 brought to a crisis the quarrel between
the new King and his wife, and led to the resignation of
Canning in the last days of the year, and Lord Liverpool
then tried to induce Peel to enter the Cabinet in the
vacant post of President of the Board of Control. Peel,
however, refused the office, declaring that he differed
from some of the proceedings of the Ministry about the
Queen. In the summer of 1821 he again declined a similar
offer, chiefly, as it appears, on the ground of uncertain
health and of a dislike to official life which his recent
marriage had produced. But when Lord Sidmouth resigned the Home Office, Peel proved less inflexible, and
on January 17, 1822, he accepted the seals, which he held
till 1827. In August Castlereagh, or, as he now was,
Lord Londonderry, committed suicide. Lord Liverpool

saw the necessity of recalling Canning to the Cabinet as Minister of Foreign Affairs, and Canning would accept the post only as leader of the House of Commons. The King hated Canning, and would gladly have excluded him altogether from the Ministry, and Eldon and the Duke of Newcastle greatly desired that the leadership of the House of Commons should be given to Peel. Canning, however, who had been sixteen years longer in Parliament than Peel, had both the right and the power to insist upon the leadership, and Peel acquiesced in his claim with honourable frankness. Except on the Catholic question they appear to have cordially agreed, and something of the success of Canning's brilliant foreign policy is due to the loyalty with which he was supported by Peel in the Cabinet and at Court.

Space will not permit us to relate at length the history of Peel's conduct as home Minister. The Catholic question was rapidly advancing to a crisis, and the system of a divided Ministry in which it was an open question, and in which the leading Ministers took opposite sides, was becoming plainly impossible. Ireland was again in a state of anarchy bordering on civil war, and the foundation, in 1823, of the Catholic Association by O'Connell and Sheil gave a new impulse to the agitation. The Duke of Wellington, who knew the country well and was not liable to panic, predicted that the new association if it continued would lead to civil war, and declared that the organisation of the disaffected in Ireland was much more perfect than in 1798.[1] At the same time the long-protracted and increasing violence of the conflict had aroused fierce Orange passions both in the North and in Dublin, while in England the King was

[1] *Peel Correspondence*, p. 348.

embarrassing even his 'anti-Catholic' Ministers by the vehemence of his hostility to concession. He described Peel as 'the King's Protestant Minister' and Lord Wellesley as an 'enemy in the camp.' He assured Peel that, whether the Cabinet wished it or not, he would never consent to give letters of precedence to a Roman Catholic barrister, and he wrote Peel a formal letter in which he said, 'the sentiments of the King upon Catholic emancipation are those of his revered and excellent father; from those sentiments the King never can and never will deviate.' [1]

Peel, while maintaining his unflinching hostility to important concessions, tried to moderate all parties. He implored the King to make no public declaration. He wrote to Ireland strongly discouraging the violence of the Orangemen and urging that 'in this age of liberal doctrine, when prescription is no longer even a presumption in favour of what is established, it will be a work of desperate difficulty to contend against "emancipation," as they call it, unless we can fight with the advantage on our side of great discretion, forbearance, and moderation on the part of the Irish Protestants.' He recurred to his old idea of establishing a system of unsectarian national education, and he readily abandoned the corrupt and proselytising charter schools. He supported a measure of Lord Nugent, which Lord Eldon succeeded in defeating in the Lords, for extending to the English Catholics such privileges as were already possessed by Catholics in Ireland, and he fully approved of a letter written on behalf of the Cabinet to the Lord-Lieutenant urging 'that a disposition should be manifested to admit the Roman Catholics of Ireland

[1] *Peel Correspondence*, pp. 349, 358, 359, 370-371.

to a fair proportion of the emoluments and honours to which they are eligible by law,' but without issuing patents of precedence.[1]

On matters unconnected with the Catholic question his administration was skilful and, on the whole, enlightened ; and in 1823 he introduced the first of a series of important measures diminishing the enormous number of capital offences that disgraced the English criminal code, and, at the same time, doing much to simplify and consolidate that code. In this, as in most respects, there was little original in his legislation. He followed, at some distance, in the steps of Romilly and Mackintosh, and he left very much to be done, which was chiefly accomplished during the Whig ascendancy that followed the Reform Bill of 1832. It appears, from some remarkable letters in this volume, that, before Peel took up the question of criminal reform, George IV. was exceedingly sensible of the enormity of executing very young men for secondary offences, and that he was continually pressing on his Ministers a more merciful administration of the law. He sometimes found Peel by no means ready to yield. In one case Peel invoked the aid of the Cabinet to overrule the wish of the King, who desired to save two culprits from the gallows ; and, in another case, he threatened to resign his office if the King persisted in commuting the sentence of a youth who had been found guilty of uttering forged notes.[2] But Peel had at least the merit of recognising an intolerable abuse, and his legislation on the subject was skilfully framed and still more skilfully introduced and carried. In his patronage in this, as in later periods of his life, he cared much more than most English Ministers for the

[1] *Peel Correspondence*, p. 358.   [2] *Ibid.* pp. 315-317.

interests of science, literature, and art. He was by no
means indifferent to the opportunities his position gave
him of advancing his own family and friends ; but he
never, in his English patronage, forgot the character of
those whom he recommended for promotion, and he
brought forward or assisted many men of ability and
learning with whom he had no connection and no political
sympathy. The letters in this volume between Peel and
his very intimate Oxford friend Dr. Lloyd are especially
interesting and characteristic. They are in general very
honourable to Peel ; but Mr. Parker is much too indulgent
when he describes the intensely worldly letters in which
Dr. Lloyd urged his own merits and his claims to the
bishopric of Oxford as merely 'frank, and free from
affectation of the traditional *nolo episcopari.*' Both
Peel and Lord Liverpool appear to have had a much
stronger sense than most of their predecessors of the
responsibilities attaching to Church patronage and of
the duty of administering it in the public interest, and
in this respect they were broadly distinguished from
Lord Eldon.

'It is really a cruel thing,' Lord Liverpool wrote to
Peel, 'that the patronage of the Crown as to Church
matters should be divided between the Minister and the
Chancellor, and that all the public claims should fall upon
the former. The Chancellor has nine livings to the
Minister's one. With respect to these he does occasionally attend to local claims, but he has besides four
cathedrals, and to no one of these cathedrals has any
man of distinguished learning or merit been promoted.'

In the beginning of 1825 the Irish Government,
having without consulting Peel undertaken a foolish
prosecution of O'Connell for a not very dangerous speech,

received a heavy rebuff, for the Grand Jury threw out the Bill, and the prosecution of an Orange leader was equally unsuccessful. A Bill was about the same time brought in and carried, suppressing the new association; but it could not suppress the spirit which it had aroused. O'Connell, however, was thoroughly alarmed at the state of the country, and as far as possible from desiring a rebellion, and he was at this time in a very conciliatory mood. He was perfectly ready to accept an endowment for the priesthood, which would attach them to the Government, and also a considerable raising of the Irish franchise. This was the last occasion on which his party and the Catholic gentry very cordially concurred, and it was the last occasion on which the Catholic question could have been settled on a basis that would have given real strength to the Empire. A Relief Bill passed through all its stages in the Commons by considerable majorities, and it was followed by a Bill for raising the qualifications of Irish electors, and by a resolution for endowing the priesthood. O'Connell fully believed that Catholic emancipation would definitely pass in this session,[1] and he appeared to have excellent reasons for his belief. In Ireland it generally prevailed, and it exercised an immediate pacifying influence. Lord Fingall and other Catholic noblemen, in presenting an address at this time to the King, were able to say 'the whole of Ireland reposes in profound tranquillity, and the law, without the aid of any extraordinary power, everywhere receives voluntary obedience.' It was afterwards stated by Lord George Bentinck that Peel had changed his opinions about Catholic emancipation in 1825, and had communicated this change to Lord Liverpool. The letters

[1] Fitzpatrick's *Correspondence of O'Connell*, i. p. 108.

before us, however, conclusively prove that if Peel was shaken, it was not about the merits of emancipation, but about the practicability of resisting it. Having been four times defeated in the Commons on the Catholic question, he tendered his resignation, and Lord Liverpool at once declared that without his assistance he could not continue the struggle. Peel was the only Minister in the House of Commons opposed to the Catholic cause, differing on the question from all his colleagues in the House. If he had resigned, and if Lord Liverpool had followed his example, there is good reason to believe that a Government might have been formed which would have carried the measure safely and speedily with the securities that had been accepted. Most unfortunately for the Empire, the ' Protestant ' party persuaded Peel to withdraw his resignation in order to avert this surrender. In the House of Lords the Duke of York, who was the heir-presumptive to the throne, stood up and declared his unalterable opposition to the Catholic claims, ' whatever might be his situation in life, so help him God,' and the Lords rejected the Bill by a majority of 48.

The conscientious views of George III. obtained some measure of respect even from those who believed them to be most unfounded ; but no halo of sanctity dignified the scruples of George IV. or of the Duke of York. The Irish Catholics, exasperated at the present disappointment of their hopes, and at the prospect of another hostile King, flung themselves into a furious agitation, and in a few months all the progress which had been made towards pacifying the country was undone, while in England Peel had to meet a terrible commercial crisis. Seventy county banks stopped in less than a week. In dealing with questions of commerce and currency Peel

was always in his element, and his measures appear to
have been wise and skilful. A general election took
place, and he was again returned by the University of
Oxford as the uncompromising opponent of Catholic
emancipation. In England the anti-Catholic party
gained some seats, and the increasing violence in Ireland
had produced some reaction. In Ireland it was soon
apparent that what Grattan had feared had come to pass,
and that the tie which had hitherto attached the people
to their landlords was completely broken. The priests
everywhere appeared at the head of their people, and it
was at once seen that a new and terrible power was
dominating Irish politics. In Waterford, where the
Beresfords had long been omnipotent, they were totally
defeated, and Leslie Foster sent Peel a vivid description
of his own defeat in the Louth election. At the outset
of the contest, upwards of five-sixths of the votes were
promised to him ; but the whole priesthood turned
themselves into electioneering agents against him. In
every chapel there were political sermons; the priests
menaced all who voted for him with eternal damnation ;
they were present at every polling-booth to overawe their
parishioners; and their efforts were seconded by savage
mobs who waylaid and beat all opponents, and forced
multitudes of Protestants, by threats of assassination or
of the burning of their houses, to vote against their
promises and their convictions. 'In the county town
the studied violence and intimidation were such that it
was only by locking up my voters in enclosed yards that
their lives were preserved.' By these means the election
was won. What, asked Foster, will be the end of this ?
' The landlords are exasperated to the utmost, the priests
swaggering in their triumph, the tenantry sullen and

insolent. Men who, a month ago, were all civility and submission now hardly suppress their curses when a gentleman passes by. The text of every village orator is, "Boys, you have put down three lords; stick to your priests, and you will carry all before you." '

The letters of Goulburn, the Chief Secretary, show that the picture was not overcharged.

'Never,' he wrote, 'were Roman Catholic and Protestant so decidedly opposed. Never did the former act with so general a concert, or place themselves so completely under the command of the priesthood.' 'The priests exercise on all matters a dominion perfectly uncontrolled and uncontrollable. In many parts of the country their sermons are purely political, and the altars in the several chapels are the rostra from which they declaim on the subject of Roman Catholic grievances, exhort to the collection of rent, or denounce their Protestant neighbours in a mode perfectly intelligible and effective, but not within the grasp of the law. In several towns no Roman Catholic will now deal with a Protestant shopkeeper, in consequence of the priest's interdiction, and this species of interference, stirring up enmity on one hand and feelings of resentment on the other, is mainly conducive to outrage and disorder. . . . The first vacancy on the Roman Catholic bench is to be supplied by Dr. England from America, a man of all others most decidedly hostile to British interests and the most active in fomenting the discord of this country. . . . With such leaders it is reasonable to anticipate the worst. It is impossible to detail in a letter the various modes in which the Roman Catholic priesthood now interfere in every transaction of every description, how they rule the mob, the gentry, and the magistracy, and how they impede the

administration of justice.' Their power is greater than
any other in the State, 'and they love to display it, and
omit no opportunity of taunting their adversaries.' 'The
state of society here is so disorganised, and the Government
has so inferior an authority to other powers acting on the
people, that the opinion formed to-day may be quite
changed to-morrow.' [1]

The election of 1826 virtually carried Catholic emancipation, for it reduced Ireland to a state in which it was
impossible long to resist it. Clear-sighted men had no
difficulty in perceiving that the policy of Peel had failed
to avert it, though it had succeeded in making impossible
the securities which Grattan and the wisest men of his
generation had pronounced indispensable for its safe
working, in kindling religious hatreds as intense as in the
darkest period of the eighteenth century, in breaking
down that healthy relation and subordination of classes
on which beyond all other things the future well-being
of Ireland depended. Peel was not wholly blind to
what was happening. 'A darker cloud than ever,' he
wrote, 'seems to me to impend over Ireland, that is if
one of the remaining bonds of society, the friendly connection between landlord and tenant, is dissolved.' [2]
He still persuaded himself, however, that the political
power of the priests was transient, and that a
reaction would set in that might destroy it. The
defeat of the Catholic question in the new Parliament by a majority of four encouraged him in his
resistance. In January 1827 the death of the Duke of
York removed one serious obstacle to the Catholic cause,
and six weeks later Lord Liverpool, who had so long
held together the divided Ministry, was struck down by

[1] *Peel Correspondence*, pp. 416, 418, 419, 422.   [2] *Ibid.* pp. 413, 420.

apoplexy. Peel would gladly have continued in his
present position if a peer of real weight who held his
opinions on the Catholic question was appointed to the
vacant place. But there was no such peer, except
Wellington, to be found, and under Wellington Canning
refused to serve. Canning had, indeed, now fully resolved
to be at the head of the Administration, and Peel refused
to serve under him.

With his opinions on the Catholic question it is
impossible to blame him, and the letters which passed
between the two statesmen are very honourable to both,
and show clearly that in spite of great divergence of
opinion, character, and interests, each could recognise
the good faith of the other. In a letter written to one of
his brothers Peel describes his position with complete
frankness :

'I am content with my position in the Government,
and willing to retain it—willing to see Mr. Canning
leader of the House of Commons, as he has been. But
giving him credit for honesty and sincerity, if he is at the
head of the Government, and has all the patronage of the
Government, he must exert himself as an honest man to
carry the Catholic question ; and to the carrying of that
question, to the preparation for its being carried, I never
can be a party. Still less can I be a party to it for the
sake of office.'

These words were written little more than a year
before Peel undertook, as Minister of the Crown, to
introduce a measure of Catholic emancipation. But if
they do little credit to his prescience, no one can mistake
the accent of sincerity in what follows :

'I do not choose to see new lights on the Catholic
question precisely at that conjuncture when the Duke of

York has been laid in his grave and Lord Liverpool struck dumb by the palsy. Would any man, woman, or child believe that after nineteen years' stubborn unbelief I was converted, at the very moment Mr. Canning was Prime Minister, out of pure conscience and the force of truth ?' [1]

With the resignation of Peel and the other anti-Catholic members of Lord Liverpool's Government, and the formation of the short Canning Ministry, this instalment of Peel's letters comes to an end. [2] We rejoice that the publication of this very interesting correspondence has been entrusted to an editor who is at once so competent and so judicious.

[1] *Peel Correspondence*, p. 485.

[2] Two more volumes have been published since this Essay was written.—Ed.

EDWARD HENRY, FIFTEENTH EARL OF DERBY

THE time has not yet arrived for the publication of a full life of the late Lord Derby, but in submitting to the public a collection of his more important speeches outside Parliament, a short sketch of the chief features of his life and character may not be out of place.

Edward Henry, fifteenth Earl of Derby, was born July 21, 1826, and was educated at Rugby, and Trinity College, Cambridge, where he obtained a First Class in classics. In March 1848 he unsuccessfully contested Lancaster, and soon after started for a long and instructive journey in America and the West Indies. During his absence from England he was elected Member for Lynn Regis upon the death of Lord George Bentinck in September 1848, and he held this seat without interruption till his accession to the earldom in October 1869. His first speech in the House of Commons was delivered on May 31, 1850, on the sugar duties. The effect on the West Indies of the abolition of the preferential duty on sugar was a subject which he had specially studied during his journey, and he had published a pamphlet upon it. Sir Robert Peel greatly praised his maiden speech, and Greville describes the great impression which it made — an impression which a further knowledge of the speaker speedily confirmed.

The appearance in Parliament of the eldest son of one of the most brilliant party leaders of the age could scarcely fail to be a considerable political event, and it was soon found that the new member was not only a man of rare ability, but was also in nearly all respects very unlike his illustrious father. Never was there a more striking instance of that strange freak of heredity by which an able son is sometimes much less the continuation than the complement of an able father, exhibiting in strongly contrasted lights both opposite qualities and opposite defects. The fourteenth Earl was a great orator. He was one of the greatest debaters who have ever lived. He was a party leader of extraordinary power, delighting in political conflict; throwing into it much of the fire and passion which he displayed in his sporting contests; little fitted to conciliate opponents, but eminently fitted to win the enthusiastic loyalty of his followers, to rally a dispirited minority, to lead a party attack. His keen and rapid judgment; his perfect command of pure and lucid English; his unfailing readiness in argument, invective, sarcasm, and repartee; his indomitable courage, and the somewhat imperious dignity of his manner, all marked him out for the position which he held. If there was some truth in the common taunt that he was more a party leader than a statesman, it must at least be remembered that he has identified his name with several important measures, and that during most of his career he was in a hopeless minority. His enemies accused him of rashness, arrogance, and some superficiality, both of thought and knowledge. They alleged that he carried too much of the sporting spirit into politics; that his naturally excellent judgment was often deflected by the passions of the fray; that he was accustomed to judge measures more by their party advantages than by their intrinsic merits, and to care more for an immediate triumph than for ultimate results. His son was made in a very different mould. Though like most able and clear-headed men he acquired by much practice a respectable facility in purely extemporaneous argument, he was never a great debater. His speeches were very carefully prepared, and they possessed conspicuous merits of form as well as of matter, but they were not the speeches of a brilliant orator. No one could reason more clearly, more powerfully, or more persuasively. He was a supreme master of terse, luminous, weighty, and accurate English. He had much skill in bringing into vivid relief the salient points of an obscure and complicated subject, condensing an argument into a phrase, and illustrating it by graphic felicities of language that clung to the memory. But he hated rhetoric. His enunciation was faulty and unimpressive. He appealed solely to the reason, and never to passion or to prejudice, and he had nothing of the fire and temperament of a party orator. Very few politicians mastered so thoroughly the subjects with which they dealt. No politician of his time retained so remarkably, amid party conflicts, the power of judging questions from all their sides ; of balancing judicially opposing considerations ; of looking beyond the passions and interests of the hour ; of realising the points of view of those to whom he was opposed. Declamation, clap-trap, evasion, ambiguities of thought and expression, empty plausibilities, unfair, partial, and exaggerated statements, were all essentially repugnant to that clear and sceptical intellect, to that sound, cautious, practical judgment. His business talents were very great, and they were assiduously culti-

vated. His appetite for work was insatiable. No one
knew better how to administer a great department or
preside over a Parliamentary Committee, or arbitrate in
a difficult controversy, or give wise and timely advice to
an inexperienced organisation. It was in these fields
that his influence was, perhaps, most deeply felt. His
success in them did not depend merely on his unflagging
industry and his excellent judgment, it was also largely
due to his eminently conciliatory character. The uniform courtesy which he displayed to men of all ranks
and opinions is happily no rare thing among his class,
but everyone who was brought in contact with Lord
Derby soon felt that he was in the presence of one who
tried to understand his position, to estimate his arguments
at their full worth, to find some common ground of
agreement. If it were possible in a bitter controversy
to arrive at reasonable compromise, Lord Derby was
most likely to effect it. He had a curious talent of
making speeches with which everyone must agree, and
which at the same time were never commonplace.
Their secret lay in the habit of mind that led him
always to seek out the common grounds of principle or
fact that underlie every controversy, and which in the
heat of the conflict the disputants had often failed to
recognise.

It was not difficult to forecast the place which a
statesman of this kind was likely to fill in English politics.
He was plainly wanting in many of the qualities of a
party leader, and in most of the qualities of a parliamentary gladiator, and he was not likely to succeed in all
forms of statesmanship. He would certainly not prove

> A daring pilot in extremity,
> Pleased with the danger when the waves went high.

His clear perception of the objections to any course, combined with a very deep sense of responsibility, not unfrequently enfeebled his will in moments when bold and decisive action was required, and there were times when the love of compromise which was so useful an element in his character seemed to his best friends too closely allied to weakness. But he probably saved every party with which he acted from many mistakes. He brought to every Government which he joined a very eminent administrative capacity. He defended every policy that he espoused with a persuasive reasoning that few men could equal. He was a supremely skilful detector of false weights and of false measures. Every fad, every new-born enthusiasm, every crude ill-digested theory, found in him the calmest and most penetrating of critics, and he inspired the great body of moderate men of all parties with a deep confidence in his patriotism and in his judgment.

His political position was marked out by the fact that his father had recently broken away from the Whig connection which had hitherto been that of his family, and was now the leader of the Conservative party. The son naturally took his place under his father's banner, but I much question whether he would have done so if no family influence had interfered. It was not that he at any time changed considerably his views. As Macaulay has truly said—while the extremes of the two English parties are separated by a wide chasm, there is a frontier line where they almost blend; and Lord Derby when a Conservative always represented the Liberal, and when a Liberal the Conservative wing of his party. But his mind had much of the Whig character; his judgment was very independent; and on

Church questions especially he was never fully in harmony with his party. He was appointed Under-Secretary of State for Foreign Affairs in his father's first short Ministry in March 1852, at a time when he was travelling in India, and he left office with his father in December of the same year. In 1853 he made a remarkable speech on Indian affairs, in some degree foreshadowing the Indian policy which he was afterwards destined to take such a large part in carrying into effect. During the next few years he spoke frequently on Indian and Colonial questions, on questions connected with education, factories, and other working-class interests, and he supported—often in opposition to the majority of his party—a large number of reforms which have since been accomplished. He advocated the introduction of competitive examinations, first of all into the Diplomatic, and then into most branches of the Civil Service. He spoke against the system of purchase in the army, and served on a Royal Commission on the subject. He supported a motion for securing to married women their property and earnings. He took a decided part in opposition to Church rates. He voted for the emancipation of the Jews. He voted and spoke in favour of the Maynooth grant. He was an early advocate of the opening of museums on Sundays, and of a conscience clause to be enforced in all schools receiving State assistance. He supported the establishment of the Divorce Court, and clearly showed that preference for social as distinguished from political questions which he retained through his whole life. He delighted in placing himself in touch with working men. Mechanics' institutes, free libraries, almost every movement for the education and improvement of the working class, found in him a steady friend.

He once wrote to Lord Shaftesbury : ' We are both public men deeply interested in the condition of the working class, and for my own part I would rather look back on services such as you have performed for that class than receive the highest honours in the employment of the State.' On working-class questions he was often accused of Radicalism, but it was Radicalism of the old school, which relied mainly for reform on spontaneous effort, on moral improvement, and extended education, and was very jealous of State interference, compulsion, and control. He had a great admiration for Mill's writings, and especially for his treatise on Liberty, which he described as ' one of the wisest books of our time.' Mill fully reciprocated the feeling. He once spoke of Lord Stanley as ' one of the very few English public men who hold that a politician's opinions ought to be founded on principles.'

' Our party,' wrote Lord Malmesbury in 1853, ' are angry with Disraeli, which is constantly the case, and they are also displeased with Lord Stanley, suspecting him to be coquetting with the Manchester party.' Greville, nearly at the same time, expressed his belief that Lord Stanley was taking ' a wise and liberal line,' and that he was ' pretty sure to act a conspicuous part.' In November 1855 there was a critical moment in his career, when Lord Palmerston, on the death of Sir William Molesworth, offered Lord Stanley the post of Secretary of State for the Colonies. He at once went down to Knowsley to consult his father, who put a strong veto on the proposal, and the offer was refused, but in terms which showed that it had been far from unacceptable. It is probable that the refusal was a wise one, for although on many home questions Lord Stanley would

have found himself more in harmony with moderate
Liberals than with his own party, he would certainly
have dissented from Lord Palmerston's foreign policy.
During the Crimean war he seems to have sympathised
with the views of Bright and Cobden. He took an
active part in an able but now nearly forgotten Tory
paper called 'The Press,' which was opposed to the war,
and his extreme horror of war and of every policy which
could possibly lead to war was one of his strongest
characteristics. Responsibility in office never weighed
lightly upon him, but responsibility for measures which
led or might lead to bloodshed was more than he could
bear.

At the time when this offer of Lord Palmerston was
made, Lord Stanley was little more than twenty-nine.
Greville considered that he had acted wisely in refusing,
and he has given us an interesting account of the light in
which the young statesman then appeared to experienced
political judges. 'His position and abilities,' he said, 'are
certain before long to make him conspicuous, and to
enable him to play a very considerable part. He is exceedingly ambitious, of an independent turn of mind,
very industrious, and has acquired a vast amount of
information. Not long ago Disraeli gave me an account
of him and of his curious opinions—exceedingly curious
in a man in his condition of life and with his prospects.
Last night Lord Strangford (George Smythe) talked to
me about him, expressed the highest opinion of his capacity and acquirements, and confirmed what Disraeli had
told me of his notions and views even more, for he says
that he is a real and sincere democrat, and that he would
like if he could to prove his sincerity by divesting himself of his aristocratic character, and even of the wealth

he is heir to. How far this may be true I know not. . . .
Nothing appears to me certain but that he will play a
considerable part for good or for evil, but I cannot pretend
to guess what it will be. At present he seems to be more
allied with Bright than with any other public man, and
as his disposition about the war and its continuance is
very much that of Bright it would have been difficult for
him to take office with Palmerston.'

Lord Stanley had not long to wait for high office.
His father formed his second Administration in February
1858, and Lord Stanley was made Colonial Secretary. He
appears to have accepted the office with some reluctance,
and only because Sir E. Bulwer, for whom it was at first
intended, found that he could not secure his re-election.
The Government was a very weak one, and it opened with
the worst prospects. It was a Government in a minority.
Its very existence depended on the dissensions between
Lord Palmerston and Lord John Russell, and its first
steps met with little favour either in the House or in the
country. The Indian Mutiny was now nearly suppressed,
and Lord Palmerston shortly before quitting office had
pledged the House of Commons to the policy of withdrawing the Government of India from the East India
Company and placing it directly under the Crown. To
carry this policy into effect was the first task of the new
Government. They introduced an Indian Bill which they
were compelled to withdraw, and then substituted for it
a new Bill founded on resolutions which were carried
through the House of Commons. In May the Government almost fell on account of the indiscreet publication
of a despatch of Lord Ellenborough, condemning a Proclamation of the Governor-General, Lord Canning. A
vote of censure was moved and would certainly have been

carried if Lord Ellenborough had not saved his colleagues by resigning. He was President of the Board of Control, the Office which then directed Indian affairs, and Lord Stanley took his place, piloted the Indian Bill successfully through the House of Commons, and when the measure became law, was the first Secretary of State for India, and undertook the very important and responsible task of beginning the new system of Indian Government.

'The Times' noticed the singular good fortune of Lord Derby in being able at this very critical moment to place his eldest son in one of the most important Cabinet offices in his Ministry without incurring from any side the smallest imputation of nepotism, and the skill and success of the new administration of the India Office was speedily and generally recognised. Greville tells us that Lord Stanley 'gained golden opinions and great popularity at the India House'; and he gives a striking instance of the firmness with which he maintained the full authority of the new Council over Indian affairs. He adds: 'I was prepared to hear of his ability, his indefatigable industry, and his business qualities; but I was surprised to hear so much of his courtesy, affability, patience, and candour; that he is neither dictatorial nor conceited, always ready to listen to other people's opinions and advice, and never fancying that he knows better than anyone else. I afterwards told Jonathan Peel what I had heard and he confirmed the truth of this report and said he was the same in the Cabinet.' 'Lord Stanley,' Greville said, 'is so completely *the man* of the present day, and in all human probability is destined to play so important and conspicuous a part in political life, that the time may come when any details, however minute, of his early career will be deemed worthy of recollection.'

P

It is a characteristic fact that Lord Stanley offered a seat on the Indian Council to John Stuart Mill, which, however, that great writer declined.

The disturbance in European politics which culminated in the French declaration of war against Austria contributed to weaken still further the feeble Ministry of Lord Derby. The Reform Bill caused profound divisions in its ranks. Mr. Walpole and Mr. Henley resigned, and the Government Bill was defeated in the spring of 1859. Lord Malmesbury mentions that in the Cabinet divisions on that question Lord Stanley supported the more democratic view, and that on one occasion he threatened to resign if the measure were not made more liberal. He defended the Bill in an elaborate speech, advocating such an introduction of the working class to the franchise as would give them a considerable but not a preponderating power. A general election followed, and the Government gained several seats, but not sufficient to give it a majority. The different fractions of the Opposition drew together; on June 11 a vote of want of confidence was carried by a majority of 13, and Lord Derby immediately resigned.

In opposition Lord Stanley devoted himself chiefly to the class of questions that had occupied him before his accession to office. He served on the long Cambridge University Commission, and supported the admission of Nonconformists to Fellowships. He was also warmly in favour of the measure which made it possible for clergymen to free themselves from their Orders and to adopt other professions. He presided over the Commission on the Sanitary State of the Indian Army and over the Commission on Patents. Like Disraeli, he displayed during the American Civil War a reticence and reserve which contrasted very favourably with the rash language of other leaders.

In 1862 a curious episode occurred which showed at least the widespread reputation that he had acquired. Prince Alfred having refused the throne of Greece, the idea was for a short time entertained of offering it to Lord Stanley. ' If he accepts,' Disraeli wrote to his friend Mrs. Willyams, ' I shall lose a powerful friend and colleague. It is a dazzling adventure for the house of Stanley, but they are not an imaginative race, and I fancy they will prefer Knowsley to the Parthenon and Lancashire to the Attic Plains.' ' The Greeks really want to make my friend Lord Stanley their king. This beats any novel ; but he will not. Had I his youth I would not hesitate, even with the earldom of Derby in the distance.'

It does not appear that this proposal ever took a very serious form, and if it had been made there is little doubt that Disraeli formed a just forecast of what would have been the result. The death of Lord Palmerston on October 18, 1865, gave a new turn to the political kaleidoscope: Lord Russell became Prime Minister ; the policy of reform was pushed into the forefront, and the Reform Bill of 1866 speedily produced a secession in the Liberal ranks and led to the downfall of the Ministry. The feature of the Bill which specially lent itself to attack was that it dealt solely with reduction of the franchise, leaving the question of the distribution of seats to subsequent legislation, and an amendment was moved by Lord Grosvenor to the effect that no Bill for the reduction of the franchise should be discussed till the whole scheme was before the House. This amendment was seconded by Lord Stanley in a speech which Lord Malmesbury

pronounced to be 'the finest and most statesmanlike
speech he ever made.' In June the Government were
beaten by a small majority on an amendment of Lord
Dunkellin substituting rating for rental; a few days
later Lord Russell resigned and Lord Derby for the third
time became Prime Minister.

As on the two former occasions he was in a minority,
though the temporary secession of a portion of the
Liberal party gave him a precarious power. Once more,
too, he took office amid the convulsions of a European
war, for the war of Prussia and Italy with Austria had
just begun. In the new Ministry Lord Stanley was
Secretary for Foreign Affairs. In his election address
he gave the keynote of his policy by insisting in the
strongest terms that England should observe a strict
neutrality in European controversies. Her vast Indian
and Colonial Empire, he said, made her a world apart and
threw upon her duties and responsibilities that taxed all
her energies. She had duties also to her poorer classes
at home, whose condition was not what we could desire ;
and by simply existing as a free, prosperous, and self-
governed nation, we should do more for the real freedom
of Europe than by any policy of meddling or war.

As far as his own department was concerned Lord
Stanley's administration during this short Ministry was
both eminently consistent and eminently successful. It
is true that this pacific Minister made the Abyssinian
war for the release of some imprisoned British subjects,
but he only did this after every peaceful effort to procure
their release had proved abortive, and it was almost
universally recognised that there was no honourable
alternative open to him. During his ministry the
Luxemburg question brought France and Prussia to the

very verge of war. It fell to the task of Lord Stanley to mediate between them, and he did so with a success which certainly adjourned, though it could not ultimately avert, the great catastrophe that burst upon Europe in 1870. No success could have been more gratifying to him, and he was fond of repeating the saying of Canning that ' If a war must come sooner or later, for my part I prefer that it should come later than sooner.' Lord Russell bore an ungrudging testimony to the ' tact and discretion ' Lord Stanley displayed in this negotiation. In the same spirit he refused to take part in a conference of European Powers which the French Emperor desired to convene to settle the Roman question, declaring that this question was one with which England should in no way meddle, and that a conference would be useless and dangerous unless a basis were laid down before. He refused to interfere in any way with the Cretan rebellion, and with the impending disputes between Turkey and Greece. His abstention on this question was blamed by some, but it met with the full approbation of his great opponent, Lord Russell, who declared that 'he had acted with much prudence and discretion.' He laid the foundation also of the settlement of the long outstanding difficulty with America by proposing to refer the Alabama question to arbitration, and he negotiated a treaty on the subject, which, however, the Senate refused to ratify.

In all this he was very consistent. The same consistency cannot be claimed for his support of a Reform Bill far more Radical than that which his party had so recently rejected. In my own judgment it is impossible to defend with success the conduct of the Derby Ministry on this question, and although Lord Stanley took only a subsidiary part in it, he cannot escape his share of the

responsibility. The difficulty of the position of the
eldest son of the Prime Minister who was taking this
' leap in the dark ' was very great, and it must be remembered that he had long been identified with the more
democratic wing of his party. After the great agitation
that followed the downfall of the Russell Ministry, he
probably regarded a democratic measure as inevitable,
and it was the character of his mind to be very ready
to accept what he considered the inevitable, and to
endeavour by timely compromise to mitigate its effects.
Lord Derby's health was now completely broken, and
on February 24, 1868, he resigned office, and Disraeli
became Prime Minister.

Mr. Gladstone soon re-united the sundered sections
of the Opposition by raising the question of the Disestablishment of the Irish Church. The resolutions
asserting the expediency of this policy were introduced
into the House of Commons in April. Lord Stanley was
put forward as the principal opponent. His amendment
expressed no opinion about the merits of the proposed
policy, but simply affirmed that it was a question which
ought to be reserved for a new Parliament which was
soon to be elected under an altered franchise. In his
speech he disclaimed any wish to maintain that the
Irish Church Establishment was what it ought to be, but
urged that in the condition of Ireland a merely destruc-
tive measure would do nothing but harm, that it would
serve no good purpose to attack the Establishment without laying down the lines of a definite, constructive
ecclesiastical policy, and that it was absurd to launch
such a question in the last session of an expiring Parliament. The more ardent spirits of the Tory party
strongly censured the ambiguity of this defence, and the

Government were beaten by majorities of 56 and 60. The House of Commons was dissolved in the autumn and a large Liberal majority returned. Disraeli at once resigned without waiting for the assembling of Parliament.

In October 1869 the death of Lord Derby terminated the career of his son in the House of Commons, and the following year added very greatly to the happiness of his life by his marriage with the Dowager Marchioness of Salisbury. His attitude in opposition is clearly shown in his published speeches. He had no wish to see the Conservative party again in office till they possessed an assured and homogeneous majority, and he maintained that it should be their main object to strengthen the influence of the more moderate section in the Government. He believed that by habitually pursuing this policy they would best prevent revolutionary changes, mitigate by wise compromises measures which they did not wholly approve, secure the continuance of the harmony of classes, on which more than on any other condition the prosperity of England depends, and gradually strengthen their own hold on the confidence of the country. It was also his earnest desire that English politics should be turned as much as possible from a policy of organic change to a policy of administrative reform. He considered it a great evil that public men had acquired the habit of continually tampering with the existing legislative machinery instead of wisely using it for the benefit of the whole nation. The party system, as he always thought, had falsified the perspective of English politics, bringing into the foreground comparatively unimportant questions which were well suited to rally parties and win majorities ; thrusting into the

background others which were immeasurably more
important, but which were less available for party
purposes. What Carlyle called 'The Condition of
England Question' was always in his thoughts. No
one would accuse him of under-rating the evils of war,
but he questioned whether the most sanguinary battle
which had ever been fought carried off nearly as many
human beings as die in England every year from purely
preventible causes. He threw the whole force of his
clear and penetrating intellect into such questions as
sanitary reform, the regulation of mines, the promotion
of education and especially technical education, the organisation of charities, the treatment of juvenile offenders,
the diffusion of wise methods of encouraging saving
among the poor. The overcrowding of the great cities,
and the vast masses of insanitary dwellings, seemed to him
one of the most pressing dangers of the time, and he was
a prominent member of nearly every important company
and association in England for improving the houses
of artisans. He had no puritanism in his nature and was
very anxious, by the establishment of free libraries and
people's parks, and Sunday opening of museums, to
extend the range of innocent pleasure. 'Men die,' he
once said, 'for want of cheerfulness, as plants die for
want of light.' He did not believe in the repression of
drunkenness by coercive legislation like the Local Veto
Bill, but he believed that its true root lay in overcrowding, ignorance, insanitary conditions of life, the want of
innocent means of enjoyment, excessive hours of labour.
'When you have to deal with men in masses,' he said, 'the
connection between vice and disease is very close. With
a low average of popular health you will have a low
average of national morality and probably also of national

intellect. Drunkenness and vice of other kinds will flourish on such a soil, and you cannot get healthy brains to grow on unhealthy bodies. Cleanliness and self-respect grow together, and it is no paradox to affirm that you tend to purify men's thoughts and feelings when you purify the air they breathe.' He supported liberally the movement for establishing coffee-houses, and he looked with great hope to the co-operative movement as averting or mitigating industrial conflicts. 'The subject of co-operation,' he said, 'is in my judgment more important as regards the future of England than nine-tenths of those which are discussed in Parliament, and around which political controversies gather.' As the possessor of one of the largest properties in England he was excellently informed on all agricultural questions, and he exercised a great influence upon them. Among other services he dispelled many misrepresentations by obtaining an accurate return of the numbers of owners of land in the United Kingdom, and of the quantity of land which they owned.

With the single exception of Lord Shaftesbury, I believe no conspicuous English public man devoted so much time and labour as Lord Derby to the class of questions I have described. He brought to their discussion an almost unrivalled fulness of knowledge. His purse was liberally opened in such causes, and the speeches in which he examined what Government can do and what it cannot do for the material well-being of the poor, are in my judgment among the most valuable contributions to political thought that have been furnished by any English statesman during the present century.

The election of 1874, bringing the Conservative party again into power, called him to other fields, and he became for the second time Foreign Secretary under Disraeli, and was soon involved in that Eastern Question which led to his severance from the Conservative party. It would answer no good purpose in a short sketch like the present to rake up the still smouldering ashes of that controversy. The time will come when it will be reviewed in the calm light of history, and with the assistance of materials that are not now before the public. I shall here content myself with a mere sketch. In the earlier stages of their foreign policy the Government appear to have been perfectly agreed. Lord Derby fully concurred in the purchase of the Khedive's shares in the Suez Canal, which was one of the most successful strokes of policy of the Government, though he defended it on somewhat more prosaic grounds than some of its supporters, and was careful to explain that it was essentially a measure of self-defence, and not connected with any project for the dismemberment of Turkey or the establishment of an English protectorate in Egypt. When the insurrection broke out in 1875 in Herzegovina and Bosnia, neither Lord Derby nor any of his colleagues believed it to be more than a mere passing disturbance. But the feebleness manifested by the Turkish army in suppressing the insurrection, and the partial bankruptcy of the Government at Constantinople, contributed with many elements of race and religious dissension, with foreign intrigue and local misgovernment, to aggravate the sore, and the movement soon acquired the dimensions of a great European danger. In sending an English Consul in conjunction with the Consuls of the other Powers to the scene of insurrection, in order, if possible, to arrive at a mediation; in the acceptance of the Andrassy Note, by which the three Imperial Powers laid down the reforms which they considered urgently necessary; in the rejection of the

Berlin Memorandum, on the ground that the Porte could
not or would not carry out its demands, and that it would
almost certainly lead to an armed intervention; and
finally, in sending the British fleet to Besika Bay for the
purpose of protecting English and Christian interests at
Constantinople, at a time when that city was in a state
of almost complete anarchy, the Government were fully
agreed, and they carried with them an immense majority
in Parliament and in the country. For some time, also,
the country seemed to approve of the policy which Lord
Derby uniformly avowed and steadily observed, of maintaining a strict neutrality in the contest that was raging;
doing all that could be done by advice, remonstrance,
mediation, and moral influence to induce the Porte to
carry out internal reforms; warning the Turkish Government in clear terms that under the circumstances of the
case they must not look for any military assistance from
England, but at the same time discouraging as much as
possible the active interference of other Powers in the
affairs of Turkey, and abstaining rigidly from any step
that would involve the use of force or the chance of war
unless some serious English interest was affected. He
believed that the integrity of the Turkish Empire was
a vital English interest, and that any attempt to substitute a Slavonic for a Turkish Empire would bring upon
Europe calamities the extent of which it was impossible
to exaggerate or to foresee. Russia and Austria would at
once come into collision; England would almost certainly
be drawn into the war, and all the fierce elements of race
hatred and religious fanaticism would be let loose.

For a time most English politicians seem to have agreed
with him, and his one great object was to bring about
an armistice, a mediation, and a peace. But the popular

agitation which arose in England on the subject of the
Bulgarian atrocities in the summer and autumn of 1876
added enormously to his difficulties, and the danger was
the greater because some skilful party management
was blended with much genuine philanthropy. The
speeches addressed by Lord Derby to the successive
deputations that came to him, give the best explanation
and defence of his position during this critical period,
and the interruptions to which he had to reply give
a vivid picture of the state of feeling that had arisen.
The Crimean war was now deplored as a calamity,
if not a crime. The Turks were described on high
political authority as 'the one great anti-human specimen
of humanity.' The Ministers were accused of com-
plicity in the Bulgarian massacres; they were urged
to cast neutrality to the wind; to adopt a policy of
armed coercion in Turkey; even to assist Russia in
driving the Turks out of Constantinople. It had become,
as Lord Derby sarcastically said, a very unpopular thing
for an English Minister to talk of English interests in
connection with the Eastern Question—almost dangerous
for any man at a public meeting to express in plain terms
his doubt of the disinterested philanthropy of Russia.

Lord Derby had at this time to encounter much
unpopularity. He was accused of an undue leaning
towards the Turkish Government, and an inadequate
sympathy with the Christian populations, and it was
alleged that if he had acted in firm concert with the other
Powers in coercing the Porte—if he had not proclaimed
so loudly and constantly his determination to abstain
from all active interference and compulsion—his remonstrances would have had more effect, and he might
have averted or restricted the calamities that had occurred.

But a great change soon took place. The first object of the Government was to prevent the Turkish disturbance from leading to a European war, and in this object they failed. On April 24, 1877, Russia, in spite of English remonstrances, declared war against Turkey. On the same day a Russian army crossed the Pruth, and the Eastern Question entered into a new and dangerous phase.

To a statesman like Lord Derby, who maintained that war, unless it is a necessity, is a crime; that the maintenance of peace is beyond all comparison the greatest of British interests, the months that followed were extremely trying. His first object was to limit the war, and to safeguard English interests, and for this purpose he drew up on May 6, 1877, a Note defining the English interests that were vital in the East. He warned the Russian Government that an attempt by Russia to blockade the Suez Canal, an attack on Egypt, a Russian occupation of Constantinople, or an alteration of the existing arrangements for the navigation of the Bosphorus or the Dardanelles might compel England to abandon her neutrality. Russia accepted these conditions, and for some time there appeared every prospect of limiting the war. But in the beginning of 1878 a period of extreme danger undoubtedly arrived. Plevna had fallen. The Turkish resistance had collapsed. A Russian army, flushed with victory, had advanced to near Constantinople. The treaty of San Stephano was signed ; which in the opinion of most European statesmen placed Turkey at the feet of Russia, and Russia at first refused to submit its terms to a conference of European Powers. Public feeling in England now ran strongly in a direction almost opposite to that in which it had been running eighteen months before, and the nation was extremely alarmed at the danger of Constantinople becoming speedily and irremediably a Russian port. On the other hand, the national and military pride of the conquering Power was aroused, and it was felt that a single false step, a single imprudent menace, might lead to war.

It was one of those moments in which men's judgments are largely affected by their temperaments, and it soon became evident that the Cabinet was seriously divided. Disraeli had now become Lord Beaconsfield, and sat with his Foreign Secretary in the House of Lords. With his character it was inevitable that he should meet the danger by a bold, decisive, and even aggressive, policy. It was no less natural that Lord Derby should have persistently leaned towards the side of caution and shrunk from any measure that could cut short negotiation and diminish the chances of peace. The order given that the British Fleet should enter the Dardanelles, first produced the inevitable schism, and Lord Derby and Lord Carnarvon resigned. The order was countermanded, and Lord Derby, for a short time, resumed his post. He acquiesced, but with great reluctance, in the vote of credit for six millions which was at once brought before the House of Commons, but he was soon convinced that measures he did not approve of were impending, and when orders were given for calling out the reserves he definitely resigned.

He announced his resignation on March 28, 1878, in terms of much dignity and moderation. He believed, he said, that his colleagues desired peace as truly as himself, and he did not maintain that their later measures led inevitably to war, but he considered that they were neither necessary nor 'prudent in the interests of

European peace.' He agreed that the terms of the
treaty should be submitted to a European Congress,
in which England should take part. On minor matters
he thought it his duty to waive his own opinion, but he
could not do so on a question involving the momentous
issue of peace or war. The threat involved in the last act
of the Government, he said, in a later speech, would make
it more difficult for Russia to modify her policy, and he
believed that without a threat such a modification of the
treaty of San Stephano could be obtained as would make
it acceptable. He had been accused of indecision and
even of cowardice. For his own part he thought it
needed more courage to stand up in his place to express
views which he knew to be unpopular among the great
body of his friends, than to sit at a desk in Downing
Street and issue orders which would bring no danger
or unpopularity to himself, but might bring about a
European war.

The short speech in which Lord' Beaconsfield
accepted the resignation, and dwelt on the long friendship, personal as well as political, that bound him to
Lord Derby, seems to me a perfect model of good feeling
and good taste. Unfortunately the example of the Prime
Minister was not followed, and words used in a later
debate went far to make the breach irrevocable.

Lord Derby for a short time maintained a neutral
position, but the foreign policy of Lord Beaconsfield was
in the highest degree distasteful to him. A wave of
Chauvinism was passing over England, which was
utterly opposed to his views, and he believed that a
section of the Conservative party encouraged it in order
to divert the thoughts of men from internal reforms. He
objected to the acquisition of Cyprus, to some of the

responsibilities assumed by England under the treaty of Berlin, and very strongly to the Afghan war; and in the beginning of 1880 he formally attached himself to the Liberal party, on the ground of his objections to the foreign policy of the Government. His speeches in his new capacity differed very little from those which he had formerly delivered, but he said that he had learnt to see more clearly the uselessness of attempting to resist popular ideas, and to think 'more highly of the moderation, the fairness, and the general justice with which masses of men, including all conditions of life, are disposed to use their power.' He thought that England should mix herself as little as possible with 'the sanguinary muddle' of European diplomacy; that she should avoid increasing her responsibilities; that she should take stringent measures to reduce her debt; that she should pay much more attention than she was accustomed to do to the condition of her own poorer population; and that it should be the object of her statesmen to meet every great popular demand by wise and equitable compromise. One of the greatest dangers, he said, that could befall the country, would be 'a state of things in which the comparatively harmless antagonism of parties would be replaced by the far more serious and dangerous war of classes. From that danger more than from any other it is the business of a well-considered Liberalism to protect us.'

In 1882 he accepted the Colonial Office from Mr. Gladstone, and held it until the fall of the Government in the summer of 1885. His ministry was not a very eventful one, and it was marked by that steady adherence to a middle line which had always characterised him. He congratulated the country that the indifference to our colonies which had prevailed during his youth had passed away, but he was by no means favourable to extensions of the Empire. 'We have quite black men enough,' he was accustomed to say ; and he believed that any increase of our responsibilities was likely to endanger the Empire, and to divert the energies of politicians from pressing home questions. He did not condemn the policy which led to the occupation of Egypt by England, but he declared that even if it was inevitable it was a misfortune, and that we ought to 'see that we do not on any pretext, however plausible, get that Egyptian millstone tied permanently round our necks.' He was very sceptical about Imperial Federation, and entirely incredulous about the possibility of an Imperial Zollverein. He deplored the protectionism of the colonies, but was himself a strict free-trader of the school of Cobden, and utterly opposed to any attempt to negotiate treaties with the colonies on a basis of preferential tariffs. On the other hand, he showed himself quite ready to favour Confederation in Australia, and he accepted gratefully Australian help in the Soudan, but he was much alarmed by tendencies in some colonies which might lead to complications with foreign Powers, and he incurred considerable unpopularity in Australia by refusing to consent to the annexation by Queensland of New Guinea.

There is, however, one incident in the colonial administration of Lord Derby on which it is necessary to dwell at somewhat greater length, for subsequent events have given it an unfortunate prominence and it has thrown some discredit on his statesmanship. I allude, of course, to the convention with the Transvaal in 1884. In the preceding convention, which had been signed in

August 1881, complete self-government had been granted by England to the Transvaal 'subject to the suzerainty of her Majesty' and her successors, and also to a large number of carefully specified reservations and limitations. They comprised the complete control of the external relations of the Transvaal, including the conclusion of treaties and the conduct of diplomatic intercourse with foreign Powers, which could only be carried on through her Majesty's officers ; the right of moving British troops in case of necessity through the Transvaal ; a power of veto over all legislation affecting the interests of the native population. A number of articles prohibited slavery in the new State ; protected with much detail the interests of the native population ; secured complete religious liberty ; established the right of all persons other than natives who conformed themselves to the laws of the State, to enter, travel, and reside in any part of the Transvaal, to acquire property and to carry on their business without being subject to any other taxation than that which was imposed on the citizens of the Transvaal ; and placed British imports and exports on the same plane as those of the most-favoured nations. The limits of the new State were carefully defined and a British Resident was established in the Transvaal to superintend the carrying out of these provisions. There was no express provision in the convention for the political privileges of the English residents in the Transvaal, but the Government appear to have relied on a not very explicit verbal assurance given to the British Commissioners by President Kruger in May 1881. Asked about the rights of British subjects to complete free trade throughout the Transvaal, President Kruger answered that before the annexation 'they were on the same footing

as the burghers '; that ' there was not the slightest difference in accordance with the Sand River convention';
that this state of things would be continued and that
' there would be equal protection for everybody.' Sir
Evelyn Wood then added, ' and equal privileges ?' ' We
make no difference,' answered President Kruger, ' so far
as burgher rights are concerned. There may perhaps be
some slight difference in the case of a young person who
has just come into the country.' It was subsequently
explained that the words ' young person ' did not refer to
age, but to the time of residence in the Republic—
according to the old Transvaal Constitution, a year's
residence in the Republic was necessary for naturalisation. With this assurance the Government of 1881
appears to have been content. They believed in words
expressly sanctioned by Mr. Gladstone, that the concession of limited independence to the Transvaal by the
convention of 1881 would ' provide for the full liberty
and equal treatment of the entire white population, guard
the interests of the natives, and promote harmony and
good-will among the various races in South Africa.' [1]
As a matter of fact, the only change in the political
position of the English residents in the Transvaal was
that the period of naturalisation was extended from one
to five years—a change which appears to have produced
little or no commotion in the Republic.

The convention of 1881 was, however, extremely unpopular among a large section of the Boer population.
Complete independence was ·their avowed object, and in
order to attain it their first task was to abolish the
suzerainty of Great Britain. Almost immediately after

[1] See, on this subject, Cook's *Rights and Wrongs of the Transvaal
War*, pp. 260–265.

the convention was signed, the limitations of the Transvaal established by the convention were flagrantly disregarded by Transvaal filibusters, who proceeded with the tacit and even with the avowed countenance of their Government to place new sections of native territory under the exclusive protectorate of the Transvaal Government ; [1] and a deputation, headed by President Kruger, came to England in 1883 for the purpose of negotiating with the Colonial Office for the abolition of the chief articles of the convention of 1881.   They avowed with complete frankness that absolute independence would alone satisfy them, and that their desire was to revert to the Sand River convention of 1852, by which this independence had been recognised.   This demand was absolutely rejected by the Imperial Government, but Lord Derby attempted to meet the objections of the Transvaal leaders by substituting for the articles of the convention of 1881 new articles in several respects more favourable to the pretensions of the Boers.

He, in the first place, made a sentimental concession to which it is probable he attached little importance, but which was regarded by the Boer population as a considerable step towards the achievement of their independence. The term 'Transvaal State,' which was accepted in the convention of 1881 as the designation of the new State, was dropped and the old title of ' South African Republic ' was revived and recognised.   The question of suzerainty was dealt with in a somewhat ambiguous fashion.   The new convention purported only to substitute new articles in the place of those of the preceding convention ; and it was afterwards argued that the old preamble, which asserted at once the internal independence of the Transvaal

---

[1] See Westlake's *L'Angleterre et les Républiques Boers*, pp. 30-31.

and the suzerainty of Great Britain, remained in force,
In fact, however, this preamble was neither reprinted nor
replaced in the new convention, and the term 'suzerainty,'
which occurred in the original draft of the document,
was deliberately expunged—it is said by Lord Derby
himself. He considered the term wholly wanting in the
precision which is desirable in a treaty arrangement, that
it was capable of many different degrees of extension, and
that the fact of the paramountcy of Great Britain over
the new State might be sufficiently established without
the use of an ambiguous word which excited the most
bitter hostility in the Transvaal. His own words in defending his conduct in the House of Lords are perfectly
clear. 'The word suzerainty,' he said, 'is a very vague
word, and I do not think it is capable of any precise legal
definition. Whatever we may understand by it, I think
it is not very easy to define. But I apprehend whether
you call it a protectorate, or a suzerainty, or the recognition of England as a paramount Power, the fact is that a
certain controlling power is retained when the State which
exercises this suzerainty has a right to veto any negotiation into which the dependent State may enter with foreign
Powers. Whatever suzerainty meant in the convention
of Pretoria (1881), the condition of things which it
implies still remains; although the word is not actually
employed, we have kept the substance. We have abstained
from using the word because it was not capable of legal
definition, and because it seemed to be a word which was
likely to lead to misconception and misunderstanding.'
     The articles of the previous convention relating to
slavery, to native rights, to free trade, to religious liberty,
to the rights of residence of foreigners in the Transvaal,
reappear in the new convention, and the limits of the

State were somewhat more fully defined, but the controlling power of Great Britain over the foreign policy of the Transvaal, though clearly reasserted, was somewhat limited in its scope. It was provided that the South African Republic should conclude no treaty or engagement with any State or nation other than the Orange Free State, or with any native tribe to the eastward or westward of the Republic, until the same had been approved by the Queen; that every such treaty should be at once submitted to her Majesty's Government for her consent, but that this consent should be presumed to have been granted if no notification to the contrary was received within six months. The desire of the Transvaal authorities to be recognised as representing an independent sovereign power was thus distinctly rejected, and the English Government positively refused a proposal to admit foreign arbitration in cases of dispute between England and the Transvaal.

This convention has been severely censured by later writers on the ground of the insufficiency and ambiguity of its assertion of the paramount authority of Great Britain over the Transvaal, and of its failure to do anything to supply the great deficiency in the preceding convention by an article securing political equality for the British population within it. A few years later, when an immense English immigration had taken place, not only with the consent but at the express invitation of the Transvaal Government; when the English element formed a large majority of the inhabitants of the State; when they paid an enormous preponderance of its taxation, and were the chief agents in developing its wealth and raising it from the position of a very poor pastoral community into that of a great and wealthy State, the

Transvaal Government proceeded to impose upon the new emigrants disqualifications and disabilities which were utterly unknown when England conceded self-government to 'the inhabitants of the Transvaal.' They completely deprived the vast majority of political power or local self-government, and surrounded them at every turn with the most irritating disabilities. The Transvaal became the one part of South Africa where one white race was held in a position of inferiority to another. At a time when perfect equality was enjoyed by the Dutch population in our own colonies, the political disqualification of the English race was made the very corner-stone of the policy of the Transvaal Government. An annual revenue greatly in excess of what was required for its internal government was raised almost entirely from the taxation of an unrepresented class, to whom the prosperity of the State was mainly due, and it was employed in accumulating a great armament which could only be intended for use against England and for maintaining the subjection of an English population.

This was the position to which the paramount Power in South Africa, the Power which of its own free will had conceded a limited independence to the Transvaal, found itself reduced. And yet it was possible for the Boer Government to maintain that there was nothing in all this legislation which was inconsistent with the terms of the convention of 1884.

I do not think that the justice of this criticism can be wholly denied. The Transvaal authorities had already given clear intimation of their desire to emancipate themselves from all British control, and especially of their determination to disregard the limitations which had been imposed on the expansion of their State.

There is, however, one very material fact to be remembered in judging the policy of Lord Derby. At the time of the convention of 1884 the English population in the Transvaal was a small, scattered, and powerless minority, and as their numbers were far too scanty to make them a danger to the State, there was not much reason to believe that the Transvaal authorities would repudiate their own assurances and subject them to oppressive disabilities. It was not until two years after the convention that the vast gold-mines of the Transvaal were discovered and all the conditions of the South African problem fundamentally changed. The gigantic immigration that ensued reversed the proportion between the two races. The revenue and the expenditure of the State multiplied more than fifteen fold in little more than ten years.[1] The Transvaal became the most powerful and wealthy State in South Africa, and the great preponderance of the Outlander element in numbers, wealth, energy, and industry rendered a conflict of races almost inevitable. No statesman could have foreseen this change, and a convention that might have allayed discontent if the gold-mines had never been discovered, proved wholly inefficient to meet it.

Though in a politician of the stamp of Lord Derby the change from a very liberal conservatism to a very conservative liberalism involved little real modification of opinion, it necessarily involved some change of attitude, and on some questions he spoke with a freedom which would have been impossible as a member of the Conservative party. On Church questions, for example, while strongly maintaining that the country was not ripe

[1] See the table of revenue and expenditure in Fitzpatrick's *Transvaal from Within*, p. 71.

for the disestablishment of the Church in England, he declared that in his opinion the exclusive alliance of one religious denomination among many with the State could not be permanently maintained side by side with a democratic representation—that disestablishment and at least partial disendowment must ultimately come; that if the representatives of Scotland desired the disestablishment of their Church, it was not for Englishmen to oppose them; and that Wales had a strong claim to be separately dealt with. 'The Welsh people constitute in many respects a distinct nationality, and I do not see why we should refuse to Welsh loyalty what we have granted to Irish sedition.' On the subject of endowments indeed as early as 1875 his view was that of most moderate Liberals. 'To my mind, so far as right is concerned, the Legislature may do what it chooses in regard to any endowment, without injustice, provided only that the rights of living individuals are respected. How far it is politic to use that power is another matter. . . . Respect the founder's object, but use your own discretion as to the means. If you don't do the first, you will have no new endowments. If you neglect the last, those which you have will be of no use.' [1] He maintained that the question of local government had in England become one of pressing importance, and that the administration of county affairs must be put into the hands of elective bodies. He would give those local parliaments very large power—but he most urgently insisted on the importance of one restriction. The new bodies must not be given an unlimited power of mortgaging the future. The gradual reduction of the National Debt had been for some years one of the chief aims of enlightened politicians, but all

[1] Inaugural address at Edinburgh University.

that had been done in this direction would be undone if, side by side with the National Debt, there grew up a municipal debt of perhaps equal amount. In this tendency to municipal extravagance he saw one of the gravest menaces to property. ' The growth of Socialism throughout Europe has followed very closely on the gigantic increase of national indebtedness during the present century, and men who begin to feel the pressure intolerable are apt to raise questions, more easily stated than solved, as to the right of any State to impose burdens in perpetuity for the benefit of one generation.' He urged that every local body which contracted a debt should be under a statutory obligation to provide for its repayment in fifty or sixty years at latest.

The growth of municipal indebtedness ; the excessive tendency to increase the functions of the State ; the disaffection of Ireland and the contingency of an isolated and disloyal body of some eighty Irish representatives offering their services to any party which would consent to carry out their designs, appeared to Lord Derby the chief dangers of English domestic politics. The last danger was very speedily realised, and the sudden conversion of Mr. Gladstone to Home Rule produced one more change in the attitude of Lord Derby. On this question he had never flinched or wavered, and he at once took his place in the front rank of the Liberal Unionists, whom for some time he led in the House of Lords. I do not know that the Unionist case has ever been more powerfully put forward than in his speeches on the subject, and the eminently judicial character of his mind, and his entire freedom from all mere party bias, gave a special weight to his advocacy. With this exception he took little part in party politics during the last years of his life, but he devoted himself largely to social questions, and among other things served with great assiduity and ability on the Labour Commission. His last speech was delivered at Manchester on the unveiling of the statue of Mr. Bright in October 1891. His last public work was that of presiding over the Labour Commission in May 1892. In the preceding year an attack of influenza, followed by a relapse, had shattered a health which had hitherto been robust. Other complications ensued, and he passed away at Knowsley on April 21, 1893, in his sixty-seventh year.

The foregoing sketch will, I hope, have given a sufficient idea of his public character. Few men have made a greater sacrifice of ambition to a conscientious conviction than he did, when, rather than support a measure which might lead to war, he abandoned the Conservative Ministry in 1878. He was then the fully recognised successor of Lord Beaconsfield, and if he had adopted a different course he would in a short time have been, beyond all doubt, Prime Minister of England. On the whole, however, the severance from old friends cost him, I believe, far more than the sacrifice of his political prospects. Whatever he may have been in his youth, he was certainly not in mature life an ambitious man. With the great position he held in England the world had little to offer him, and the self-knowledge which was not the least of his many remarkable gifts showed him that party conflict was not the sphere in which Nature intended him to move. With many of the qualities of the highest statesmanship he wanted some necessary ingredients of a great statesman. He wanted the power of appealing to the imagination and moving the passions. He wanted more decision of character, more power of initiative, more capacity of bearing lightly

the weight of a great responsibility. His belief that the
House of Lords must always ultimately yield to the
House of Commons aggravated a weakness of resolution
which was deeply rooted in his nature. There were
moments when his inveterate moderation tended to ex-
asperate, and he was accused, not altogether without
reason, of sometimes making admirable speeches, pointing
out in the clearest terms all the evils and dangers of a
measure, and then concluding by exhorting the House of
Lords to vote for it, introducing mitigating amendments
in Committee. The measures he treated in this way
usually, as he had predicted, became law, but this was
not the attitude of a great leader. During a considerable
part of his career, like a very large proportion of moderate
men in England, he was in the embarrassing position of
agreeing substantially with the home policy of one party
and with the foreign policy of the other. After the death
of Lord Palmerston an element of passion was infused
into public life which was very uncongenial to his temperament, and English politics passed into phases in
which caution, character, judgment, and knowledge were
less prized than brilliant strokes that appealed to the
popular imagination, clever coalitions, a skilful barter of
principles for votes. In spheres governed by such methods
Lord Derby was very useful, but he was not likely to play
a foremost part.

To few men who have taken a conspicuous part in
active politics was the excitement of such an existence
so little necessary. Happy in his domestic life and in
a companionship and sympathy which were all-sufficient
to him, he was not less happy in the wide range
of his interests and duties. The administration of
his vast estate would have been more than sufficient

to tax the energies of most men, and it was, I believe,
universally acknowledged that it was admirably administered. In the everyday affairs of practical life he
had no indecision, and he judged swiftly with the
clearest of judgments. Nothing about him was more
remarkable than the apparent ease and the absence of
all hurry and confusion with which he could deal with
many different forms of work. His study in its perfect
neatness was more like a lady's boudoir than the workshop
of a very busy man. *Ohne Hast, ohne Rast,* might have
been his motto. He had much belief in the future of
English land, and was not, I think, at all exempt from
the great English landlord's foible of adding field to field.
In the long period of agricultural depression it was easy
for a rich man to do so. 'In my experience,' he used
to say, 'in nine cases out of ten it is Naboth who comes
to Ahab and begs him to buy his vineyard.' Certainly
no one had reason to complain, for there were few better
or more popular landlords than Lord Derby. In many
long walks with him through his property I was always
struck with the evident pleasure with which he was
welcomed by his people, the fulness of knowledge and
the kindness of interest with which he inquired into
the circumstances of every tenant. It is characteristic
of him that only two days before his death he was giving
instructions for building a hospital for the sick poor of
Knowsley. I have known few men in whom the desire
to make everyone about them happy was so strongly
and so clearly marked. He was fond of looking minutely
into the circumstances of men of different classes, and
comparing their wants with their means, often with
somewhat whimsical results. There was a tradesman
who made regularly 5*l.* a week; who was accustomed

every week to devote 2*l.* to his household expenses, to lay by 2*l.*, and to employ the remainder in getting drunk. He was, Lord Derby thought, the only man he had ever known who satisfied all his wants with 40 per cent. of his income, who always laid by 40 per cent., and who expended 20 per cent. on his pleasures.

Outside his property Lord Derby had strong county interests. With perhaps the exception of Birmingham there is no part of England where a distinctive local patriotism is so intensely developed as in Lancashire, and Lord Derby in tastes and character was pre-eminently a Lancashire man, very proud of the greatness, and deeply concerned in the interests, of his county. In all the vicissitudes of his career, Liverpool, I believe, never wavered in its attachment to him. He contributed to the many charitable and philanthropic works with which he was concerned not only much money, but also—what in so rich a man was far more meritorious —an extraordinary amount of time and patient super- vision. Among the many offices he accepted, was presi- dent of the Literary Fund for dispensing charity to needy authors, and on the committee of that charity I had, during many years, ample opportunity of observ- ing how far he was from treating a presidential position as a sinecure. The regularity of his attendance, the constant attention he paid to every detail of the charity; the infinite pains which he would bestow upon obscure cases of distress, marked him out as a model president, and many of those whom our rules did not allow us to help were assisted by his bounty. He contributed with a large but discriminating generosity to many causes that were conspicuous in the eyes of the world, but his special bias was towards unostentatious and unobserved benevolence, and crowds of obscure men in obscure positions were assisted by him.

Those who did not know him, and those who had come in merely casual contact with him, sometimes formed a false impression of his character. He had a great deal of natural shyness. He had very little of the gift of small talk. On occasions of mere show and in uncongenial atmospheres he was apt to be awkward and embarrassed, and when walking by himself he was extremely absent and quite capable of brushing against his oldest friend with a complete unconsciousness of his presence. These traits sometimes gave rise to natural misinterpretations, which a fuller knowledge always dispelled. No one who knew Lord Derby could fail to feel that his nature was one of the most genuine and transparent simplicity, singularly free from all tinge of arrogance, superciliousness, and acrimony. His personal tastes were exceedingly simple, and there was not a particle of ostentation in his character. He delighted in a quiet country life and had a strong sense of natural beauty. In his youth he had been an ardent mountaineer, and in later life he had few greater pleasures than to watch the growth of his plantations. He calculated that he had planted in his lifetime about two million of trees.

He was among the best-read men I have ever known. His private library was one of the finest in England, and he took a keen interest in it. A love of sumptuous, large-paper editions was indeed one of the very few luxuries in which from mere personal taste he greatly indulged. Like all men of literary tastes he had his limitations. German was a closed book to him. Theology and metaphysics were conspicuous by their absence. He was certainly not drawn to the mystical,

the unintelligible, or the morbid, either in imaginative
or speculative literature, and although he was a great
lover and great buyer of water-colour pictures, I do not
think he had much real sense or knowledge of art. But
he had read very extensively and with great profit and
discrimination in many widely different fields, and his
memory was unusually retentive. He was an excellent
literary critic, and if clear thought and accurate knowledge were what he most valued, it would be a complete
mistake to suppose that he was insensible to the poetic
and imaginative side of literature. He could repeat long
passages from ' Childe Harold,' and I can well remember
the delight which he took in the picturesque narrative of
Mr. Froude, and in the fiery verses of Sir Alfred Lyall.

He was one of the kindest and most gracious of hosts,
and his genuine unforced good nature and good humour
drew to him many whose tastes and sympathies were
widely different from his own. Nature certainly never
intended him for a sportsman, but he preserved game
extensively and until the last years of his life usually
went out with his guests. ' I rather like shooting,' he
once said to me, ' it prevents the necessity of general
conversation.' Among kindred spirits, however, his own
conversation was eminently attractive. His wide knowledge both of books and men, his vast range of political
anecdote, his experience of so many statesmen and offices
and departments of life, made it singularly instructive.
He was a very shrewd, and at the same time a very kind,
judge of character ; and he had a power, which is certainly
not common, of fully appreciating merits that are allied
with great and manifest defects. He had much quaint,
dry humour, and a great happiness of expression ; and
one always felt that his opinions were genuinely thought
out—that they were voices and not echoes. His private

conversation had the quality that I have noticed in his public speeches, of grasping at once the essential elements of a question and disencumbering it from accessories and details. It is one of the qualities that add most to the charm of conversation, and, with the exception of Lord Russell, I do not think I have met with anyone who possessed it to a greater degree than Lord Derby. He delighted in long walks with one or two friends, and he might be seen to great advantage in some small dining-clubs which play a larger part than is generally recognised in the best English social life of our time. He had been a member of Grillion's for thirty-seven years, but the society to which he was most attached was, I think, 'The Club' which was founded by Johnson and Reynolds. During the nineteen years of which I can speak from personal experience, he was an almost constant attendant, and certainly no other member enjoyed a greater popularity in it, or contributed more largely to its charm.

He hated cant of all kinds, and had a great distrust of ostentatious professions of lofty motives. He disliked, I think greatly, the habit of dragging sacred names into party speeches, and attributing every party manœuvre to a solemn sense of duty. Language of this kind will never be found in his speeches, but I have known few men who were governed through life more steadily though more unobtrusively by a sense of duty. He always tried to look facts in the face, and to promote in the many spheres which he could influence the real happiness of men. There have been statesmen among his contemporaries of greater power and of more brilliant achievement. There has been, I believe, no statesman of sounder judgment and more disinterested patriotism; there have been very few whose departure has left a void in so many spheres.

HENRY REEVE, C.B., F.S.A., D.C.L.

ALTHOUGH it has never been the custom of the 'Edinburgh Review' to withdraw the veil of anonymity from its writers and its administration, it would be mere affectation to suffer it to appear before the public without some allusion to the great editor whom we have just lost,[1] and who for forty years has watched with indefatigable care over its pages.

The career of Mr. Henry Reeve is perhaps the most striking illustration in our time of how little in English life influence is measured by notoriety. To the outer world his name was but little known. He is remembered as the translator of Tocqueville, as the editor of the 'Greville Memoirs,' as the author of a not quite forgotten book on Royal and Republican France, showing much knowledge of French literature and politics; as the holder during fifty years of the respectable, but not very prominent, post of Registrar of the Privy Council. To those who have a more intimate knowledge of the political and literary life of England, it is well known that during nearly the whole of his long life he was a powerful and living force in English literature; that few men of his time have filled a larger place in some of the most select circles of English social life; and that he exercised during many years a political influence such as rarely falls to the lot of any Englishman outside Parliament, or even outside the Cabinet.

[1] Mr. Reeve died October 21, 1895. — ED.

He was born at Norwich in 1813, and brought up in a highly cultivated, and even brilliant, literary circle. His father, Dr. Reeve, was one of the earliest contributors to the 'Edinburgh Review.' The Austins, the Opies, the Taylors, and the Aldersons were closely related to him, and he is said to have been indebted to his gifted aunt, Sarah Austin, for his appointment in the Privy Council. The family income was not large, and a great part of Mr. Reeve's education took place on the Continent, chiefly at Geneva and Munich. He went with excellent introductions, and the years he spent abroad were abundantly fruitful. He learned German so well that he was at one time a contributor to a German periodical. He was one of the rare Englishmen who spoke French almost like a Frenchman, and at a very early age he formed friendships with several eminent French writers. His translation of the 'Democracy in America,' by Tocqueville, which appeared in 1835, strengthened his hold on French society. Two years later he obtained the appointment in the Privy Council, which he held until 1887. It was in this office that he became the colleague and fast friend of Charles Greville, who on his death-bed entrusted him with the publication of his 'Memoirs.'

Mr. Reeve had now obtained an assured income and a steady occupation, but it was far from satisfying his desire for work. He became a contributor, and very soon a leading contributor, to the 'Times,' while his close and confidential intercourse with Mr. Delane gave him a considerable voice in its management. The penny newspaper was still unborn, and the 'Times' at this period was the undisputed monarch of the Press, and exercised an influence over public opinion, both in England and on the Continent, such as no existing paper can be said to

possess. It is, we believe, no exaggeration to say that
for the space of fifteen years nearly every article that
appeared in its columns on foreign politics was written
by Mr. Reeve, and the period during which he wrote for
it included the year 1848, when foreign politics had the
most transcendent importance.

The great political influence which he at this time
exercised naturally drew him into close connection with
many of the chief statesmen of his time. With Lord
Clarendon especially his friendship was close and confidential, and he received from that statesman almost
weekly letters during his viceroyalty in Ireland and
during others of the more critical periods of his career.
In France, Mr. Reeve's connections were scarcely less
numerous than in England. Guizot, Thiers, Cousin,
Tocqueville, Villemain, Circourt—in fact, nearly all the
leading figures in French literature and politics during
the reign of Louis Philippe were among his friends or
correspondents. He was at all times singularly international in his sympathies and friendships, and he
appears to have been more than once made the channel
of confidential communications between English and
French statesmen.

It was a task for which he was eminently suited.
The qualities which most impressed all who came into
close communication with him were the strength, swift-
ness, and soundness of his judgment, and his unfailing
tact and discretion in dealing with delicate questions.
He was eminently a man of the world, and had quite as
much knowledge of men as of books. Probably few
men of his time have been so frequently and so
variously consulted. He always spoke with confidence
and authority, and his clear, keen-cut, decisive sentences,

a certain stateliness of manner which did not so much claim as assume ascendancy, and a somewhat elaborate formality of courtesy which was very efficacious in repelling intruders, sometimes concealed from strangers the softer side of his character. But those who knew him well soon learnt to recognise the genuine kindliness of his nature, his remarkable skill in avoiding friction, and the rare steadiness of his friendships.

One great source of his influence was the just belief in his complete independence and disinterestedness. For a very able man his ambition was singularly moderate. As he once said, he had made it his object throughout life only to aim at things which were well within his power. He had very little respect for the judgment of the multitude, and he cared nothing for notoriety and not much for dignities. A moderate competence, congenial work, a sphere of wide and genuine influence, a close and intimate friendship with a large proportion of the guiding spirits of his time, were the things he really valued, and all these he fully attained. He had great conversational powers, which never degenerated into monologue, a singularly equable, happy, and sanguine temperament, and a keen delight in cultivated society. These characteristics showed conspicuously in two small and very select dining-clubs which have included most of the distinguished English statesmen and men of letters of the century. He became a member of the Literary Society in 1857 and of Dr. Johnson's Club in 1861, and it is a remarkable evidence of the appreciation of his social tact that both bodies speedily selected him as their treasurer. He held that position in 'The Club' from 1868 till within a year of his death, when failing health and absence from London obliged him to relinquish it.

The French Institute elected him 'Correspondant' in 1863 and Associated Member in 1888, in which latter dignity he succeeded Sir Henry Maine. In 1869 the University of Oxford conferred on him the honorary degree of D.C.L.

It was in 1855, on the death of Sir George Cornewall Lewis, that he assumed the editorship of the 'Edinburgh Review' which he retained till the day of his death. Both on the political and the literary side he was in full harmony with its traditions. His rare and minute knowledge of recent English and foreign political history; his vast fund of political anecdote; his personal acquaintance with so many of the chief actors on the political scene, both in England and France, gave a great weight and authority to his judgments, and his mind was essentially of the Whig cast. He was a genuine Liberal of the school of Russell, Palmerston, Clarendon, and Cornewall Lewis. It was a sober and tolerant Liberalism, rooted in the traditions of the past, and deeply attached to the historical elements in the Constitution. The dislike and distrust with which he had always viewed the progress of democracy deepened with age, and it was his firm conviction that it could never become the permanent basis of good government. Like most men of his type of thought and character, he was strongly repelled by the later career of Mr. Gladstone, and the Home Rule policy at last severed him definitely from the bulk of the Liberal party. From this time the present Duke of Devonshire was the leader of his party.

His literary judgments had much analogy to his political ones. His leanings were all towards the old standards of thought and style. He had been formed in the school of Macaulay and Milman, and of the great French writers under Louis Philippe. Sober thought, clear reasoning, solid scholarship, a transparent, vivid, and restrained style were the literary qualities he most appreciated. He was a great purist, inexorably hostile to a new word. In philosophy he was a devoted disciple of Kant, and his decided orthodoxy in religious belief affected many of his judgments. He could not appreciate Carlyle; he looked with much distrust on Darwinism and the philosophy of Herbert Spencer and he had very little patience with some of the moral and intellectual extravagances of modern literature. But, according to his own standards and in the wide range of his own subjects, his literary judgment was eminently sound, and he was quick and generous in recognising rising eminence. In at least one case the first considerable recognition of a prominent historian was an article in the 'Edinburgh Review' from his pen.

He had a strong sense of the responsibility of an editor, and especially of the editor of a Review of unsigned articles. No article appeared which he did not carefully consider. His powerful individuality was deeply stamped upon the Review, and he carefully maintained its unity and consistency of sentiments. It was one of the chief occupations and pleasures of his closing days, and the very last letter he dictated referred to it.

Time, as might be expected, had greatly thinned the circle of his friends. Of the France which he knew so well scarcely anything remained, but his old friend and senior Barthélemy Saint-Hilaire visited him at Christ Church, and he kept up to the end a warm friendship with the Duc d'Aumale. He spent his eightieth birthday at Chantilly, and until the very last year of his life he was never absent when the Duke dined at 'The Club.' In

Lord Derby he lost the statesman with whom in his later years he was most closely connected by private friendship and political sympathy, while the death of Lady Stanley of Alderley deprived him of an attached and lifelong friend.

Growing infirmities prevented him in his latter days from mixing much in general society in London, but his life was brightened by all that loving companionship could give; his mental powers were unfaded, and he could still enjoy the society of younger friends. He looked forward to the end with a perfect and a most characteristic calm, without fear and without regret. It was the placid close of a long, dignified, and useful life.

HENRY HART MILMAN, D.D., DEAN OF ST. PAUL'S.

THE great prominence which the High Church movement has assumed in the ecclesiastical history of England during the second and third quarters of the nineteenth century, and the extraordinary success with which it has permeated the Established Church by its influence, have led some writers to exaggerate not a little the place which it occupied in the general intellectual development of the time. In the universities, it is true, it long exercised an extraordinary influence, and Mr. Gladstone, who was by far the most remarkable layman whom it profoundly influenced, was accustomed to say that for at least a generation almost the whole of the best intellect of Oxford was controlled by it. It possessed in Newman a writer of most striking and undoubted genius. In an age remarkable for brilliancy of style he was one of the greatest masters of English prose. His power of drawing subtle distinctions and pursuing long trains of subtle reasoning made him one of the most skilful of controversialists, and he had a great insight into spiritual cravings and an admirable gift of interpreting and appealing to many forms of religious emotion. But though he was a man of rare, delicate, and most seductive genius, we have sometimes doubted whether any of his books are destined to take a permanent and considerable place in English literature. He was not a great scholar, or an original and

independent thinker. Dealing with questions inseparably
connected with historical evidence, he had neither the
judicial spirit nor the firm grasp of a real historian, and
he had very little skill in measuring probabilities and
degrees of evidence. He had a manifest incapacity, which
was quite as much moral as intellectual, for looking facts
in the face and pursuing trains of thought to unwelcome
conclusions. He often took refuge from them in clouds
of casuistry. The scepticism which was a marked feature
of his intellect allied itself closely with credulity, for it
was directed against reason itself; and though he has
expressed in admirable language many true and beautiful
thoughts, the glamour of his style too often concealed
much weakness and uncertainty of judgment and much
sophistry in argument.

Many of those who co-operated with him were men of
great learning and distinguished ability. No one will
question the patristic knowledge of Pusey, the meta-
physical acumen of Ward, the genuine vein of religious
poetry in Keble and Faber, the wide accomplishments
and scholarly criticism of Church. But on the whole
the broad stream of English thought has gone in other
directions. In politics the Oxford movement had brilliant
representatives in Gladstone and Selborne, but the ideal
of the relations of Church and State and the ideal of
education to which the Oxford school aspired, have been
absolutely discarded. The universities have been
secularised. The Irish Established Church, which it was
one of the first objects of the party to defend, has been
abolished by Gladstone himself, and although the English
Established Church retains its hold on the affections of
the nation, it is defended by its most skilful supporters
on very different grounds and by very different arguments

from those which were put forward by the Oxford divines. Among the foremost names in lay literature during the fifty years we are considering, it is curious to observe how few were even touched by the movement. Froude is an exception, but he speedily repudiated it. The mediæval sympathies that were sometimes shown by Ruskin sprang from a wholly different source. Macaulay, Carlyle, Hallam, Grote, Mill, Buckle, Tennyson, Browning, and the great novelists, from Dickens to George Eliot, all wrote very much as they might have written if the movement had never existed. An unusual proportion of the best intellect of England passed into the fields of physical science, and the methods of reasoning and habits of thought which they inculcated were wholly out of harmony with the school of Newman, while both geology and Darwinism have made serious incursions into long-cherished beliefs. Even in the Church itself, though the High Church movement was stronger than any other, great deductions have to be made. The school of independent Biblical criticism, which in various degrees has come to be generally accepted, certainly owed nothing to it, and several of the most illustrious Churchmen of this period were wholly alien to it. Thirlwall and Merivale were conspicuous examples, but they devoted themselves chiefly to great works of secular history. Arnold—who was one of the strongest personal influences of his age, and whose influence was both perpetuated and widened by Dean Stanley—and Whately, who was one of the most independent and original thinkers of the nineteenth century, were strongly antagonistic. In the field of ecclesiastical history it might have been expected that a school which was at once so scholarly and so wedded to tradition would have been pre-eminent, but no ecclesiastical histories which England has produced can, on the whole, be placed on as high a level as those which were written by the great Broad Church divine whose name stands at the head of this article. Milman was, indeed, a man well deserving of commemoration on account of the works which he produced, yet it is perhaps not too much to say that to those among whom he lived the man seemed even greater than his works. For many years he was a central and most popular figure in the best English literary society, and he reckoned most of the leading intellects of his day among his friends. He was in an extraordinary degree many-sided, both in his knowledge and his sympathies. He was an admirable critic, and the eminent sanity of his judgment, as well as the eminent kindness of his nature, combined with a great charm both of manner and of conversation. Few men of his time had more friends, and were more admired, consulted, and loved.

Mr. Arthur Milman has sketched his father's life in one short volume,[1] written in excellent English and with uniformly good taste. We have read it with much interest, yet in laying it down it is impossible not to be sensible how much of the personal charm which was so conspicuous in its subject has passed beyond recovery. More than thirty years have gone by since the old Dean was laid in his grave, and but few of those who knew him intimately survive. He appears to have kept no journal. He wrote nothing autobiographical, and he had a strong sense of the chasm that should separate private from public life. It was wholly contrary to his unegotistical nature to make the great

---

[1] *Henry Hart Milman, D.D., Dean of St. Paul's.* A Biographical Sketch by his son, Arthur Milman, M.A., LL.D.

public the confidant of his domestic affairs or of his inner feelings, and he was deeply sensible of the injustice which is so often done by biographers in printing unguarded, unqualified opinions and judgments, expressed in the freedom of private correspondence. He acted sternly on this view. Many of the foremost men in England were among his correspondents, but he deliberately burnt their letters. ' I could never bear,' we have heard him say, ' that what was written to me by dear friends in the most unreserved and absolute confidence should, through my fault, be one day dragged before the public.' This reticence and this strong feeling of the sanctity of friendship and private correspondence, which is now becoming very rare, was one of his most characteristic traits, but it has necessarily deprived his biography of many elements of interest.

He was the youngest son of Sir Francis Milman, the well-known physician of George III. He was born in 1791, and educated at Eton and Oxford, where he soon distinguished himself as one of the most brilliant of students. He won the Newdigate in 1812, the Chancellor's prize for Latin verse in 1813, the prize for English and Latin essays in 1816. He obtained a first class in classics, and in 1815 he was elected a Fellow of his college. He was ordained in the following year, and a year later Lord Eldon, who was then Chancellor of the university, nominated him to the vicarage of St. Mary at Reading, where he spent eighteen happy and fruitful years. Like most young and brilliant men, he first turned to verse, and for several years he poured out in rapid succession a number of dramas and poems which have been collected in three substantial volumes. The tragedy of ' Fazio ' was written when he was still at

Oxford, and it was speedily followed by a long and
ambitious epic poem called ' Samor, Lord of the Bright
City ' ; by three elaborate sacred dramas, the ' Fall of
Jerusalem,' the ' Martyr of Antioch,' and ' Belshazzar ' ;
and by an historical tragedy on ' Anne Boleyn,' as well as
by a few minor poems.

Some of these works had considerable popularity.
' Fazio ' for many years held its place on the stage.
Byron, in one of his letters to Rogers, speaks of its
' great and deserved success ' when it was brought out at
Covent Garden.   Its heroine was a favourite part of Miss
O'Neil and of Fanny Kemble.   It was translated into
Italian by Del Ongaro for Ristori, who acted it with
admirable power, and there was also a French translation
or adaptation in which Mademoiselle Mars took part.
The ' Fall of Jerusalem ' was never intended for the
stage, but it had a great literary success.   Murray, who
had given only a hundred and fifty guineas for ' Fazio,'
gave five hundred for the ' Fall of Jerusalem,' and he
gave the same sum both for the ' Martyr of Antioch ' and
for ' Belshazzar,' which succeeded it.   Neither of these,
however, proved as popular as the ' Fall of Jerusalem,'
but the ' Martyr of Antioch ' contains that noble funeral
ode beginning ' Brother, thou art gone before us, and thy
saintly soul is flown,' which is familiar to numbers who
are probably not aware of its authorship.   It is worthy
of notice that as recently as 1880 Sir Arthur Sullivan set
the ' Martyr of Antioch ' to music and brought it out at
the Leeds Festival, where it achieved an immediate and
brilliant success, and was frequently performed.[1]   On the
other hand, ' Samor ' and ' Anne Boleyn ' were almost
absolute failures, and, on the whole, the longer poems of

[1] Laurence's *Life of Sir A. Sullivan*, p. 310.

Milman have not retained their popularity, and probably now rarely find a reader.

Those who turn to them will certainly be struck by the command of language and metre they display. It was shown both in rhyme and in blank verse. Many fine odes are scattered through them, and in the octo-syllabic verse Milman always appears to us peculiarly happy. But his poetry, like most of the poetry that was written under the Byronic influence, was rather the poetry of rhetoric than of imagination, and it wanted both the intensity and the concentration of the great master. Stately, sonorous, fluent, unfailingly lucid, it was too lengthy and too artificial, and Lockhart was not wholly wrong in pronouncing that it showed 'fine talents, but no genius,' and in urging that prose rather than poetry was the vehicle in which its author was destined to succeed. In addition, however, to the funeral ode to which we have referred, Milman has written many hymns, and some of these are of singular beauty. They appeared originally in the collection of that other great hymn-writer, Bishop Heber, who was one of his dearest friends, and one of the men to whose memory he looked back with the fondest affection. The Good Friday hymn, 'Bound upon th' accursèd tree,' the Palm Sunday hymn, 'Ride on, ride on in majesty,' and perhaps still more that exquisitely pathetic hymn (so often misprinted in modern hymn-books) beginning

> When our heads are bowed with woe,
> When our bitter tears o'erflow,

have long since taken their permanent place in devotional literature.

In another and very different field of poetry also he greatly excelled. He was an admirable example of that highly finished and fastidious classical scholarship which is, or was, the pride of our great public schools, and he took great pleasure in translations from the classics. He translated into verse the 'Agamemnon' of Æschylus, and the 'Bacchanals' of Euripides, and also a great number of small and much less known poems. He held the professorship of poetry at Oxford from 1821 to 1831, and as his lectures, according to the custom which then prevailed, were delivered in Latin, he had the happy thought of diversifying them by English metrical translations of the different poems he treated. They range over a wide field of obscure Greek poets, as well as of epitaphs, votive inscriptions, and inscriptions relating to the fine arts, and in addition to these there are translations from Sanscrit poetry—a branch of knowledge which was then very little cultivated, and to which Milman was greatly attracted. These poems the author published in 1865, but the lectures in which they were produced he committed to the flames. They had, in his opinion, lost their value through the subsequent publication of the works on the history of Greek literature by Bode, Ulrici, Otfried Müller, and Mure.

In prose his pen was exceedingly active. In 1820 he began his long connection with the 'Quarterly Review,' which continued, with occasional intervals, through more than forty years. His articles extended over a great variety of subjects, but most of them were essentially reviews and essentially critical. The fact that he was both a poet and an accomplished critic of verse caused some persons to ascribe to him the authorship of two articles which had an unhappy reputation—the criticism which was falsely supposed to have hastened the death of Keats, and the attack upon the 'Alastor' of Shelley, a poet for whom Milman had a special admiration. It is now well known that neither of these articles was by him, but it is characteristic of his loyalty to his colleagues that he never disclaimed the authorship. This loyalty was indeed not less conspicuous in his nature than the singular kindness of disposition with which he ever shrank from giving pain. After his death a few of his many essays in the ' Quarterly ' were collected in one volume. Among them there is an admirable account of Erasmus, with whom in mental characteristics he had considerable affinity.

In 1829 appeared his first historical work, the ' History of the Jews,' a work which excited a violent storm of theological indignation. The crime of Milman was that he applied to Jewish history the usual canons of historical criticism—sifting evidence, discriminating between documents, pointing out the parallelisms between Jewish conditions and those of other Oriental nations, and attempting to separate in the sacred writings the parts which were essential and revealed from those which were merely human and fallible. In a remarkable preface to a revised and enlarged edition of this work, which was published thirty years later, he laid down very clearly the principles that had guided him. The Jewish writers, in his opinion, were ' men of their age and country who, as they spoke the language, so they thought the thoughts of their nation and their time. . . . They had no special knowledge on any subject but moral and religious truth to distinguish them from other men, and were as fallible as others on all questions of science, and even of history, extraneous to their religious teaching. . . . Their one paramount object being instruction and enlightenment in religion, they left their hearers uninstructed and

S

unenlightened as before in other things. . . . In all other
respects society, civilisation, developed itself according to
its usual laws. The Hebrew in the wilderness, excepting
as far as the law modified his manners and habits, was
an Arab of the desert. Abraham, except in his worship
and intercourse with the one true God, was a nomad
Sheik. . . . The moral and religious truth, and this alone,
I apprehend, is "the word of God" contained in the
sacred writings.'

It must also, he contended, be always remembered
that the Semitic records are of an 'essentially Oriental,
figurative, poetical cast,' and that it is therefore wholly
erroneous to suppose that every word can be construed
with the precision of an Act of Parliament or of a simple
modern historical narrative.

His attitude towards the miraculous was carefully
defined. He observed the absolute impossibility of
evading the conclusion that the Jewish writers, whether
eye-witnesses or not, implicitly believed in 'the super-
naturalism, the divine or miraculous agency almost
throughout the older history of the Jews,' and that it is
'an integral, inseparable part of the narrative.' Sometimes it is possible 'with more or less probability to detect the naked fact which may lie beneath the imaginative
or marvellous language in which it is recorded; but even
in these cases the solution can be hardly more than
conjectural.' In other cases 'the supernatural so entirely
predominates and is so of the intimate essence of the
transaction that the facts and the interpretation must be
accepted together or rejected together.' In such cases
it is the duty of the historian simply 'to relate the facts
as recorded, to adduce his authorities, and to abstain from
all explanation for which he has no ground.'

The distinction between the providential and the strictly miraculous appears to him impossible to draw. ' Belief in Divine Providence, in the agency of God as the Prime Mover in the Natural world as in the mind of Man, is an inseparable part of religion. There can be no religion without it.' But in numerous cases, to distinguish between the simply providential and the strictly miraculous implies a knowledge of the working of natural causes greater than we possess; and in certain stages of civilisation, and very eminently in the Jewish mind, there is a marked tendency to suppress secondary causes, and to attribute not only the more extraordinary but also the common events of life to direct divine agency. The possibility and the reality of the miraculous he emphatically asserts.

' The palmary miracle of all, the Resurrection, stands entirely by itself. Every attempt to resolve it into a natural event, a delusion or hallucination in the minds of the disciples, the eye-witnesses and death-defying witnesses to its truth, or to treat it as an allegory or figure of speech, is to me a signal failure. It must be accepted as the keystone—for such it is—and seal to the great Christian doctrine of a future life, as a historical fact, or rejected as a baseless fable.'

But great numbers of what were deemed miracles may be explained by natural causes, by figurative modes of expression which were common in Oriental nations, by the tendency of the human mind to embellish or exaggerate surprising facts, or invent supernatural causes for what it is unable to explain, by the retrospective imagination which seeks to dignify the distant past with a supernatural halo. The early annals of all nations are strewn with pretended miracles which no one will

now maintain, and Milman shows in a powerful passage
how the idea of the miraculous has been steadily con-
tracting and receding; how dangerous it is to base the
defence of Christianity on the evidence of miracles rather
than on appeals to the conscience, the moral sense, the
innate religiousness, the deep spiritual cravings of human
nature.

Such views, though now sufficiently commonplace,
seemed very novel in England when Milman wrote. Dean
Stanley described his work as 'the first decisive inroad
of German theology into England; the first palpable
indication that the Bible could be studied like another
book; that the characters and events of sacred history
could be treated at once critically and reverently.' But
though Milman was very well acquainted with German
theology, he resented the notion that he was its in-
terpreter or representative. He contended that in
restricting the province of inspiration to the direct
inculcation of religious truth he was following a sound
Anglican tradition. He quoted the authority of Paley
and Warburton, of Tillotson and Secker. In such
principles of interpretation he said he had found 'a
safeguard during a long and not unreflective life against
the difficulties arising out of the philosophical and
historical researches of his time.' They had enabled him
'to follow out all the marvellous discoveries of science,
and all those hardly less marvellous, if less certain,
conclusions of historical, ethnological, linguistic criticism,
in the serene confidence that they are utterly irrelevant
to the truth of Christianity.' 'If on such subjects,' he
concluded, 'some solid ground be not found on which
highly educated, reflective, reading, reasoning men may
find firm footing, I can foresee nothing but a wide,

a widening—I fear, an irreparable—breach between the thought and the religion of England. A comprehensive, all-embracing, truly Catholic Christianity which knows what is essential to religion, what is temporary and extraneous to it, may defy the world.'

These words are taken from the later preface to which we have referred. In the same preface, and also in his ' History of Christianity,' may be found some interesting remarks on the German school of Biblical criticism, the greater portion of which has arisen since the original publication of the ' History of the Jews.' In many of its conclusions he had anticipated it, and he was quite as sensible as the German writers of the hopelessness of seeking scientific revelations in the Biblical narrative ; of the worthlessness of most of the common schemes for reconciling science and theology; of the untrustworthy character of Jewish chronology and Jewish figures ; of the grave doubts that hang over the authorship and the date of some of the books ; of the necessity of making full allowance, when reading them, for human fallibility and inaccuracy. At the same time, his admiration for the German critics was by no means unqualified. While fully admitting their extraordinary learning, industry, and ingenuity, he complained that their too common infirmity was ' a passion for making history without historical materials,' basing the most dogmatic and positive statements upon faint indications, or upon ingenious conjectures that could not legitimately go beyond a very low degree of probability. The assurance with which these writers undertook by internal evidence to decompose ancient documents, assigning each paragraph to an independent source; the decisive weight they were accustomed to give to slight improbabilities or coincidences, and to small variations of style and phraseology; the confidence with which they put forward solutions or conjectures which, however ingenious or plausible, were based on no external evidence as if they were proved facts, appeared to him profoundly unhistorical.

It must have been somewhat irritating to one who clung so closely to University life, and who had been justly regarded as one of the most brilliant of Oxford scholars, to find that his own University was prominent in the condemnation of the 'History of the Jews.' Only two years before he had preached with general approbation the Bampton Lectures in defence of Christianity. His new work was again and again condemned from the University pulpits, and among others by the Margaret Professor of Divinity and by the Hulsean lecturer for 1832. The clamour was naturally taken up in many other quarters, and especially by the religious newspapers. It was noticed that 'Milman's History' appeared in the window of Carlisle, the infidel bookseller.

'I only wish,' wrote Milman, when the fact was brought to his notice, 'all Carlisle's customers would read it. A noble lord once wrote to the bishop of a certain diocese to complain that a baronet who lived in the same parish brought his mistress to church, which sorely shocked his regular family. The bishop gravely assured him that he was very glad to hear that Sir —— brought his naughty lady to church, and hoped that she would profit by what she heard there and amend her ways. So say I of Carlisle's customers.' [1]

The opinions expressed in this, as in his later works, no doubt in some degree obstructed the promotion of

[1] Smiles' *Memoirs of John Murray*, ii. p. 300.

Milman in the Church, but he had no reason to regret it. Of all men, he once said, he thought he owed most to Bishop Blomfield, for there was once a question of offering him a bishopric, and it was a remonstrance of the Bishop of London that prevented it. 'I am *afraid*,' he said, 'that if it had been offered me I should have accepted it, and I should then never have written my "Latin Christianity."' But, though he escaped the fate which has cut short the best work of more than one distinguished historian, his conspicuous position among the scholars and writers in the Church was widely recognised, and he was soon transferred from a provincial town to a central position in the Metropolis. In 1835 Sir Robert Peel made him Rector of St. Margaret's, Westminster, and Prebendary in the Abbey. Though continuing without intermission his historical work, he appears to have discharged with exemplary vigour the duties of a large and poor parish until 1849, when Lord John Russell appointed him Dean of St. Paul's. The position was exactly suited to him. It was one of much dignity, but also of much leisure, and it gave him ample opportunities of pursuing the studies which were the true work of his life.

The great subject of the history of Christianity was, indeed, continually before him. Among other things, he studied minutely both the text and the authorities of Gibbon, for whom he had a deep and growing admiration. An excellent edition of Gibbon was one of the first results. Milman's notes have been included in Smith's later edition, and, though a large proportion of them were naturally somewhat controversial, being devoted to refuting some of the conclusions of the fifteenth and sixteenth chapters, it is impossible to read them without recognising the candour as well as the learning and the acumen of the critic. Few things that Milman has written are finer than the preface in which, in ten or twelve masterly pages, he sums up his estimate of his great predecessor.

The three volumes of the 'History of Christianity,' dealing with its early history up to the period of the abolition of Paganism in the Roman Empire, appeared in 1840, and they were followed by the six large volumes of the 'History of Latin Christianity,' carrying the history of the Western Church to the end of the Pontificate of Nicholas V. in 1455. This great work was published in two instalments—the first three volumes in 1854, and the remaining three in the following year—and it gave its author indisputably the first place among the ecclesiastical historians of England and a high place among the historians of the nineteenth century. He possessed, indeed, in an eminent degree some of the qualities that are most rare, and at the same time most valuable, in ecclesiastical history. A large proportion of the most learned ecclesiastical historians have been men who have devoted their whole lives to this single department of knowledge, who derived from it all their measures of probability and canons of criticism, and who, treating it as an isolated and mainly supernatural thing, have taken very little account of the intellectual and political secular influences that have largely shaped its course. Most of them also have been men who undertook their task with convictions and habits of thought that were absolutely incompatible with real independence and impartiality of judgment in estimating either the events or the characters they described. Milman was wholly free from these defects. His wide knowledge, his cool, critical, admirably trained judgment, were never better shown than in the many pages in which he has pointed out the analogies or resemblances between Jewish and other Oriental beliefs; the manner in which national characteristics or secular intellectual tendencies affected theological types; the countless modifications in belief or practice which grew up, as the Church accommodated itself to the conditions of successive ages and entered into alliance or conflict with different political systems; the many indirect, subtle, far-reaching ways in which the world and the Church interacted upon each other in all the great departments of speculation, art, industry, social and political life. A certain aloofness and coldness of judgment in dealing with sacred subjects was the reproach which was most frequently brought against him. As he himself said, he wrote rather as an historian than a religious instructor, and he dealt with his subject chiefly in its temporal, social, and political aspects. Justice and impartiality of judgment to friend and foe he deemed one of the first moral duties of an historian, and Dean Church was not wrong in ascribing to him a quite 'unusual combination of the strongest feeling about right and wrong with the largest equity.' 'What a delightful book, so tolerant of the intolerant!' was his characteristic eulogy of the work of another writer, and it truly reflects the turn of his own mind. Provost Hawtrey, who was no mean judge of men, said, after an intimacy of nearly fifty years, that he had never known a man who possessed in a greater degree than Milman the virtue of Christian charity in its highest and rarest form. It was a gift which stood him in good stead in dealing with the very blended characters, the tangled politics, the often misguided enthusiasms of ecclesiastical history. While he was constitutionally extremely averse to the moral casuistry which confuses the boundaries of right and wrong, he had too sound a grasp of the evolution of history to fall into the common error of judging the acts of one age by the moral standards of another. His history was eminently a history of large lines and broad tendencies. The growth, influence, and decline of the Papacy—the distinctive characteristics of Latin and Teutonic Christianity; the effect of Christianity on jurisprudence ; the monastic system in its various phases; the rise and conquests of Mohammedanism; the severance of Greek from Latin Christianity; Charlemagne, Hildebrand, the Crusades, the Templars, the Great Councils; the decay of Latin and the rise of modern languages; the influence of the Church on literature, painting, sculpture, and architecture—are but a few of the great subjects he has treated, always with knowledge and intelligence, often with conspicuous brilliancy.

In so vast a field there were, no doubt, many subjects which have been treated with a greater fulness and completeness by other writers. There are some in which subsequent research has gone far to supersede what Milman has written, and inaccuracies of detail not unfrequently crept into his work; but in the truthfulness of its broad lines, in the sagacity of its estimates both of men and events, it holds a high place among the histories of the world. Very few historians have combined in a larger measure the three great requisites of knowledge, soundness of judgment, and inexorable love of truth. The growth and modifications of doctrines and the minutiæ of religious controversies were, however, subjects in which he took little interest, and though they could not be excluded from an ecclesiastical history, they

are dealt with only in a slight and cursory manner.
Those who desire to study in detail this side of ecclesiastical history will find other histories much more
useful. It has been said that his work is imperfect as a
book of reference, for while the great events and personages are discussed with a fulness that leaves little to be
desired, many of the more insignificant transactions or
more obscure periods are passed over or barely noticed.
Critics of different religious schools have also complained
that his mind was essentially secular ; that he had a low
sense of the certainty and the importance of dogma ; that
there were some classes of ecclesiastical writers who have
been deeply revered in the Church with whom he had no
real sympathy ; that the spirit of criticism was stronger
in his book than the spirit of reverence ; that he did not
do full justice to the spiritual and inner side of the religion
he described. He looked upon it, they said, too exter-
nally. He valued it as a moral revolution, the introduction of new principles of virtue and new rules for
individual and social happiness. Much of this criticism
would probably have been accepted with but little
qualification by Milman himself. He would have said
that what these writers complained of was in the main
inseparable from an historical as distinguished from a
devotional treatment of his subject. He would have
added that no form of human history reveals so clearly as
ecclesiastical history the fallibility, the credulity, the
intolerance of the human mind, or requires more im-
peratively the constant exercise of independent judgment
and of fearless and unsparing criticism, and that, if the
history of the Church is ever to be written with profit, it
must be written in such a spirit. Of his own deeper
convictions he seldom spoke ; but in the concluding page

of his ' Latin Christianity ' there is a passage of profound
interest.   Leaving it, as he says, to the future historian
of religion to say what part of the ancient dogmatic
system may be allowed to fall silently into disuse, and
what transformations the interpretation of the Sacred
Writings may still undergo, he adds these significant
words :

'As it is my own confident belief that the words of
Christ, and his words alone (the primal indefeasible truths
of Christianity), shall not pass away, so I cannot presume
to say that men may not attain to a clearer, at the same
time more full, comprehensive, and balanced sense of
those words, than has as yet been generally received in
the Christian world.   As all else is transient and mutable,
these only eternal and universal, assuredly whatever light
may be thrown on the mental constitution of man, even on
the constitution of nature and the laws which govern the
world, will be concentered so as to give a more penetrating
vision of those undying truths. . . . Christianity may yet
have to exercise a far wider, even if more silent and un-
traceable influence, through its primary, all-pervading
principles, on the civilisation of mankind.'

Macaulay, speaking of the ' History of Latin Christianity' in his Journal, says, ' I was more impressed than
ever by the contrast between the substance and the style :
the substance is excellent ; the style very much otherwise.'   Looking at it from a purely literary point of view
it had undoubtedly great merits.   Milman had an admirable sense of proportion—a rare quality in history.
He was invariably lucid, and it is easy to cull from his
history many characters excellently drawn, many pages of
vivid narrative, or terse and weighty criticism.   Still, on
the whole his historic style is on a lower level than that

of Macaulay, Buckle, and Froude, though it will compare, I think, not unfavourably with that of Hallam and Grote. The points of controversy are usually relegated to his notes, which contain a great mass of curious learning and excellent criticism. The reader who turns to them from works of the German school will be struck by his strong English common-sense and grasp of facts, and his dislike of subtle far-fetched ingenuities of explanation. He has the crowning merit of being always readable, and his strong sane moral sense never left him. He was probably at his best in the later volumes, when he could treat his subject like secular history and was free from the embarrassing theological difficulties of the earlier portion, and he is especially admirable in those chapters which give scope to his wide literary and artistic sympathies. He was an excellent Italian scholar and keenly sensible of the beauties of Italian literature, and his love of the ancient classics never left him. There was something at once characteristic and amusing in the delight which he again and again expressed, after the termination of his History, at being able to return to them after spending so many years in reading bad Latin and Greek. In taste and character he was indeed pre-eminently a man of letters, and as such he ranks in the first line among his contemporaries.

The outburst of indignation that in some quarters had greeted the first appearance of the ' History of the Jews ' was not repeated when that work was republished in an enlarged form. Nor does it appear to have arisen on the appearance of the two later histories. Newman reviewed the ' History of Early Christianity ' at great length, speaking with much personal respect of the writer, though he was naturally extremely hostile to its spirit.

The difference between the High Church sentiment and the mind of Milman was indeed organic. Milman's own type of thought was formed before the Tractarian movement had begun; the sacerdotal spirit was thoroughly alien to him, and his profound study of ecclesiastical history had certainly not tended to attract him to it. He fully recognised both the abilities and the piety of Newman, and he described his secession as perhaps the greatest loss the Church of England had experienced since the Reformation; but he disliked his opinions, he profoundly distrusted the whole character of his mind and reasonings, and he early foresaw that he could never find a permanent resting-place in the English Church. In the posthumous volume of Essays there will be found a full and most searching examination of Newman's ' Essay on Development,' in which these points of difference are clearly shown. For Keble, Milman entertained warmer feelings. They were contemporaries, and at one time most intimate friends. In the field of sacred poetry they had been fellow-labourers. Keble had succeeded Milman as professor of poetry, and Milman had been one of the few persons who had read the ' Christian Year ' in manuscript. When, after Keble's death, a committee was appointed to erect a memorial to his memory, Milman was much hurt at finding that it was determined to give it a distinctly Tractarian character, and that his own name was deliberately excluded. In Milman's last years the Oxford movement had begun to assume its ritualistic form, and questions of vestments and ceremonies and candles came to the forefront. With all this Milman had no sympathy. ' After the drama,' he said of it, ' the melodrama ! '

It was a remarkable coincidence that for some years

the two deaneries of London were both held by brilliant men of letters and by men with the strongest theological sympathy. A feeling of warm personal affection united Milman and Stanley, and there was something peculiarly touching in the almost filial attitude which Stanley assumed towards his older colleague. In one point, however, they differed greatly. Stanley was a keen fighter. He threw himself into the forefront of ecclesiastical controversies, and was never seen to greater advantage than when leading a small minority, defying inveterate prejudice, defending an unpopular cause. Milman could seldom be tempted to follow his example. He pleaded old age and declining strength, but, in truth, though he never flinched from the avowal of his own opinions, he had a deep and increasing distaste for religious controversies and Church politics. He was rarely seen in Convocation, and he always regarded its revival as a misfortune. He proposed, however, in it a petition for the discontinuance of the use of the State services commemorating the martyrdom of Charles I., the restoration of Charles II., the discovery of the gunpowder plot, and the Revolution of 1688; and Parliament soon after adopted his view. He also sat on the Royal Commission in 1864 for considering the subject of clerical subscription. He took on this occasion a characteristic line, advocating a complete abolition of the subscription of the Articles, and desiring that the sole test of membership of the Church should be the acceptance of the Liturgy and the Creeds. In 1865 he received an invitation, which greatly gratified him, to preach before the University of Oxford the annual sermon on Hebrew prophecy. The sermon was delivered in the pulpit of St. Mary's, where many years before he had been so vehemently condemned for views on the same subject, no one of which, as he truly said, he had either recanted or modified. His sermon was afterwards printed, and would form a worthy chapter of his 'History of the Jews.' In the Colenso controversy he had no great sympathy with either side. Many of Bishop Colenso's arguments appeared to him crude or exaggerated, and he dissented from many of his conclusions, but he considered that he had been treated with gross injustice and intolerance, and he accordingly subscribed to his defence fund. For the rest, he confined his ecclesiastical life as much as possible to his own cathedral, where he presided over the State funeral of the Duke of Wellington, and where he introduced the custom of throwing open the nave to evening services. His last and unfinished work was his 'Annals of St. Paul's,' investigating its history and portraying with his old learning and with much of his old felicity the lives of his predecessors.

It was however in secular literary society that he was most fitted to shine, and there he passed many of his happiest hours. The usual honours of a distinguished man of letters clustered thickly around him. He was a trustee of the British Museum; an honorary member of the Royal Academy; a correspondent of the French Institute. He was also a member of 'The Club'—the small dining-club which was founded in 1764 by Sir Joshua Reynolds and Dr. Johnson, and which since then has included in its fortnightly dinners the great majority of those Englishmen who in many walks of life have been most distinguished by their genius or their accomplishments. He was elected to it in 1836, three years before Macaulay, and he became one of its most constant attendants. In 1841 'The Club' made him its treasurer, and he held that position for twenty-three years, and presided over the centenary dinner in 1864. He was also an original member of the Philobiblion Society, which has brought together many curious and hitherto unknown documents, and he wrote for it a short paper on Michael Scott the Wizard, who, as he showed, had been once offered the Archbishopric of Cashel. He was never a keen politician, but he was intimate with a long succession of leading statesmen, and he contributed to Sir Cornewall Lewis's 'Administrations of Great Britain' a full and valuable letter on the relations of Pitt and Addington, which was largely based on his own recollections of the latter statesman.

London society in the middle of the nineteenth century was much smaller and less mixed than at present, and there was then a distinctively literary or at least intellectual society which can now hardly be said to exist. The most eminent men of letters came more frequently together. Criticism was in fewer and perhaps stronger hands, and was to a larger extent representative of the opinions expressed in such social gatherings. In this kind of society Milman was long a foremost figure. He had all the gifts that fit men for it—not only brilliancy, knowledge, and versatility, but also unfailing tact, a rare charm of courtesy, a singularly wide tolerance. He was quick and generous in recognising rising talent, and he had that sympathetic touch which seldom failed to elicit what was best in those with whom he came in contact. Few men possessed more eminently the genius of friendship—the power of attaching others—the power of attaching himself to others. In the long list of his intimate friends Macaulay, Sir Charles Lyell, and Sir George Cornewall Lewis were conspicuous. Like most

T

men of this type, he found the multiplying gaps around him the chief trial of old age. Not long before he died there was an exhibition of contemporary portraits, but though Milman went to it he could not go through it. 'When I found myself,' he said, 'surrounded by the likenesses—often the miserable likenesses—of so many I had known and loved, it was more than I could bear.'

An admirable portrait by Watts which is now in the National Portrait Gallery will recall to those who knew him his appearance in old age—his strong masculine features beaming with intelligence, his grand shaggy brows, his bright and penetrating eyes. An illness affecting the spine had bowed him nearly double, and there are still those who will remember how his bent figure seemed projected, almost like a bird in its flight, across the dinner-table, while his eager brilliant talk delighted and fascinated his hearers. In his last years increasing deafness obliged him to narrow the circle of his social life, but he retained to the end all the vividness of his mind and sympathies, and when at length death came in his seventy-eighth year, it found him in the midst of unfinished work. His life was not of a kind to win wide popularity and to give him a conspicuous place among the great masses of his nation, but few English clergymen of his generation made so deep an impression on those who came in contact with them or have left works of such enduring value behind them.

QUEEN VICTORIA AS A MORAL FORCE

AT a time when the unprecedented increase of gigantic and rapidly acquired fortunes has deeply infected both English and American society with the characteristic vices of a Plutocracy, the profound feeling of sorrow and admiration elicited by the death of Queen Victoria is an encouraging sign. It shows that the vulgar ideals, the false moral measurements, the feverish social ambitions, the love of the ostentatious and the factitious, and the disdain for simple habits, pleasures, and characters so apparent in certain conspicuous sections of society, have not yet blunted the moral sense or perverted the moral perceptions of the great masses on either side of the Atlantic. To this type, indeed, we could scarcely find a more complete antithesis than in the life and character of the great Queen who has passed away. Nothing more deeply impressed all who came in contact with her than the essential simplicity and genuineness of her nature.

She was a great ruler, but she was also to the last a true, kindly, simple-minded woman, retaining with undiminished intensity all the warmth of a most affectionate nature, all the soundness of a most excellent judgment. Brought up from childhood in the artificial atmosphere of a Court, called while still a girl to the isolation of a throne ; deprived, when her reign had yet forty years to run, of the support and counsel of her husband, she might well have been pardoned if she often found herself out of touch with large sections of her people, and had viewed life through a false medium or in partial aspects. Yet Lord Salisbury probably in no degree exaggerated when he said that if he wished to ascertain the feelings and opinions of the English people, and especially of the English middle classes, he knew no truer or more enlightening judgment than that of the Queen. She thought with them and she felt with them; she shared their ambitions; she knew by a kind of intuitive instinct the course of their judgments; she sympathised deeply with their trials and their sorrows.

She could hardly be called a brilliant woman. It is difficult indeed to judge the full social capacities of anyone who lives under the constant restraints of a royal position, but I do not think that in any sphere of life the Queen would have been regarded as a woman of striking wit, or originality, or even commanding power. The qualities that made her so successful in her high calling were of another kind : supreme good sense; a tact in dealing with men and circumstances so unfailing that it almost amounted to genius; an indefatigable industry which never flagged from early youth till extreme old age; a sense of duty so steady and so strong that it governed all her actions and pleasures, and saved her not only from the grosser and more common temptations of an exalted position, but also in a most unusual degree from the subtle and often half-concealed deflecting influences that spring from ambition or resentment, from personal predilections and personal dislikes. It was these qualities, combined with her unrivalled experience of affairs, and strengthened by long and constant intercourse with the foremost English statesmen of two generations, that made her what she undoubtedly was—a perfect model of a constitutional Sovereign.

The position of a Sovereign under a parliamentary government like ours is a singular and difficult one. There was a school of politicians who were much more prominent in the last generation than in the present one, who regarded the Sovereign, in political life at least, as little more than a figure-head or a cipher, absolved from all responsibility, but also divested of all power, and fulfilling functions in the Constitution which are little more than mechanical. This view of the unimportance of the Monarchy will now be held by few really intelligent men. Those take but a false and narrow view of human affairs who fail to realise the part which sentiment and enthusiasm play in the government of men ; and no one who knows England will question that the throne is the centre of a great strength of personal attachment which is wholly different from any attachment to a party or a parliament.

In India and the Colonies this is still more the case. It is not the British Parliament or the British Cabinet that there forms the centre of unity or excites genuine attachment. The Crown is the main link binding the different States to one another, and the pervading sentiment of a common loyalty unites them in one great and living whole. In foreign politics it cannot be a matter of indifference that a Sovereign is closely related to nearly all the greatest rulers in the world, and in frequent, intimate, unconstrained correspondence with them. This is a kind of influence which no Minister, however powerful, can exercise, and it was possessed by Queen Victoria probably to a greater degree than by any

Sovereign on record, for there has scarcely ever been one who included among her relations so many of the Sovereigns of the world. Future historians will no doubt have ample means of judging how frequently and how judiciously it was employed in assuaging differences and promoting European peace. All the great offices in Church and State, all the great distributions of honours were submitted to her ; and though in a large number of cases this patronage is purely Ministerial or professional, there are many cases in which the Sovereign had a real voice, and a strong objection on her part was usually attended to. In Church patronage and in the distribution of honours she is known to have taken a great interest, and to have exercised a considerable influence.

The one subject on which the Queen was not always in harmony with her people was that of foreign politics. She and the Prince Consort took a keen interest in them, and during his lifetime she followed very implicitly his guidance. The strong German sympathies she imbued from her own marriage were much intensified by the marriages of her children, and especially by that of her eldest daughter to the heir of the Prussian throne. The influence also of Stockmar, who was the closest adviser of her early married life, was not wholly for good, and the theory which the Prince held that the direction of foreign affairs is in a peculiar degree under the care of the Sovereign, and that the Prince, her husband, should be regarded as 'her permanent Minister,' created during many years much friction. In a constitutional country, where the responsibility of affairs rests wholly on the Minister, who is doubly responsible to the Cabinet and to the Parliament, such a theory can only be maintained with great qualifications,

On the other hand, the government of the country was carried on in the name of the Queen. Foreign despatches were addressed to her and could only be answered with her sanction. The right of the English Sovereigns to be present at the Cabinet Councils of their Ministers was abdicated when George I. came to the throne, but every important departure in policy was submitted to the Queen and required her assent. The testimony of Ministers of all shades of policy supports the belief that this was no idle form. The Queen, though always open to argument and tolerant of contradiction, had her own decided opinions; she exercised her undoubted right of expressing and defending them, and even apart from her royal position, her great experience and her singular clearness and rectitude of judgment made her opinion well worth listening to.

The claim put forward by the Queen in her famous memorandum of August 1850, can, I think, hardly be pronounced excessive. She demanded only that before a line of policy was adopted and brought before her she should be distinctly informed of the facts of the case and of the motives that inspired it; that when she had given her sanction to a measure it should not be arbitrarily altered or modified by the Minister; that she must be kept acquainted with all important communications between foreign Ministers and her own Foreign Secretary, and that the drafts of foreign despatches must be sent to her for her approval in sufficient time for her to make herself acquainted with them. She complained that Lord Palmerston was accustomed to send despatches to the Continent without submitting them, in their last revise, to the Sovereign; that in one case he retained without her knowledge a passage which the Prince Consort had deleted; that he paid little or no attention to the numerous memoranda which were drawn up by the Prince for his instruction; that he of his own will and without any consultation committed his Government, in a conversation with the French Ambassador, to an approbation of the *coup d'état* of Napoleon III. If the general line of his policy had been in accordance with the royal wishes, indiscretions of detail could probably have been overlooked, but the Queen and Prince were both undoubtedly on many occasions—and especially in 1848 and 1849—strongly opposed to the policy of Lord Palmerston. In the interests of peace they objected to the remarkably provocative character of his despatches, which excited a degree of animosity and resentment among the Governments of the Continent that has rarely been paralleled—on two, if not three, occasions it brought England into grave danger of a war with France—and which aroused a very widespread indignation among statesmen of his own party at home.

The widely different tone which was adopted by Lord Clarendon and Lord Granville, the open breach between Palmerston and Lord John Russell on account of the way in which the former conducted his foreign policy without consultation with the Cabinet, and the refusal of Lord Grey, in a most critical moment, to take office in a Government in which Lord Palmerston held the seals of the Foreign Office, show how fully in this respect the sentiments of the Queen accorded with those of many of Lord Palmerston's own colleagues. But in addition to mere questions of manner and procedure, there was much in the substance of the policy of Palmerston to which the Queen objected. Her dislike to the Revolutionary element on the Continent, which Lord Palmerston either encouraged or viewed with indifference, her sympathy with the old governments and dynasties, that were so gravely shaken in the year of the Revolution, were very marked. In the disputes between Germany and Denmark on the Schleswig-Holstein question her sympathies, unlike those of her people, were decidedly with Germany, and although she was fully sensible of the misgovernment of some of the Italian States, she was not favourable to that cause of Italian unity which Lord John Russell and Lord Palmerston so strenuously upheld. Her nature, which was very frank, made it impossible for her, even if she desired it, to conceal her opinions, and she devoted much time and pains to making herself acquainted with the details of every question as it arose. She made it a rule to sign no paper that she had not read. She did not hesitate fully to apprise her Ministers of her views when they differed from their own, and she enforced her views by argument and remonstrance. She more than once drew up memoranda of her dissent from the opinions of her Foreign Minister, and insisted on their being brought before the Cabinet for consideration. In the formation of a new Ministry she more than once exercised her power of deciding to whom the succession of the first places should be offered. After an adverse vote of the House of Commons, she considered herself fully authorised to decide whether she would accept the resignation of a Minister or submit the issue to the test of a dissolution, and there were occasions on which she remonstrated with her Ministers on their too ready determination to resign.

At the same time it is certain that the Queen fulfilled with perfection that most difficult duty of an able constitutional Sovereign—the duty of yielding her convictions to those of her responsible Ministers and acting faithfully with Ministers she distrusted. To a Sovereign with clear views and a more than common force of character this must often have been very painful, and to have fulfilled it faithfully and with no loss of dignity is no small merit. It is the universal testimony of all who served her, that no Sovereign ever supported her successive Ministers with a more perfect loyalty or held the scales between contending parties with a more complete impartiality. No one understood better to what point a constitutional Sovereign may press her opinions and at what point she is bound to give way ; and while maintaining her rightful authority she never in any degree transgressed its bounds. In the very beginning of her reign she showed this quality in a high degree. She looked up to Lord Melbourne with an almost filial affection, and there were peculiar reasons why his great opponent, Sir Robert Peel, should have been distasteful to her. The dispute about the removal of her Ladies of the Bedchamber, and still more the conduct of Sir Robert Peel in supporting the reduction of the income which the Whigs had proposed for Prince Albert, must have touched her feelings on the most sensitive points, and the stiff, formal, somewhat awkward manner of Peel seemed very little fitted to ingratiate him with a young Sovereign. Yet when the change of Ministry arrived, Peel found no trace of resentment in the Queen. She gave him her complete confidence, and she fully estimated his great qualities. Of all the Ministers who served her there is indeed none of whom she has written in warmer terms. When Lord Palmerston became Prime Minister in 1855 it was contrary to her earnest desire, but when the change was made Palmerston himself acknowledged that he had ' no reason to complain of the least want of

cordiality or confidence on the part of the Court.' At the
time when she was most opposed to her Ministers, she
fully acquiesced in the principle that she must submit all
letters on public affairs to them and frame her replies
upon their advice. There were constant attempts on the
part of foreign Sovereigns who were connected with her to
carry on affairs by correspondence with her without the
knowledge and sanction of her Ministers, but the Queen
steadily resisted them. Anything, indeed, that in any
way savoured of intrigue was in the highest degree
repugnant to her nature.

She acted in the same way in internal affairs. Few
measures that were carried in her time were more repugnant to her than Gladstone's disestablishment of the
Irish Church. It abolished an institution of which she
was herself the head and which a special clause in the
Coronation Oath required her to uphold, and she foretold,
not without good reason, that it would not pacify Ireland
but would be an encouragement to further agitation.
The question, however, had been submitted at a general
election to the decision of the country, and after that
decision had been unequivocally given in favour of the
policy of Gladstone, she frankly accepted it with the assent
of the Prime Minister. When a great danger of a conflict
between the two Houses of Parliament had arisen, she
devoted herself actively in preventing it. She employed
for that service the instrumentality of Archbishop Tait—
a great statesman-prelate, whose promotion to the see
of Canterbury was due to her own personal initiative,
contrary to the wish of Lord Beaconsfield, but most fully
justified by the result—and it was largely due to the intervention of the Queen that the Church Bill was not thrown
out in the House of Lords. She acted in a somewhat

similar way with reference to the Franchise Bill of 1884, though on this occasion she does not seem to have disliked the measure, which she urged the House of Lords to accept.

On three very memorable occasions the intervention of the Queen had probably a great effect on English politics. It is well known that at the time when the issue of peace or war with the United States was trembling in the balance on account of the seizure of the Southern envoys on the 'Trent,' the Queen, acting in accordance with the Prince Consort, by softening and revising the language of an English despatch to America, did very much to prevent the dispute from leading to a great war; that in the proclamation which was issued to the Indian people after the Sepoy Mutiny, she insisted on the excision of some most unfortunate words that seemed to menace the native creeds, and on the insertion of an emphatic promise that they should in no wise be interfered with, and thus probably prevented a new outburst of most dangerous fanaticism; that at the time of the Schleswig-Holstein dispute she contributed powerfully and actively to give a turn to the negotiations that averted a war with Prussia and Austria, which, as is now almost universally recognised, could only have led to a great catastrophe.

Whatever opinions may be formed of the merits of the dispute between Denmark and the German powers about Schleswig-Holstein, few persons who judge by the event can doubt that an isolated intervention of England on behalf of Denmark against the combined forces of Austria and Prussia would have been absolutely impotent to effect the object that was desired, and that even if France had consented to join in the struggle it would have led to a military disaster hardly less than that of the war of Sedan. If, contrary to all probability, the combined forces of France and England had proved stronger than those of Austria and Germany, the result could have hardly failed to be that France would have been established on the left bank of the Rhine, and that the treaty of Vienna, which it was one of the great objects of English policy to maintain, would have been torn into shreds.

The dangers, however, of conflict arising from the extreme irritability of English public opinion against Germany on the Danish question, were very great, and there can be little doubt that the personal influence of the Queen with the German Sovereign was an appreciable influence, and it was her desire that a paragraph in the Queen's Speech opening Parliament in February 1864 was erased. Words which contained at least a veiled or attributed threat to Germany were omitted, and instead of them an inoffensive paragraph was inserted expressing the Queen's ardent desire for peace and recording the earnest efforts she had made to maintain it.[1] At the same time when, by the Convention of Gastein in August 1865, the Duchies were severed from the Danish throne and placed in the virtual possession of Prussia and Austria, the protest of Lord Russell against so flagrant a violation of public right, and especially of the right of the people to be consulted on their own destiny, was drawn up with her full assent and indeed in a great measure at her suggestion.[2]

On other occasions her remonstrances were disregarded, and courses were pursued to which she strongly objected.

---

[1] *Queen Victoria*, by Sidney Lee, p. 349.
[2] Ollivier, *L'Empire Libéral*, vii. p. 455.

The surrender after Majuba was in her opinion a pusillanimous abandonment of the English flag, and it was with extreme reluctance that she acquiesced in it. Still more vehement were her feelings about the long abandonment of General Gordon in the Soudan. She had been indefatigable in urging on the Ministry of Gladstone the duty of speedy measures for his rescue, and when, owing to the long delay of the Ministry, the most heroic of modern Englishmen perished at Khartoum, her indignation knew no bounds. In a letter to his sisters, burning with mingled pity and indignation, she pronounced his 'cruel though heroic fate' to be 'a stain left upon England,' which she keenly felt. This was one of the few occasions in which she allowed her sentiments in hostility to the policy of her Ministers to appear publicly before the world. In general, she had a profound distrust of the policy and judgment of Mr. Gladstone, and she fully shared the dread with which the great body of English statesmen looked upon the Home Rule policy. It was no new sentiment on her part, for she had lived through the Repeal agitation of O'Connell, and as far back as 1843 Sir Robert Peel had somewhat unconstitutionally declared in Parliament that he was authorised by the Queen to state that she, like her predecessor, was resolved to maintain the Union inviolate by all the means in her power.

There can now be no harm in saying—what when both parties were alive was naturally kept in the background—that the relations of the Queen with Mr. Gladstone were usually of a very painful character. She had personally not much to complain of. The skill and firmness with which Mr. Gladstone resisted the attempts to diminish the parliamentary subsidies for her family were fully and gratefully recognised by the Queen, but the main course of his politics, both foreign and domestic, filled her with alarm, and she never appears to have experienced the attraction which his great personal gifts exercised over most of those with whom he came in immediate contact. The extreme copiousness of his vocabulary, the extreme subtlety of his mind and reasoning, and the imperiousness of temper with which he seldom failed to meet opposition, were all repugnant to her. To those who have experienced the sustained emphasis of language with which Mr. Gladstone was accustomed in conversation to enforce his views, there is much truth as well as humour in the saying which was attributed to the Queen, 'I wish Mr. Gladstone would not always speak to me as if I was a public meeting'; and a little episode which is related by Sir Theodore Martin illustrates the irritation which Mr. Gladstone's methods of business must have caused to a very busy and overworked lady who always loved few words and simple and direct arguments.[1] At all times the Queen had decided political opinions, and the experience of a long reign had given her a large measure of not unjustifiable self-confidence. Few persons had studied as she had during all those years the various political questions that arose, and she had had the advantage of discussing them at length with a long succession of the leading statesmen of England. Under such circumstances her opinions had no small weight, and although in the Liberal Government she gave her full confidence to Lord Clarendon and Lord Granville,

[1] Sir Theodore Martin was asked by the Queen to give her a *précis* of a very long and unintelligible letter of Mr. Gladstone purporting to explain the Irish Church Disestablishment Bill (*Queen Victoria as I knew Her*, by Sir Theodore Martin).—ED.

she looked with the gravest apprehension on the policy of Mr. Gladstone.

It was a painful and irksome position, but it did not lead the Queen to any unconstitutional course.   No public act or word ever disclosed her feelings.   It was indeed in most cases very slowly, and in small circles and through private channels, that the convictions of the Queen became known.

At the close of the second Ministry of Mr. Gladstone she at once offered him an earldom, which he refused, and on his death she fully acquiesced in the public funeral in Westminster Abbey, and the Prince of Wales attended it as her representative.   In an autograph letter to Mrs. Gladstone she spoke with the deep and genuine warmth that was never wanting in her letters of condolence of her sympathy with the bereavement of that lady. She spoke of his illustrious gifts and of his personal kindness to herself, but it was noticed that no sentence in the letter intimated any approbation of his general policy. 'Truth in the inmost parts' was indeed a prominent characteristic of the Queen, and she wrote nothing which was not in accordance with her true convictions.

There were occasions when she took independent steps, and some of these had a considerable influence on politics.   Louis Napoleon was one of the few great Sovereigns who were not related to her, and to few persons could the *coup d'état* which brought him to the throne have been more repugnant, but the cordial personal relations she established with him undoubtedly contributed considerably to the good relations which for many years subsisted between England and France. Bismarck detested English Court influence and was greatly prejudiced against her, but he has left a striking testimony to the favourable impression which her tact and good sense made upon him when he first came into contact with her. She possessed to a high degree the power of choosing the right moment and striking the true chord, and she appears to have been an excellent judge not only of the feelings of large bodies of men, but also of the individual characters of those with whom she dealt. She had a style of writing which was eminently characteristic and eminently feminine, and it is easy to trace the letters which were entirely her own. Her letters of congratulation, or sympathy, or encouragement on public occasions scarcely ever failed in their effect and never contained an injudicious word. The same thing may be said of her many beautiful letters to those who were suffering from some grievous calamity. Whether she was writing to a great public character like the widow of an American President, or expressing her sorrow for obscure sufferers, there was the same note of true womanly sympathy, so manifestly spontaneous and so manifestly heartfelt, that it found its way to the hearts of thousands. The tact for which she was so justly celebrated, like all true tact, sprang largely from character, from the quick and lively sympathies of an eminently affectionate nature. No one could have been less theatrical, or less likely in any unworthy way to seek for popularity ; but she knew admirably the occasions or the methods by which she could strike the imagination and appeal most favourably to the feelings of her people. She showed this in the very beginning of her reign when she insisted, in defiance of the opinion of the Duke of Wellington, on riding herself through the ranks of her troops at her first review. She showed it on countless other occasions of her long

U

reign—pre-eminently in her two Jubilees and in her last visit to Ireland. It is well known that this visit was entirely her own idea. To many it seemed rash or even positively dangerous. They dwelt upon the bitter disaffection of a great portion of the Irish people, upon the danger of mob outrage or even assassination, upon the extreme difficulty of preventing a royal visit to Ireland from taking a party character and being regarded as a party triumph or defeat. But the Queen, as Sir William Harcourt once truly said, 'never feared her people,' and nothing could be more happy than the manner in which she availed herself of the new turn given to Irish feeling by the splendid achievements of Irish soldiers in South Africa, to come over, as if to thank her Irish people in person, and at the same time to repair in extreme old age a neglect for which she had been often, and not altogether unjustly, blamed. There never indeed was a more brilliant and unqualified success. To those who witnessed the spontaneous and passionate enthusiasm with which she was everywhere greeted, it seemed as if all bitter feeling vanished at her presence ; and the Irish visit, which was one of the last, was also one of the brightest pages of her reign. The credit of its most skilful arrangements belongs chiefly to the officials in Dublin, but the Irish people will long remember the patient courage with which the aged Queen went through its fatigues ; the tactful kindness and the gracious dignity with which she won the hearts of multitudes who had never before seen her or spoken to her ; the evident enjoyment with which she responded to the cordiality of her reception. One feature of that visit was especially characteristic. It was the Children's Review in Phœnix Park, where, by the desire of the Queen, some fifty thousand children were brought together to meet her. No act of kindness could have gone more directly home to the hearts of the parents, and it left a memory in many young minds that will never be effaced. It is rather, however, by the example of a life than by any public acts that a constitutional Sovereign can impress her personality on the affections of her people. Of the reign of Queen Victoria it may be truly said that very few in English history have been so blameless as this, which was the longest of all. Her Court was a model of quiet dignity and decorum, singularly free from all the atmosphere of intrigue and from all suspicion of injudicious or unworthy favouritism. She managed it as she managed her family, with a happy mixture of tact and affection; and though she gave her confidence to many she gave it to such persons and in such a way that it seemed never to be abused. No domestic life could in all its relations have been more perfect, and her love of children amounted to a passion. Among the great female rulers it would be difficult to find one less like Queen Victoria than the Empress Catherine of Russia, but they had this common trait of an intense love of children and a great power of winning their affection. There is a charming letter of Catherine to Grimm, describing her life among her grandchildren, which might almost have been written by the English Queen. Her vast family, spread through many countries, was her abiding interest and delight, and although she had to pay in full measure the natural penalty of many bereavements, she at least never knew the dreary loneliness that clouded the last days of her great predecessor, Elizabeth.

In the early years of her reign she fully filled her place as the leader of English society. In the plays she patronised, in the art she preferred, in the restrictions of her Drawing Rooms, in the fashions she countenanced, in the intimacies she selected or encouraged, her influence was always healthy and pure, and for some years it powerfully affected the tone of English society. Unfortunately, after the great calamity of her widowhood the nerves of the Queen seem to have been shaken, and though she never intermitted her political duties and spent daily many hours over her correspondence, she allowed her social duties to fall too much and too long into abeyance. She still, it is true, occasionally appeared in public ceremonies. She laid the first stones of several hospitals and infirmaries. She presided over the inauguration of several great industrial enterprises. She sometimes opened Parliament in person, and was sometimes present at military and naval reviews. But she scarcely ever appeared in London, except for a few days. She never appeared in a London theatre. She shrank from great crowds and large social gatherings, and buried herself too much in her Highland home. This is one of the few real reproaches that history is likely to bring against her. Her influence on English society was never wholly lost, and it was always an influence for good, but for many years it was exerted less frequently and less powerfully than it should have been, and the tone of large sections of society lost something by her retirement.

It may be doubted, however, whether this long retirement really injured her in the minds of her people. Her rare occasional appearances had a greater weight, and the depth of feeling exhibited by her long widowhood became a new title to respect. The transparent simplicity and unselfishness of her character were now generally appreciated, and her own books contributed

greatly to make her people understand her. It is in
general far from a wise thing for royal personages to
descend into the arena of literature unless they possess
some special aptitude for it. They expose themselves to
a kind of criticism wholly different from that which
follows them in their public lives—a criticism more
minute and often more deliberately malevolent than that
to which an ordinary writer is subject. The Queen
wrote pure and excellent English and she had a good
literary taste, but she certainly could never have become
a great writer; and the complete frankness and unreserve
of her Journals, as well as their curious homeliness of
thought and feeling, were not viewed with favour in some
sections of the fashionable and of the literary world.
There were circles in which the word 'bourgeois,' and
there were others in which the word 'commonplace,' was
often pronounced. Yet in this, as on nearly all occasions
when the Queen acted on her own impulse, she acted
wisely. Her books had at once an enormous circulation,
and there can be no doubt that they contributed very
widely to her popularity. Multitudes to whom she had
before been little more than a name, now realised that
she was one with whom they had very much in common.
Her evident longing for sympathy produced an immediate
response. Her deep domestic affection, her constant
interest in her servants, her high spirits, her love of
scenery, her love of animals, her power of taking delight
in little things, appeared vividly in her pages and came
home to the largest classes of her people.

In some respects the Queen was an eminently
democratic Sovereign. While maintaining the dignity of
her position, rank and wealth were in her eyes always
subordinate to the great realities of life and to true

human affections. In no one was the touch of Nature that makes the whole world kin more constantly visible. She was never more in her place than in visiting some poor tenant on the morrow of a great bereavement, or uttering words of comfort by the sick bed of some humble dependant. Men of all ranks who came in contact with her were struck with her thoughtful kindness, and her royal gift of an excellent memory never showed itself more frequently than in the manner in which she remembered and inquired after the fortunes and happiness of obscure persons related to those with whom she spoke.

Her religious opinions were brought very little before the public. Beyond a deep sense of Providential guidance and of the comforting power of religion, little is to be gathered from her published utterances; but she seemed equally at home in the Scotch Presbyterian and the Anglican Episcopal Church, and her marked admiration for such men as Dean Stanley and Norman Macleod, and for the preaching of Principal Caird, gives some clue to the bias of her opinions. Her mind was not speculative but eminently practical, and while she patronised good works of the most various kinds, there is reason to believe that those which most appealed to her personal feelings were those which directly contributed to alleviate the sufferings, or promote the material welfare, of the poor. She devoted the greater part of her Jubilee present to institutions for providing nurses for the sick poor, and this is said to have been one of the charities in which she took the warmest and most constant interest.

She is said not to have had any sympathy with the movement for the extension of political power to women, which became so conspicuous in her reign; but her own

success in filling for sixty-three years the highest
political position in the nation will always be quoted
in its support. Considering, indeed, how comparatively
small has been the number of reigning female Sovereigns,
it is remarkable how many in modern times have shown
themselves pre-eminently capable. Isabella of Spain,
Catherine of Russia, Maria Theresa of Austria, and our
own Elizabeth, all rise far above the level of ordinary
Sovereigns. Some of these seem figures of a larger and
stronger mould than Queen Victoria, but they governed
under very different constitutional conditions, and, with
one exception, there are serious blots on their memory.
There are few sadder facts in history than that the pure
and tender-hearted Spanish Queen should have been
deeply tinged with the persecuting fanaticism of her age
and country ; that she should have consented to the
establishment of the Inquisition in Castile, to the
expulsion of the Moors from her dominions, to the first
law in Europe establishing a practical censorship of
the Press. The unscrupulous ambition, the shameless
favouritism, the gross personal vices of Catherine, are as
conspicuous as her high intelligence, her indomitable
will, her majestic commanding power. The reign of
Elizabeth is perhaps the most glorious in English
history, but the character of that great Queen is
lamentably tarnished by waywardness and caprice.
Among purely constitutional Sovereigns Queen Anne
holds a respectable, though certainly not a brilliant,
place, and it may be added that much of the merit of the
very constitutional though not very glorious reign of
George II. is due to the excellent sense and judgment of
Queen Caroline. In spite of the saying of Burke, the age
of chivalry is not wholly dead. The sex of Queen

Victoria no doubt gave an additional touch of warmth to the loyalty of her people, and many of the qualities that made her most popular are intensely, if not distinctively, feminine. They would not, however, have given her the place she will always hold in English history, if they had not been united with what men are accustomed to regard as more peculiarly masculine—a clear, well-balanced mind, singularly free from fanaticisms and exaggerations, excellently fitted to estimate rightly the true proportion of things.

In the last years of her reign the political horizon greatly cleared. Lord Beaconsfield, during his later Ministries, obtained not only her fullest political confidence, but also won a warmer degree of personal friendship than she had bestowed on any Minister since the death of Lord Melbourne; and her relations with his successor, Lord Salisbury, appear to have been perfectly harmonious. The decisive rejection by the country of the Home Rule policy removed a great incubus from her mind, and she was fully in harmony with the strong Imperialist sentiments which now began to prevail in English thought, and especially with the warmer feeling towards our distant colonies which was one of its chief characteristics. Her own popularity also rapidly grew. She had keenly felt and bitterly resented the reproaches which had at one period been frequently brought against her for her neglect of social and ceremonial duties during many years of her widowhood. Her censors, she maintained, made no allowance for her loneliness, her advancing years, her feeble health, the overwhelming and incessant pressure of her more serious political duties. But her two Jubilees, bringing her once more into close touch with her people, put an end to these reproaches.

The Queen found with pleasure and perhaps with surprise how capable she still was of performing great public functions, and the vast outburst of spontaneous loyalty and affection of which she became the object gave her deep and unconcealed pleasure. To those, however, who were closely in connection with her it was touching to observe the gracious and unaffected modesty with which she received the homage of her subjects. Flattery was one of the things she disliked the most, and all who knew her best were struck with the singularly modest view she always took of herself. But blending with this modesty, and even with a shyness which she never wholly conquered, was the craving of a deeply affectionate and womanly nature for sympathy, and this craving was now abundantly gratified.

Still, with all this there was much that was melancholy in her later days. She had survived nearly all the intimacies of her youth. Death had made—especially in very recent times—many gaps in the circle of those who were nearest to her, and several of her children and of her children's husbands had preceded her to the tomb. Her sight had greatly failed. She was bowed down by physical infirmity, and her last year was saddened by a long, sanguinary, and inglorious war. Yet almost to the very end she continued with unabated courage to fulfil her daily task, and there was no sign that she had lost anything of her quick sympathy and her admirable judgment and tact. Her life was a most harmonious whole in which mind and character were happily attuned,

Like perfect music set to noble words.

OLD-AGE PENSIONS

THERE are many signs that the question of old-age pensions is destined to assume a great prominence in England; although it is probable that the large increase of national expenditure which is certain to follow the unhappy war in South Africa may, for some time, postpone actual legislation on the subject. The generation has passed away which witnessed the enormous abuses of Poor Law relief that existed, under the old English Poor Law, before 1834, and the rapid diminution of pauperism that was effected by the sterner administration introduced in that year.

The principles of poor-law relief which were then recognised by the best minds in England have been somewhat forgotten. These principles were that, while in England provision is made for the support of all who are absolutely destitute, it is of the utmost importance that on the whole the condition of the pauper should be a less eligible one than that of an independent labourer; that nothing should be done that could diminish habits of thrift, forethought, and steady industry among the poor; nothing that could weaken their sense of the necessity of providing for their latter days, or of their duty of supporting, when they have the means, their aged parents and relations. In accordance with these principles it was laid down that outdoor relief should be either absolutely refused to the able-bodied or only granted under most exceptional circumstances; that the workhouse test, with its stringent, deterrent discipline, should be steadily maintained; that relaxations and special favours granted out of public funds should be limited, as far as possible, to cases of special calamity which it was impossible for any prudence or foresight to have averted.

It would certainly be a great exaggeration to say that these principles have disappeared. Indeed, the robust, independent, self-respecting character which it was the object of the Manchester School to encourage is abundantly displayed in the gigantic Friendly and other working-class Co-operative Societies which have so largely increased in England during the last half-century. Two of these Friendly Societies—the Manchester Unity and the Foresters—have each of them more than seven hundred thousand members on their roll. At the same time, it is equally certain that in many quarters a different, and, in my opinion, very dangerous, spirit prevails. In England as elsewhere there is an increased tendency to aggrandise the functions of the State and to look to State aid or State control rather than individual or co-operative effort as the remedy of every evil. Social questions have assumed a greater prominence in politics; and, with the lowering of the franchise, the vague State Socialism, which, in different degrees, pervades most working-class politics, has given a bias to both parties in the State. It has become prominent in every election and has produced many rash pledges.

The close connection between taxation and representation, which was once considered the cardinal principle of English Liberalism, has, in a marked degree, diminished, both in Imperial and local taxation. It used to be contended that those who chiefly paid should chiefly regulate, and that taxation should be as much as possible the voluntary grant of the taxpayers, restricted to their common purposes. But in many quarters a different belief has grown up. It is held that in the hands of a democracy taxation should be made the means of redressing the inequalities of fortune, ability, or industry; the preponderant class voting and spending money which another class are obliged to pay. The income-tax is so arranged that a large majority of the voters are exempt from its burden; a highly graduated system of death duties is now nearly the most prominent of our Imperial taxes; and the Local Government Act of 1894 has placed local taxation on the most democratic basis. The latter has given the power of voting rates to many who do not pay them; and, by abolishing the nominated, or ex-officio, guardians, and the plural voting of the larger ratepayers, it has almost destroyed the influence of property on local taxation.

At the same time the doctrine has arisen, and is now sedulously propagated in England, that the State ought to undertake to provide at the public expense for all old persons, or at least for all deserving old persons, who have not succeeded in obtaining a sufficient livelihood for themselves; that this provision should not be regarded as an eleemosynary grant, but as a positive right; and that, in order to free it from the taint of pauperism, and take away from the recipient all reluctance to receive it, a new fund should be created, entirely distinct from poor-law relief, and administered by some other tribunal than the poor-law guardians.

The claim has been supported on another ground. The immense improvement of the material condition of the

English working classes during the last half-century is beyond all question; but it is much more evident among the young and the strong than among the old. The intense competition of modern industry, stimulated to the highest point by free trade, by the factory system, and by the vast development of machinery, has expelled the old and feeble from some of its most important fields; and the influence of trade-unions in enforcing, in each trade which they can control, a uniform and minimum wage, has obliged the employer to employ only the most efficient labour.

The old man who could once easily obtain a little work at low wages now finds it much more difficult; and the recent legislation compelling the employer to compensate his workmen for all accidents that take place in his employment, even when those accidents are in no degree due to any negligence on his own part or on that of his servants, has acted in the same direction. Such serious obligations have been thrown on the employer in the more dangerous trades, that he is obliged in self-defence to restrict himself to the workmen who are least liable to accidents; and they are naturally those whose strength, activity, and eyesight are at their best. Among the recipients of poor-law relief the proportion of men over sixty-five is enormously great; and some figures which, in 1893, were brought before the Commission on the Aged Poor, made a great impression on the country. It was stated that in a single year 29·3 of the whole population over sixty-five were in receipt of poor-law relief in England and Wales; and assuming that a third part of these old persons belonged to the well-to-do, it was calculated that not much less than three in seven must fall into the ranks of pauperism.

302   HISTORICAL AND POLITICAL ESSAYS

There has been much controversy about the accuracy
of this statement; and, even if it be admitted, a good deal
has been said to attenuate its force. In the poor-law
system as it was reformed in 1834, it was a first principle
that the workhouse, with its painful and degrading
associations, was to be the chief form of poor-law relief,
and that outdoor relief should only be granted on exceptional occasions and on stringent conditions. This
provision has been gradually relaxed. Outdoor relief,
which, in the eyes of the poor, carries with it very little
of the discredit and dislike that gathers round the workhouse, is now by far the larger part of poor-law relief;
and in many districts it is administered with great laxity.

It has been proved by the clearest evidence that the
immense majority of the aged and deserving poor who are
in receipt of poor-law relief only receive it in the form of
outdoor relief, and very often only in the form of medical
relief, and that if they go to the workhouse it is only
when their peculiar circumstances make it desirable for
them to do so. Wherever a more stringent system of
relief is imposed, pauperism invariably and rapidly de-
creases; and Mr. Loch, the Secretary of the Charity
Organisation Society, has collected much evidence to
show that, on the whole, old-age pauperism is diminishing, though it has not been diminishing at the same rate
as pauperism under the age of sixty. The administration
of the workhouses has also greatly improved; and the
poor-law infirmaries are becoming hospitals which are
largely resorted to in time of sickness by many who
might easily avoid them. On the whole, old-age destitution is, and must be, a grave question for philan-
thropists; but there has been great exaggeration about
its magnitude and its hardships.

The expediency of devising a new and better method
of providing for the destitute aged poor of deserving
character has long been smouldering obscurely in English
politics; but it obtained a real importance for the first
time when a very strong Royal Commission, under the
presidency of Lord Aberdare, was appointed, at the beginning of 1893, to inquire into the question. After long
and careful inquiry, and after hearing a great multitude
of witnesses, this Commission reported in the spring of
1895. The majority of the members, while recommend-
ing various reforms in the administration of the poor-
law, reported decisively against any system of old-age
pensions, either in the form of endowment or assisted
assurance, as likely to do more harm than good; but
a minority, which derived special importance from the
presence of Mr. Chamberlain, refused to accept this
decision as final, and urged that the question should be
submitted to a smaller body of experts. In the election
which took place in 1895 the question appeared frequently
upon the platform, and many members on both sides of
politics pledged themselves on the subject.

The weight which is always attached to the speeches
of Mr. Chamberlain gave a great impulse to the movement. He never countenanced the idea of universal old-
age pensions, which was already advocated by many;
but he strongly maintained that special provision, apart
from the poor-law and in the shape of pensions, might,
and ought to, be made for the old and deserving poor ; he
expressed his belief that such a measure ' would do more
than anything else to secure the happiness of the working
classes ' ; and he suggested as the most feasible scheme
that ' whenever a man acquires for himself in a Friendly

Society or any other society a pension of 2s. 6d. a week
the State should come in and double that pension.'   Mr.
Chamberlain, however, did not insist on this precise
proposal ; but he gave the question a great prominence ;
and among politicians on both sides there was a manifest
tendency to make party capital out of it.

A purely non-party Committee, presided over by Lord
Rothschild, and consisting mainly of distinguished
financial authorities connected with the permanent Civil
Service, and therefore removed from active politics, was
appointed in 1896, in accordance with the recommendation
of the Aberdare Commission, to inquire especially into
the question of old-age pensions ; and it reported in a
document of conspicuous ability.   It was unanimous in
condemning as impracticable or dangerous all the schemes
for such pensions that were brought before it ; and it
fully confirmed the views of the preceding Commission.
The report, and the evidence on which it is based, clearly
show the ways in which measures intended for the benefit
of the working class may prove in the highest degree
injurious to them.

If the matter could have been decided by pure reasoning, this report might have been generally accepted as
decisive.   But many of the supporters of the Government
had at the election made speeches in favour of old-age
pensions.   One of its most powerful members had thrown
his weight into the scale.   The idea had taken hold of
great sections of the working classes.   The trade-unions,
that see in increasing old-age poverty the chief drawback
to their policy of enforcing in each trade a uniform and
minimum wage, were naturally delighted that the State
should undertake, out of public funds, to remove their

difficulty. A number of Bills dealing with the question had been introduced into the House of Commons by private members; and the reluctance of the Government to take it up had become a favourite form of party attack. The Government acted as perhaps most Governments, under the circumstances, would have done. While refusing to give any pledge, and repudiating any sympathy with the idea of universal pensions, and insisting that an encouragement of thrift should be an essential condition of any old-age pension scheme, they refused to admit that a false departure had been made; and they appointed a new Committee—of which the writer of these lines was a member—to report upon the best means of improving the condition of the aged deserving poor, and upon the feasibility of dealing with their case by old-age pensions.

Mr. Chaplin, the President of the Local Government Board, an experienced and very popular member of the Cabinet, presided over the Committee; and the fact that he drew up the report of the majority gave that report its chief political importance. The Committee consisted largely of members who had already committed themselves deeply in favour of old-age pensions; and it will hardly be disputed in England that it carried with it much less financial and political weight than its predecessors; and that the majority report—which was carried by 9 to 4—is more remarkable for the boldness of its recommendations than for the cogency of its reasoning. It completely, and almost contemptuously, discarded the conclusions of the majority of the Aberdare Commission, and the unanimous opinion of the Rothschild Committee; and it recommended that old-age pensions, derived in part from Imperial and in part from local sources, and varying from 5s. to 7s. a week, should be granted to all the deserving poor who had attained the age of sixty-five and whose incomes did not exceed 10s. a week. It proposed that these pensions should be granted by committees established in every poor-law union and elected by the poor-law guardians ; that they should be revised every three years ; and that they should be distributed through the agency of the post-office.

On the great difficulties that seemed so formidable to its predecessors it touched very lightly. How many of the poor were likely under the proposed system to become pensioners, and what burden of taxation was likely to be thrown on the State, were questions that were put aside as irrelevant to the inquiry. To meet the enormous difficulty of deciding upon the real merits, and of investigating the real circumstances, of the great masses of independent and industrious labourers who live in the manufacturing towns, or are constantly moving from one great centre of population to another, and circulating in quest of work through the whole extent of the Empire, it was suggested that the relief be confined to those who were resident in a single locality; and it was pointed out that a number of charities, endowed out of old legacies or donations, and applying to particular classes or districts, had come to be administered by the Charity Commissioners, and that in this restricted field they had been able to convert a large part of the income at their disposal from doles into permanent pensions.

The thrift test and the character test, which previous inquirers had found it almost impossible to establish on a satisfactory basis, were defined on the loosest lines. The pensioner must not, during the preceding twenty years,

have been sentenced to penal servitude or imprisonment
without the option of a fine; he must not, during the
same period of time, have been in receipt of poor-law
relief 'other than medical relief or unless under circumstances of a wholly exceptional character'; and he must
have 'endeavoured to the best of his ability, by his
industry and by the exercise of reasonable providence,
to make provision for himself and those immediately
dependent on him.'

The extreme vagueness and the extreme elasticity of
such provisions are sufficiently manifest; and it is difficult
to see how they can give any real assistance in practical
legislation; while they leave the door open to the largest
and most lavish expenditure. I have endeavoured in a
minority report to deal with these questions at somewhat
greater length than my present space will admit; but a
few pages may suffice to give an outline of the case of
those who believe the new policy to be both mistaken
and dangerous.

Nothing is more certain or more cheering in the
condition of modern England than the extraordinary
diminution that has taken place, during the present
generation, in pauperism. It began with the reform of
the poor law in 1834; and although it has been found
possible to relax greatly the stringency of the poor-law
regulations that were then made, it has steadily continued.
Much of this is due to the increase in the rate of wages
which has taken place in most departments of English
industry, and which has been accompanied by a great
decrease in the cost of most of the chief necessaries of
life, as well as by a considerable reduction in the hours of
work. Sir Robert Giffen, in the very remarkable paper
which he published, in 1883, on the condition of the

working classes in England during the preceding fifty years, has shown that in every class of work in which it is possible to make a comparison the wages of the labourer have in these fifty years risen at least 20 per cent., and in most cases between 50 and 100 per cent.; and he has clearly demonstrated that no other section of the community has obtained so large a proportion of the increase of the national wealth, and improved in so great a degree in material prosperity.

But the mere increase of wages is but one element of this improvement. The very mainspring of the prosperity of the great masses of the British working classes is to be found in their increased sobriety, and in the habits of thrift and providence that have followed the spread of education. The statistics of the Friendly Societies, the Industrial and Provident Societies, the Building Societies, the savings-banks, and of countless other institutions, created by voluntary working-class effort for the purpose of insuring against sickness or death, and providing working-class investments, attest in the clearest manner the rapid growth of provident and thrifty habits among the wage-earning classes. In no other respect is the improvement of the nation so marked and so indisputable and no element in the national character is more important to its prosperity and to its enduring greatness. In the evidence that was brought before our Committee, it was shown that since 1849 the pauperism of Great Britain had been reduced from 62·7 per 1,000 to 26·2 per 1,000, if lunatics and vagrants are included, to 22·8 per 1,000, if lunatics and vagrants are excluded.

The first, and most vital, condition of any sound legislation for the relief of poverty is that it should not impair these industrial qualities, or weaken these vast voluntary organisations of self-help which are their result. Can it be said that the old-age pension policy is compatible with this condition ?

It proposes to open, in addition to the existing system of poor relief, a new fund, amounting to many millions of pounds a year, and drawn from compulsory taxation for the purpose of subsidising simple poverty ; a fund to which it is to be rather creditable than otherwise to resort ; a fund which is intended to deal, not with exceptional calamity, but with that which springs from the mere efflux of time, and which is, beyond all others, the most normal and most easily foreseen. It proposes to teach the whole working population to look to the State, and not to themselves, for the provision for their old age, and for the old age of those who might be dependent on them, and thus to destroy the most powerful of all motives to thrift—the very mainspring of productive and self-sacrificing industry. And it proposes to do this at a time when wages are higher than they have ever been before ; when voluntary societies for securing the poor from want are flourishing and increasing as they have never done before ; when the rapid decline of pauperism is one of the most marked and most universally recognised signs of national improvement. Can it be seriously believed that the addition of many millions a year to the State funds directly employed in the relief of poverty will, in the long run, tend to diminish pauperism or to encourage self-reliance and thrift ?

Mr. Chamberlain and the other more considerable advocates of old-age pensions clearly see that if such pensions are to be of real value they must discriminate between the deserving and the undeserving ; and they believe that they may have the effect of stimulating, instead of weakening, thrift. For this purpose several schemes have been devised.

The most popular Continental method of achieving this end is by a law obliging the working man in early life to insure against old age, and by supplementing the income derived from this insurance by a State subsidy. In Germany, where this system is actually carried out, the old-age pension is derived from three sources—viz. compulsory insurance by the workers, compulsory contribution by the employer, and a State subsidy. Compulsory insurance found for many years a powerful English advocate in Canon Blackley; and it has been recommended by a recent inquiry in Holland, which, however, refused to propose any system of old-age pensions. According to the best accounts, the German system has been far from successful either economically or politically; and it has certainly not prevented Socialism from becoming one of the great dangers of the State. Into this question, however, it is needless to enter, as it is now universally admitted in England that compulsory insurance for old age is an impossibility; for it would certainly be repudiated by the working classes.

A large group of proposals are to the effect that old-age pensions should be granted to all poor persons over the age of sixty-five whose total income is less than 10s. a week, provided that a certain portion of that income consists of a fixed annuity acquired by their own industry and thrift. It is urged that in most of the great branches of industry a deserving man in his earlier and stronger years could easily earn such an annuity; and it is suggested that the State should double it, or add to it sufficient to make it up to 10s. a week, or supplement it by a fixed grant of 2s. 6d., or 5s., or even 7s. a week.

The objections to such schemes are very serious. It is obvious that if they encourage a workman to save up to the amount required to secure a pension, they would have a directly opposite effect as soon as that amount had been attained. The first result of any addition to his income would then be to disqualify him for a pension. It is also obvious that the pensioner of sixty-five would have a strong inducement to abstain from the work he could easily do, and that if he continued to do it he would compete on exceptionally favourable terms with the workman who, though he had passed the prime of life, was not yet entitled to a pension, restricting his means of employment and beating down his wages. Many of the most necessitous and deserving poor would also be left unrelieved.

Although it is true that in the more flourishing trades men could easily in early life save out of their wages a sufficient sum to acquire this annuity, there are large fields of industry in which such a saving would be almost or absolutely impossible. We have had melancholy evidence of how utterly insufficient most forms of women's wages are to provide the needed margin. The same thing is true of the agricultural labourer in the more depressed districts in England and in large tracts of Ireland and Scotland. Even in the more remunerative employments innumerable special circumstances would prevent a thrifty and deserving man from obtaining this annuity. Certainly no one is more deserving of compassion and State aid than the widow and young orphans of a working man ; but the scheme we are considering would not only not help them, but would most seriously injure them. It is a direct incentive to the workman to sink his savings in an annuity which would terminate with his own life.

The whole policy, indeed, of attempting to turn all working-class savings into this one channel is a false one; and it has been shown that no kind of saving is in fact less popular among working men than the purchase of a deferred annuity. I may here be allowed to quote a few lines from my own report:

'In the infinitely various conditions of a working-man's life thrift will take many forms, and an attempt to prescribe a single form is eminently injudicious. The whole life-plan of a farmer whose farm will remain with him to the end will be different from that of an artisan or a domestic servant whose power of earning a livelihood depends entirely upon his physical strength. The former will probably find it most profitable to expend his savings on the improvement of his farm. Where the system of peasant proprietorship prevails most agricultural thrift is directed to the purchase and enlargement of farms. In Ireland it is largely directed to the purchase of tenant right, or to enabling the younger members of the family to emigrate.

'Nor is it true that even the artisan will find the purchase of an annuity the best thing to be aimed at. To buy a house or some furniture; to start a small business; to expend his savings in tiding over periods of slack or failing work; to avail himself of the advantage which some fluctuation in the market gives to the man who can transport himself promptly to a new locality or a new business is often far more to his advantage. Above all, money expended in settling his family is often his best policy as well as the course which is most beneficial to the community. At present a large proportion of working men look forward to their children to help them in their old age, and make it a main object of their lives to place them in a position to do so. It does not seem to me a wise thing for the State either to emancipate children from this duty or to induce every married working man to sink his savings in an annuity which will end with his life and from which his widow and children can derive no benefit. It is certainly not for the advantage of the country that in selecting between alternative ways of providing for old age he should be induced to choose that which throws the greatest burden on the State. With the vast increase of population, with the great fluctuations of modern industry, and with the rapid development of the colonies, it is extremely desirable both in the interest of the working men and of the State that they should be induced to transfer themselves from congested towns and from exhausted industries to new fields. A general pension system would certainly contribute most powerfully to prevent them from doing so.'

It has been proposed by others that the pension fund should be placed in the hands of Friendly or Benefit Societies, and that they should be intrusted with its administration, or that subscription to such societies for a certain number of years should be taken by the State as the thrift test. On the first proposal it is sufficient to say, that these great voluntary societies are themselves opposed to it ; for if they were directly subsidised by the State, they would be obliged to submit to a State control of their management and their finances which they do not desire. It is observed that only a very small proportion of the subscribers to these societies ever find it necessary to come upon the poor rates ; and if a system of old-age pensions were confined to these limits, it would act in the most unequal manner. Their members are drawn in a far larger proportion from the lucrative and flourishing trades than from those which are struggling and underpaid. Few women belong to them. In Ireland, which is the poorest part of the Empire, Friendly Societies scarcely exist; and the same thing is true of large districts in Wales and Scotland. The main result of such proposals would be to concentrate the new State fund for the relief of poverty on the richest parts of the Empire, and on the trades that need it the least.

The extreme difficulty of finding any efficient test of thrift is very evident; and those proposed by a large number of the advocates of old-age pensions are so easy as to be almost worthless. Some consider it sufficient that a man has for a certain number of years not been in receipt of poor-law relief, except medical relief or relief granted under 'exceptional circumstances.' Others would accept the mere fact that a man has lived to be sixty-five, as the drunken and disreputable workman seldom lives so long. A large number of resolutions have condemned Mr. Chaplin's report on the grounds that old-age pensions ought not to be confined to the 'deserving' poor; that they ought to begin at an earlier age than sixty-five; that they ought to be administered by a body totally unconnected with the poor law, so as to carry with them no taint of pauperism or eleemosynary relief. They ought, it is said, to be universal; to be looked on as a matter of strict right; to be considered as of the same nature as the pension given to the soldier or the Civil Servant.

It is obvious that all this may carry us very far. It is estimated that some of the most popular proposals would involve an annual expenditure of considerably more than twenty millions of pounds—making allowance for the saving that might be effected in the ordinary poor-law relief, but not counting the cost of administration. And this expenditure would be a growing one; and once accepted it could hardly be withdrawn. The vast addition to the national debt that might follow a great European war or the great shrinkage of the national income that might easily follow some revolution in trade or manufacture, might render the burden of taxation incomparably more serious than at present; but once the great mass of the population had learned to regard State support in old age as their normal prospect and their inalienable right, it would be impossible, without producing a social revolution, to recede. All the advantages gained by generations of economical administration of the national finance would be nullified; while the certain result of this crushing addition to taxation would be to weaken incalculably the spirit of thrift, providence, and self-reliance, and at the same time to lower wages, by removing one of the great considerations by which they are regulated. And this reduction of wages would fall not only on the recipient of the pension, but also on multitudes who would never live to attain it. Nothing can be more certain than that a general system of pensions attached to the labour of the wage-earner must lower wages, at least among all those who are approaching the pension age; while it would prevent or retard their natural increase over a far wider area.

It would also most certainly bring with it the gravest danger of corruption. It would not be easy to secure the pure and the impartial administration of these vast funds; but the political dangers would be much more serious. It is proposed that the pension system should be first introduced on a small scale, but gradually extended till it included all the aged poor, or at least all who were deserving. Such a question would infallibly pass into the competitions of party warfare. It would become in most constituencies one of the most prominent of electioneering tests. Rival candidates would be competing for the votes of a wage-earning electorate who had a direct pecuniary interest in increasing or extending pensions and in relaxing the conditions on which they are given. Can it be doubted that in many cases their first object would be to outbid one another, and that national and party politics would soon be forced into a demoralising race of extravagance?

I cannot conclude without protesting against the supposition that those who think with me are indifferent to the great evil of old-age destitution and propose nothing for its relief. The committees which have most clearly pointed out the dangers of old-age pensions have also urged, that within the lines of our present poor-law system it is quite possible to do much, by an improved classification, to distinguish among the recipients of poor-law relief between the respectable and the worthless. Much has already been done, and in the most important unions the guardians have introduced a large amount of classification by merit. As I have already said, the immense majority of the respectable aged poor are now relieved only in their own homes or in comfortable infirmaries. The severe test of absolute destitution has in practice been greatly relaxed; there is a legal provision preventing those who are receiving help from Friendly Societies from being disqualified for relief; husbands and wives are no longer separated in the workhouse; and in some unions of which we had evidence much more has been done. This, however, depends too much on the will of particular Boards of Guardians, and there are in consequence great inequalities of treatment. The condition of the deserving poor may be greatly improved by relaxation in points of hours, discipline, and visitors, and by workhouse arrangements securing more universally that paupers who have lived respectable lives should not be obliged to mix with the drunken, the disreputable, and the hopelessly idle. And, though extensions of outdoor relief should be carefully watched, and entail great dangers, yet under wise and strict administration something more may be done in this direction.

But all this should be regarded as essentially poor-law relief, and not as the recognition of a claim of right for services supposed to have been rendered to the community. No form of State Socialism is more dangerous than the doctrine which has been countenanced by Prince Bismarck, and which is making many disciples in England—namely, that an industrious man, who has pursued his course in life with perfect independence, made his own contracts, chosen his own work, and been paid for it by stipulated wages, is entitled, if he fails in obtaining a sufficiency for his old age, to be placed as a ' soldier of industry ' in the same category as State servants, and to receive like them, not on the ground of compassion, but of right, a State pension drawn from the taxation of the community. There is no real analogy between the relief that is very properly granted to such workmen in their destitution, and the pensions—largely of the nature of deferred pay—that are given by the State or by private employers, under the terms of distinct contracts, and for specific services duly rendered, to those who have entered into their employment and placed themselves under their control.

INDEX